Whatever It Takes

*Seven decades of true love,
hard work, and no regrets*

Also from Islandport Press

Wayfarer by James S. Rockefeller Jr.
Sea Change by Maxwell Taylor Kennedy
My Life in the Maine Woods by Annette Jackson
Hauling by Hand by Dean Lunt
Nine Mile Bridge by Helen Hamlin
Where Cool Waters Flow by Randy Spencer
How to Cook a Moose by Kate Christensen
Settling Twice by Deborah Joy Corey
Shoutin' into the Fog by Thomas Hanna
The Cows Are Out! by Trudy Chambers Price

Whatever It Takes

Seven decades of true love,
hard work, and no regrets

MAY DAVIDSON

ISLANDPORT PRESS

ISLANDPORT PRESS

Islandport Press
PO Box 10
Yarmouth, Maine 04096
www.islandportpress.com
books@islandportpress.com

ISBN: 978-1-944762-16-2
ebook ISBN: 978-1-944762-20-9
Library of Congress Control Number: 2017951784
Printed in the USA

Dean Lunt, Publisher
Cover and book design by Teresa Lagrange / Islandport Press
Photographs courtesy of the author unless otherwise noted.

To my husband, Jim, my soul mate. My Hero.

My parents, John and Jo Banis.

*Our daughter, Connie, who now owns and continues
North Country Wind Bells beyond our dreams.*

*Our daughter, Debby Jo, who has her own sheep ranch
Both daughters will write their stories one day.*

*Bill and Stacy Webster, lifelong shepherds who continue
the North Country Cheviot Sheep.*

Table of Contents

Author's Note

By the age of eight, I had made up my mind I would never live anywhere but Maine. My attachment to the state is that of a barnacle to a ledge, the pull of the moon to the earth. Maine, because of its singular and profound beauty, is a place of worship without walls. I love it so.

If you, especially young people, want to live in this great state, I encourage you to do so with all my heart.

It is certainly easier to make a living in Maine now than it was fifty or sixty years ago, especially if you have a profession. But if, as my husband Jim and I did, you wish to be self-employed, you face a more difficult situation. Particularly if you have no working capital and only a high school education. However, one message of this book is—It. Can. Be. Done.

It may take hard work, tenacity, and a strong will, but if you have the determination to stick with your goals, the rewards of living in this earthly heaven known as Maine are beyond any price paid.

Another reason I wrote this book is that every era deserves some recognition even if it is in a small place and in a quiet way. There have been enormous changes in the last eighty years. I believe my generation, the generation essentially born in the 1930s, has seen greater progress than any previous generation.

I believe a slice of that older time should be recorded and remembered. Using my husband's and my combined memories and years of notes, I have tried to write a true story of life on the coast of Maine as it was actually lived.

In living our lives, Jim and I did whatever it took to pay the bills and stay in Maine. We went lobster fishing, built a log home using twenty dollars worth of standing trees, farmed sheep, chickens and other animals, plowed snow, and sold shrimp along the roadside. We built a sawmill and employed a work force of Maine lobstermen, we drove an eighteen-wheel truck back and forth across the country, and finally we created and sold a unique craft item. We experienced folly, fear, tears, joy, and a lot of laughter along the way.

We agreed to live a life we loved and vowed to do whatever it took to survive.

And we did.

May B. Davidson

May B. Davidson
Whitefield, Maine
May 2019

Top: May at the beach in 1930 with her parents, John and Jo Banis.
Bottom: The Mayfair House as it looked in the 1930s.

Prologue

IN THE EARLY twentieth century, my parents, John Banis and Josephine Taft emigrated to this great country. They arrived when they were each sixteen, although they came at different times and did not meet until years later. They came with no money, and the relatives who welcomed them had little to offer beyond shelter.

My mother was born in Liverpool, England to Scottish parents. My mother's mother died when my mother was just five years old. Her father was a seafaring man and didn't have the time or money to care for five daughters. My mother, the youngest of the girls, entered the Bears Den School for Orphan Girls in Glasgow, Scotland in June 1910 with her sister Nell. On the carriage ride to the orphanage, Nell, who was older, sobbed the entire way, knowing the life ahead of them. My mother was too young to really understand. At the orphanage my mother learned to sew and cook, but she described the circumstances and conditions as something straight out of a nineteenth-century Charles Dickens novel. At the age of fourteen, she was sent out to homes in Scotland to work as a servant, still under the supervision of the orphanage, which also received all of her meager wages.

Meanwhile, over the years after their mother died and as money allowed, three of her older sisters had moved to America. Finally in 1920, one of her older sisters, Babs, crossed the Atlantic to get her and make the same journey. My mother was only sixteen years old, and Babs originally came for Nell. But when Nell, who by now was married and had children, decided to stay, the ticket and the opportunity fell to my mother. My mother, known as Jo or Joie, sailed from Southampton, England aboard the *Aquitania*, bound for better life. She said, "It was the twentieth of November that I got my first glimpse of America—the great land I had dreamed about so much."

Earlier, my father, who grew up on a small family farm in Lithuania during the rule of Czarist Russia, also lost his mother at an early age. He was just thirteen. His father was also sheriff of their small town and had gone to America ahead of his family looking for a way to get his family out of Europe. In 1910, during a time of turmoil and in the years before World War I, my grandfather sent for my father and my aunt. My father and his sister traveled across Lithuania, across Poland, and into Germany, where they sailed from Hamburg headed for Ellis Island. When they first arrived in America, my father and his sister spoke only Lithuanian and they didn't know anyone else who spoke the language, so the early days were quite lonely.

Once in America, the primary options for my father and my mother were to work as domestic servants. My mother first started working at a factory in New York, but soon moved on to domestic service, mostly in New England and New York. My father immediately joined his father working at a New York estate as a gardener and eventually as a chauffeur and butler.

It was fate that in the early 1920s, my mother worked at an estate near my father. By this time, she mostly worked in the huge estate kitchens learning the art of producing fine cuisine. This work provided them with both room and board so they could save their income for what they both separately dreamed of—independence in a world beyond cities.

In 1925, while working at adjoining estates along Glen Cove on New York's Long Island, my thirty-year-old father met my twenty-year-old mother and they fell in love. My mother said her first glimpse of my father was on a beach: "As I looked at him standing there, blond, broad-shouldered, and quite good looking, I was determined that I would knock the wind clear out of his sails."

She succeeded, and once together, they talked about their future and how by working and combining their savings they could some-day buy a combination farm and small inn. They just needed to find the right location.

They married in 1926, and the following year they traveled with the family they were both now working for to Hog Island in Bremen, Maine. Bremen, incorporated in 1828 and boasting a population of maybe three hundred at the time, was largely settled by German immigrants and it had developed as a farming and fishing town. My parents immediately fell in love with Maine. It was my mother's Scotland and my father's Lithuania.

They asked the boatman, Frank Lailer, who was taking them to Hog Island if there were any places for sale.

"Yes," he said. "My place."

Frank's place included a large house and fields right on Greenland Cove. He was asking $3,000. My parents found the money and bought their dream home. They moved to Maine and planned to convert the Lailer house to an inn.

The old saltwater farm featured seven bedrooms and could sleep fourteen. It included a barn and enough acreage for four cows. However, it had no electricity and no running water. My parents spent a year working to prepare it for guests. After much hard work, the old house became The Mayfair House (in later years they changed the name to Snug Harbor Inn in homage to my mother's father), an inn that became a popular destination for summer visitors. Guests had to stay a minimum of one week, and some loved it so much they returned to stay the same week every year for forty years. Lodging included meals served family style, and my parents offered nothing but the best. Guests waiting for the prime rib cooking over the fire, for example, could barely stand it knowing the delicious meal soon to follow.

I was born in the nearby town of Damariscotta on May 16, 1929 and joined The Mayfair House family.

Unfortunately, in the 1930s, there was little work in Maine after the summer ended, and my parents needed money to continue improving The Mayfair House. So for several winters during my childhood and beyond, my parents left Maine each fall to work again as domestic servants—cook and butler—at estates in places such as New York City and Mount Kisco in New York, Westport and Stamford in Connecticut, as well as places in Pennsylvania and New Jersey. One year they worked for the president of the New York Stock Exchange. They didn't want to leave Maine each year, but they didn't have any choice. They did whatever they needed to do to continue living their dream.

They were an inspiration.

As a child, I got to see these famous places and to me, there was no comparison between the freedom and beauty of Maine and the dark attic of the servants' quarters and the back stairways that led to them in these out-of-state mansions. I loved my childhood on Greenland Cove and having the woods and the shore as my playground. As I grew, I also worked at The Mayfair House washing dishes and waiting on tables. I attended the local schools, including the one-room

John Banis cooking lobster for guests of The Mayfair House. Each week the Inn provided a picnic on the shore at Greenland Cove for its guests.

Muscongus School in Bremen and later Lincoln Academy in New-castle, graduating in 1947.

In 1945, when I was sixteen I met my future husband, Jim David-son. Jim, who grew up on Staten Island, was traveling with his aunt to Nova Scotia when the two of them stopped in Bremen to stay at The Mayfair House.

We fell in love immediately.

Jim worked his entire week's vacation, mowing lawns, milking the cows, filling the woodbox, basically doing anything he could to be with me. At home, even though he was already working for the New York Central Railroad, he joined the US Army that fall after he turned eighteen. He was gone for two years, promising that he would return to Maine and me. Those two years seemed to take forever, even though Jim wrote to me every day, and when he was discharged in

May in about 1943 dressed up to serve as the piano accompanist for Lincoln Academy Glee Club. She later adapted this dress to be her wedding dress.

1947 he came straight to Maine. We were married on October 16, 1948 in a ceremony on the grounds of The Mayfair House.

As a wedding present, my parents gave us five acres of land that they carved out from their property. It was a half-mile away from their house through the woods with no good road access and no close neighbors. On that piece of land, back amongst the pines, we made plans to build a log cabin, our first home together.

And that is where our adventure begins.

October 16, 1948, Jim and May got married on the grounds of The Mayfair House. Left to Right: Jo Banis, James Davidson, Connie Davidson, Donna Grigalis, May Davidson, Jim Davidson, Arthur Davidson, John Banis, Mamie Grigalis, and Joe Grigalis.

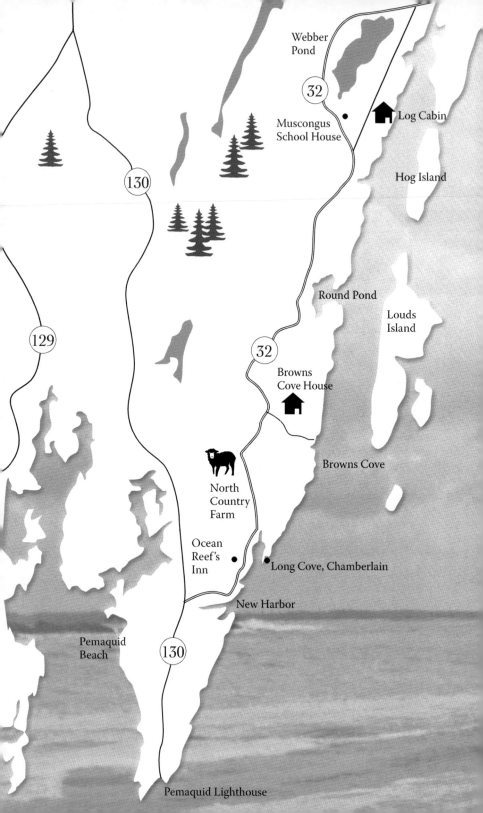

Webber
Pond

32

Muscongus
School House

Log Cabin

Hog Island

130

Round Pond

Louds
Island

129

32

Browns
Cove House

Browns Cove

North
Country
Farm

Ocean
Reef's
Inn

Long Cove, Chamberlain

New Harbor

Pemaquid
Beach

130

Pemaquid Lighthouse

Walter Watts and Jim standing amongst the unpeeled logs on the first day of building the log cabin in the fall of 1949.

CHAPTER ONE

A Cabin in the Woods

"THAT FUSE IS too short, isn't it?" I said.

"It's the last piece, so it'll have to do," Jim replied as he descended an old wooden ladder into a pit walled in by clay.

This blast was to be the last of many dynamite blasts we had detonated in recent days trying to create a well big enough and deep enough to hold our future water supply. This location, dominated by clay, was the only place on our property suitable for a well. After each explosion, Jim climbed down into the hole, loaded the loosened clumps of clay into a bucket and hauled them back to the surface using a block and tackle system hanging from a tripod that straddled the well. I grabbed the bucket when it reached the top and emptied it onto a growing pile of wet, sticky clay.

Despite our best efforts to find water, the bottom of the nearly twenty-five-foot-deep hole was not even damp. We had run out of time, money for dynamite, and now, as we dug deeper and deeper, the ladder was too short to reach from bottom to top. We knew the hole would serve as a reservoir for rainwater if nothing else.

Jim neatly buried the final three sticks of dynamite. With his jackknife, he cut a slanted end on the fuse and lit it. Before previous blasts, I had enjoyed watching the tiny flame creep along the fuse until it was within a few inches of the dynamite and then dashing for cover. This time the short fuse flamed briefly and quickly disappeared underground as it rushed for the dynamite.

"Hurry!" I shouted to Jim, who was still in the pit.

He stepped toward the ladder, looked back over his shoulder and said, "Forgot my knife."

Although I couldn't see the flame, I knew it was racing toward the dynamite.

"Never mind the knife!" I screamed, but he ignored me. He snatched up the knife and made a wild leap for the ladder to escape before the explosion. The first rung snapped under his right foot, but he was already trying to find the second rung with his left foot. That rung also broke, and I watched in horror as a third rung also snapped, dropping him back onto the clay bottom of the pit. In desperation, he jumped at the remains of the ladder, grabbed it, and rode it up out of the well just ahead of a volcanic explosion of clay clumps and, just behind, the suddenly airborne tripod.

After the explosion, he and I both lay on ground near the pit—shaken, but unhurt. We picked clay out of each other's hair and silently marveled that we had arms left to do so. As we sat, we could see and hear small bits of clay still filtering down through the leaves of the nearby oaks. And we could see pieces of the ladder scattered about the area.

We hoped this final blast would do the trick and water would rush into our well. If not, it would be painfully discouraging after so much work. We had spent the better part of our summer after-noons—after Jim finished lobster fishing for the day and while I took a two-hour break from working at The Mayfair House—slowly creating this pit. And all of a sudden here it was September of 1949 with the misty mornings promising an early fall. I was just twenty and Jim was twenty-two. We had married the previous fall and my parents had carved out this five-acre piece of land from their property in Bremen as a wedding gift. The spot where we chose to build our log cabin was about a half-mile from my parent's house, and we would not have any electricity or running water. Our heavily wooded land was located off a seldom used dirt road that had deteriorated to little more than a path as it wound up a long, steep hill and wandered easterly for three miles through thick woods until it came out on the tarred road of Route 32.

It was already September, and we still needed to built our log cabin before winter. The spruce logs we planned to use for walls were still standing as trees in the forest. We had not been able to cut them and start building because summer was really the only time we could work and earn money. We had to make as much money as we could before we could devote our days to building our new home. By stealing a few hours each day during the summer, we had dug the well, and cleared trees and underbrush from the spot where our cabin would sit.

Our part of the Old Shore Road, as it was called, had once been a main traveling route along the shore of Greenland Cove and Muscongus Bay. Old cellar holes on and around the property attested to the activity that once existed there. Just beyond the stone wall that marked the boundary of our property lay the foundation of what had once been a general store, post office, and dance hall. It was a long time ago. Forty-foot pine trees now flourished inside the foundation walls. Several hundred yards from the foundation was the cellar hole and stone arches of what was once a large farmhouse. Now, only a few old apple trees in a small patch of field, fast giving way to pine trees,

Jim and May's log cabin under construction in the fall of 1950.

was all that remained of the farmland. In springtime, the plumes of purple and white lilacs spread their fragrant glory, hiding the granite and bricks that once supported a fine home.

If we looked to the east we could see occasional glimpses of Muscongus Bay through the trees. Webber Pond was a mile through the woods to the west.

It was beautiful, but digging the well was going more slowly than we hoped. And worse, despite Jim's narrow escape following his last dynamite blast, the well was still not filling with water. We put the broken tripod and ladder remains on a brush pile to burn and we gathered the pick and shovel with which Jim had laboriously chipped away bucket after bucket of clay. We hoped maybe the lack of water was just because of the long, dry summer. Surely, fall rains would fill it. That was our hope, anyway.

Regardless, it was time to move on and start cutting the logs for the house. The following day, taking an ax and one-man cross-cut saw, Jim went to a wood lot six miles away. We had purchased the standing trees on the lot for twenty dollars. We had saved barely one thousand dollars to build and outfit our home, so finding materials to build the main part of our house for only twenty dollars was a blessing and fit nicely into our budget. We successfully found other items to fit our budget as well. Our furniture was waiting in a corner of the barn down at my parents' inn. We had ordered kitchen tools, a combination coal and wood cookstove, and material for curtains from the Sears catalog. At Robert Foster's weekly summer auctions in Round Pond, we bought a green-gold velvet-covered couch, curved at one end, for $1.25, a hand-made quilt for seventy-five cents, a huge feather-erbed mattress for $1.50, a bed and box spring for $2.00, two dining benches and a table for $6.50, and finally two chairs, some dishes, and a large wool rug for prices too small to remember. Our total furnishings cost us less than $250, leaving us $750 to spend for roofing, boards, spikes, nails, odd hardware, a brick fireplace, and a chimney (the chimney was the one thing we didn't plan to build ourselves), and a few bales of oakum for caulking the logs. It all seemed feasible.

Working afternoons that fall, Jim cut and trimmed the logs in less than two weeks. After the logs were dropped next to the ledges where we planned to build our house, it seemed our dream was truly beginning to take shape.

A good friend of ours who lived in Chamberlain, which was about twelve miles away, came to share his log cabin building knowledge with Jim. Our friend Walter Watts had built several such houses for summer people, and one of those houses was our ideal design. Walter was a short and rotund, cheery man with small merry eyes and abundant white curls above his ears, which he said, made him feel like a "Foxy Grampa." To stay within our budget, we could only hire Walter for a few days.

We built the cabin "stockade" fashion, meaning the logs stood upright, not horizontal. We felt this would better shed water that is inclined to accumulate on the surface of horizontal logs. The cabin would be roughly twenty-four feet by twenty feet.

To prepare the logs, Jim laid them on sawhorses. I straddled them and peeled off the fresh bark with a spokeshave. Meanwhile, Jim measured, cut, stood, and then bound the logs in place with twelve-inch spikes that he pounded in horizontally with a sledgehammer. At the end of each day his arms felt like they had grown longer from swinging the heavy hammer. And I was sure I would become bowlegged from sitting astride logs all day peeling the bark.

We worked dawn to dusk. At lunchtime, we leaned against the growing walls of our house to savor a peanut butter sandwich and a thermos of hot tea. We would anxiously smell the wind and scan the sky to see if the good weather would hold until we finished the roof.

By late September, tourist season had ended at my parents' inn where we were living. They were glad to rest and enjoy some freedom after working seven days a week providing meals and housekeeping for up to fourteen guests at The Mayfair House for the entire summer. Our duties at the inn were light during the fall, and our young bodies were ready to tackle the exciting task of building our dream home each day. We were both slender; I was five-feet-two and Jim stood a good six feet tall. Steady physical work each day had made us strong and fit.

Anyone who has ever built even the simplest house knows the satisfaction as every nail is pounded, and the excitement as walls rise, and as newly installed windows let in the sunrises and the light that establishes the character of each room.

Since we would have no power or running water, our progress was not slowed to deal with plumbing and wiring. The power lines were simply too far away in both price and distance to make electricity feasible, and even as fall arrived there was still no water in our well. As a back-up water plan, we painstakingly cleaned out a rocked-in well near the abandoned farmhouse foundation, maybe two hundred yards away, and thankfully some autumn rains were slowly filling it. The well wasn't actually on our property, but it was our only choice.

Five weeks out from the day we started building the house, the roof was on. Next were tedious days with caulking irons and hammers pounding the tarred oakum deep between the logs and into every crack or crevice where daylight could be seen. Jim also made two doors from split logs. A local mason built us a beautiful fireplace with a high, noble mantelpiece. In our minds, we already pictured our future children hanging stockings on it. Our white enamel coal and wood stove from Sears was hooked into the back of the same chimney that formed part of the wall between kitchen and living room. The bedroom and kitchen were the same size and took up half the cabin's floor space; the other half was our living room. Per our dreams, the living room opened to the roof cathedral-style. There was a loft formed by the ceilings over the kitchen and our bedroom. A golden stringer log ran from wall to wall in the living room, and a kerosene lantern hung from its center. The big fireplace and the kitchen stove provided our only heat. We saved all the wood we cut from clearing the land for the cabin to use that winter.

Jim built kitchen cabinets, created counter space on either side of the sink, and made a table that hinged to the wall—giving us extra floor space when it was folded up. A bucket placed under the sink and hidden behind a cabinet door served to catch everything that went down the sink drain. We had neither time nor money for a fancier setup.

When the primary structure was completed, we swept up the mortar dust, brick chips, sawdust, and bits of oakum. I scrubbed the pine floors with Fels-Naptha soap until they were white, and we spread the worn wool rug in the living room. I looped swags of red chintz dotted with blue sailboats around the windows for curtains and a dash of color. And just like that, our six weeks of building was finished.

Even though the cabin was small, there was plenty of room for my precious upright piano, given to me by a kindly music teacher, as well as our couch, a small maple chair, and the dining room benches and table.

A dresser, whose drawers opened grudgingly, a bed Jim had crafted with our auction-bought mattress, and a built-in night table furnished the bedroom. A long shelf with a pine rod under it and a curtain across it provided our clothes closet. In addition to the stove, two chairs by the folding shelf-table and dishes put away in the cabinets took care of the kitchen.

Finally, a year after we were married, our life together in our first home began on a Saturday. My Scottish mother quoted in concern an old saying, "Saturday's flitting is a quick sitting." We assured her we knew we would live there forever and we believed it. She provided a fine meal, and we ate it together in front of our fireplace, which easily overpowered the chill of the late fall evening.

The kerosene lamps were polished and glowed softly, their light reaching only partway into the velvet darkness that hung from the roof peak of the living room. Flickering flames from the open fire reflected off the tawny walls. The scent of the fresh-cut spruce and the smoky tar smell of oakum pervaded pungently and pleasantly.

A rich couple settling into their twenty-room mansion of marble and oak could not have felt more exultant than we did on that first night as we sank into the warm depths of our bed under a patchwork quilt, surrounded by walls and a roof we had built with our own hands. We listened contentedly as a spot of pitch sang in the last of the fireplace logs.

CHAPTER 2

A Long Cold Winter

WE WERE HAPPILY settled into our dream house, but an unwelcome reality soon came knocking. It seemed no matter how much we tried to stay within our budget while building the house, unforeseen expenses finally shattered it. Yes, we had our home, but our savings were gone—and we were in debt. We'd both been raised to consider the word "debt" synonymous with "failure." Our European-born parents viewed our debt status with grim disapproval. Despite their tight-lipped warnings, we knew if we hadn't borrowed five hundred dollars to finish the fireplace, we would not have any heat, and, of course, our cabin would not be habitable.

So, it was with anxiety and dry mouths that we visited the local bank to borrow money with our very first mortgage. It was scary to think we could lose our cherished home and land if we couldn't make our payments. Throughout our young lives we had paid attention to the good advice our parents had offered through the years. But we were also mavericks.

In our heart-to-heart talks at the ages of sixteen and seventeen, when we first met, we recognized in one another a yearning for the freedom to enjoy the magnificence of Maine—unhampered by mundane words like "security" and "steady job." We knew that no matter how many years of life we were granted, it would never be enough to fully savor life in Maine, and so we had best get started—money, success, and prestige were not our goals.

"As long as it's honest work, we don't care what we do to live in Maine" was our mantra. Our only wish was to live together surrounded by Maine's unmatched beauty—beauty on the sea, in the forests, and by the lakes, all far away from the drudging filth and congestion of cities.

We signed the mortgage papers and looked for jobs.

We owned a sixteen-foot dory and a five-horsepower Johnson outboard engine that weren't adequate for Jim to go lobster fishing in wintertime. Greenland Cove was frozen over anyway. Jim's wood-cutting skills netted him a job with two aspiring young men, Jeff and Paul Fortin, who were starting a small lumber mill. He started work at six in the morning and spent his days cutting great pines with an ax and crosscut saws.

The first thing he did after arriving at a woodlot each morning was light a fire from branches cut the previous day because the steel wedges and axes were so cold they needed to be heated before use or they would break. After they were properly warmed, Jim would throw the saw, ax, and wedges under the snow-laden branches that hung from a big pine or spruce. He would then crawl under himself to get at the tree's trunk. His efforts were sometimes rewarded with a frigid snow shower, the snow usually finding its way between the layers of his clothing, which then remained wet for the rest of the day.

Jim used his ax to first chop out a wedge at the base of the tree to prevent the saw from binding under the weight of the tree as he cut. Then he and another man would bring the tree down with the saw. Jim's partner was an older, wiry French-Canadian woodsman named Jacque LeBeau. The first day of work, LeBeau's dark-bearded face broke into a grin and his black eyes glinted as they each picked up their end of the saw. Jim soon found out why. Jim was young and LeBeau thought he was also green and probably good for a laugh.

Using a cross-cut saw, which features two upright handles on either end, requires teamwork to establish an effective rhythm of pushing and pulling. The effort must be equal and the down pressure not too great or the saw will stick and bend.

Jacque must have worked with men who thought they could let him do most of the pushing and pulling, and he had devised a method of hauling the saw back so swiftly that his unwary partner's knuckles were slammed into the tree. In trying to develop a smooth pattern with this new partner, Jim found his knuckles being rapped immediately in the man's swift pullbacks. It happened only a few times before Jim caught onto Jacque's game and returned the favor. By the end of the day Jacque was as happy as Jim to sharpen the saw once more, oil it, and put it away in the horse hovel.

The hovel, a shelter for the horses, was built using mill ends and poor-grade boards produced by the portable mill. It was easier to keep the log-twitching teams at the current woodlot than to transport them from home every day. When a woodlot was exhausted, the hovel and sawmill was moved to another lot. A typical lot usually lasted a winter or two.

Meanwhile, Damariscotta's Nash Telephone Company hired me as a telephone operator. I didn't have to be at work until 8 a.m. so while Jim drove our 1940 Ford Coupe to the mill, I walked a mile through the woods to Route 32 where I caught a ride with an elderly friend who passed by on his way to work. The lumber mill where Jim worked was forty miles away, so it was 6 p.m. in the evening before he could pick me up in Damariscotta to go home.

The first couple of weeks in December were better than we were able to appreciate at the time—we could drive to the door of our cabin. By late December, snow without mercy arrived and we had to leave the car parked just off Route 32 and walk the mile to get home. That mile was lined with pine, spruce and birch, its hills and curves glorious in the winter moonlight. If there was no moonlight, we carried a lantern to light the way. Before climbing the half-mile hill to the cabin there is a flat stretch that hugs Greenland Cove's edge, deeply rich with the marine smells of the tidal shore. It was usually an inspiring walk. Except, of course, when carrying sacks of groceries and the snow is knee-deep. Or when you have walked out to the car one day, and after groping through pockets, look at each other in helpless dismay and ask, "You mean you don't have the keys?"

Icy road conditions were the major reason for leaving our car out at the main road. In those days it was a long time before the town sand truck got around to the side roads. We solved our problems somewhat by using our two-passenger Flying Arrow runner sled that had brought us so much joy in past years. Basically our mile-long road was half uphill and half downhill, so we got to ride at least halfway in either direction.

The sled rides home to the cabin were the best and seemed the longest. Jim would hold the groceries between his knees, I sat behind holding him tightly. He weighed 150 pounds and I was 110 pounds, and with slick ice and a long downhill we picked up speed that barely allowed us to make the curves. As we streaked through the night the polished runners hit occasional stones and sparks streamed behind us. When we coasted to a stop at the foot of the last hill home, our

The log cabin that Jim and May built and lived in when they were first married.

cheeks were frosty white and our laughter bubbled in exhilaration. It is a small wonder we didn't end up a bundle of bones somewhere off in the woods at a straight angle to one of those curves.

Trudging the last half-mile of steep uphill while pulling the sled and groceries was less fun. There were times when keeping our footing on the ice was such a challenge that we would arrive breathless at the cabin to find that some of the grocery sacks had toppled and several items were missing. I would light the stove while Jim went back down the hill for a loaf of bread here and a bunch of carrots there. It was usually 8 p.m. at the earliest before we had supper ready; breakfast at 4:30 a.m. that morning seemed a long time ago.

We had to go to bed early every night to meet the next day's schedule, but we didn't have a radio and reading was difficult by the dim light of our kerosene lamps. We had one large mantle lamp that was brighter than the others, but we learned that trimming wicks for an even flame was an essential skill. One evening Jim fell asleep with a book in his hand, and I was so absorbed in a novel I didn't realize that the lamp was smoking until I stood up and could barely see through the black cloud. Jim's nostrils were outlined in black soot, and I had a dark greasy mustache. These were minor inconveniences compared to cleaning the smoky film that lay on the walls and other objects in the cabin. The clean-up served as a lesson in lamp care that remains with me still.

There wasn't much time for entertainment, but we appreciated even small diversions. We shared a mutual passion for cats, and one weekend Jim came home from an errand and handed me a half-grown, scrawny black cat with a white nose, chest, and paws. A lobsterman friend, Alfie Butler, had been willing to part with one of his dozen or so kitties. Joe's name had already been bestowed upon him. He had long legs, knobby knees and a long, stringy tail. He was a slouching adolescent, but he had a sweet face and charming disposition.

He was also a thief.

I made a custard pie one Saturday morning and left it on the counter to cool while we went out to cut firewood. It never occurred to me that Joe could be interested in anything but fish, meat, or milk. When we got home at lunchtime Joe was on his haunches beside the pie contentedly washing his face. His eyes were happy slits as bits of custard dripped from his whiskers. It appeared that he had eaten from the center outward, as all that remained was a narrow circle of custard around the edge. I would have been glad to give him a piece if he would have left us some too, but you can neither reason with or truly discipline cats, and we didn't try. My pies cooled behind closed doors after that.

We had jobs, but winter is the wrong time to start living in a rough cabin if one has a choice of spring and can enjoy the gentle summer months to make improvements. Fighting snow, cold, and ice enlarges each task. Our bathroom was the great outdoors. There were literally miles of forest around us with nobody in it, so privacy was no concern. The weather was.

Unlike many Maine people without indoor plumbing I could not bring myself to cope with a "slop jar" or chamber pot. I'd heard of too many accidents, and cleaning up with no running water was unappealing. We knew a couple who followed the old tradition. Nettie and Harold both worked away from home daily. While she washed the breakfast dishes, he emptied the "slops." They were running late one morning, and the outdoors was glittering after an all-night ice storm. Harold, slops in hand, moved hastily through the orchard to the wooded dumping spot. On the way he slipped, hitting an apple tree with his delicately balanced cargo, which emptied all over him on his way to the ground. It was a long while before he was fit to go to work that morning. Stories such these are immensely funny when they happen to someone else, but my sense of humor was limited when I pictured such a mishap befalling either of us with little water available for clean-up.

The outdoors remained our bathroom until a cold sunny weekend when Jim built us an outhouse. I thought it was beautiful—bright

pine boards, a roof that matched the cabin, and all just a comfortable distance away.

Jim built it so that the front was on a ledge, and the back was enclosed in an overhang beyond the edge of the ledge for easy clean-out. It was beside a massive pine tree whose branches hung just above the door, softly framing it. Inside was a neat little bench with a hinged cover and a small bag of lime. Following the pattern of the old outhouse at my parents' home, I tacked colorful calendar pictures around the inside walls.

Time proved that, outhouse or not, we still fell victim to the weather. The handsome snow-laden pine branches melted all over the doorway during the day, causing the door to freeze shut at night. We couldn't afford siding, and melting snow found its way through cracks in the walls and froze the seat cover to the bench. It was useless to visit the outhouse without a screwdriver to pry open the door and loosen the frozen seat. We kept this handy item hanging by the kitchen door.

Because of the overhang from the ledge, the distance from bench to ground below was considerable, and the enclosure acted like a chimney—the updraft was both frigid and forceful. Conversely, in summer it was a pleasant place and the wind soughing in the giant pine was soothing.

Late December snow and ice were nothing compared to the frigid polar air that clutched us in January and February. We learned the meaning of cold—its length, breadth, and intensity. Its glacial, boreal, skin-whitening, blood-slushing, bone-crunching, gut-freezing relentless eternity. In those months, a zero-degree day seemed toasty warm. Temperatures dipped to fifteen and twenty below zero, several times hitting forty below. We never had central heat in the old inn-farmhouse where I grew up, so I knew what it was like to go to bed with two hot water bottles and three sweaters on top of a flannel nightgown and still shudder under several blankets and quilts. But laying in a log cabin with half of it open to the roof was even colder. Our fireplace was lovely, but threw heat barely three feet from itself, and most of that was lost to the high ceiling.

Our kitchen stove was a malevolent beast. It provided heat in the kitchen only if we fed it with wood non-stop. It would hold a glorious coal fire, glowing with blue flame hovering over the fiery coals, but the stove guarded this treasure jealously and no heat escaped its firebox. It wouldn't boil water on its surface. Joe would creep into the open oven, left open in the wan hope of some heat emanating from it, and snuggle against the firebox. One morning when I sleepily arrived in the kitchen, I shut the oven door hoping to build up enough heat to warm some breakfast biscuits. Joe's black and white coat matched the mottled interior of the oven and I didn't notice him curled in its depth. Later when I checked for a build-up of heat, he shot out over my shoulder in a shrieking streak, legs, jaw, and eyes opened wide. Since it happened to be a coal fire, he was not overheated, but was very alarmed at the narrow, dark confinement. Thereafter I explored the oven before closing the door.

I found it a pleasure to go to work each day just to be warm. I loved being a telephone operator anyway. Jim's work was outdoors, but the action of wood-cutting all day kept him warm except when ax blows sent snow down his back.

Sleep also proved a problem, but not always from being cold. Sap in the green logs that formed our walls froze and exploded in vertical cracks. This "checking" is a natural drying process. The cracks are not deep and do no structural harm. But the explosion when they occur is like a rifle being fired past your ear. We rarely slept through the night, the noise was so sharp.

As they dried, the logs shrank just enough to let the caulking drop out. Daily we found places in the walls that afforded us an outdoor view so we regularly walked around with a hammer and caulking iron to fill them.

Webber Pond, about a mile through the woods, roared and thundered like a runaway freight train as its ice expanded and cracked. A glass of water left beside our bed would freeze and splinter by morning. We waddled to bed in all the clothes we could get on, and burrowed deeply into the feather tick, to no avail. One forty below zero night we thought the way to lick the situation was to get under the feather mattress instead of on it. It was so heavy we couldn't breathe properly; in fact, it was impossible to turn over under its weight. Feeling like two flounders, we crawled out on top of it again and tucked Joe between us for whatever warmth we could all share.

Because the kitchen stove wouldn't heat the room with coal, and somebody had to tend it constantly to keep its maw filled with wood, the cabin always felt like an ice cave when we came home at night. By late-January it seemed that cabin would never be warm again.

Getting water was another challenge. The well near the old farm foundation was six feet in diameter and a third full of water when winter arrived. It iced over in December, but with a long stout pole we kept punching a hole large enough to lower a bucket through on the end of a rope. When January's ice age came along, Jim climbed down the rock walls and chopped a hole through a foot of ice with an ax to give us access, but we were only home during daylight on weekends and it was too time consuming to spend an hour each night and morning chopping a water hole, so I brought water home in small jugs from the telephone company. I still can't believe how little water two people can get by on if necessary.

Weekends were mostly devoted to cutting wood for the following winter. There was enough hardwood on our land to last us for several winters. Although I could split wood with an ax, I didn't have what it took to chop down a tree. With several experienced swings, Jim could fell a tree in any direction he wished, and together we cut them into four-foot lengths with a crosscut saw. I learned from Jim not to push the saw into the wood but to guide it properly while letting it ride into the log by its own weight.

Jim kept it sharp and I enjoyed the teamwork as we pulled it back and forth and watched it sink into a piece of icy oak, spattering the snow with pink, bitter-sweet smelling sawdust. The best of our wood was near the sea. Salty ice cakes glistened in the thin winter sunlight, and the black spruce crests of Keene's Neck and Hog Island lay against the pale winter sky. Whenever I think my feet are cold, I remember a day on our woodlot and how cold it is possible for feet to become without actually freezing.

We were saving money to buy a new lobster boat with an inboard engine in the spring, so we cut every corner possible. My winter boots had given up, and the most complete footwear I owned in addition to what I wore to work was a pair of sneakers. Jim had two pairs of army boots from his service days, but his size elevens wouldn't fit my five and a halfs. I still love the light-footed feeling of sneakers and wear them year-round even now—but by choice, not necessity. Sneakers are not a good choice for wood-cutting at below zero temperatures. Canvas seems to conduct cold right to the inner workings of one's feet. I didn't give in that day, but I wanted to go home and stick my feet in that lukewarm oven so badly, I didn't care if we crystallized next winter without the firewood that would have been cut that day.

The depths of winter also provided splendid beauty at times. Moonlight on the pine-encircled frozen cove made it look like a great tray of glittering sugar, silvery frost crystals floating like winter fireflies in the brittle air. And the Northern Lights!

Some night I hope to see the Northern Lights again as they were on those February nights when we walked the icy road to the cabin. They flashed in ever-changing curtains turning from blue-white to brilliant red, pinks and yellows. The veils then drew together and hung in a complete and surrounding circle from a fiery dome straight above. Still shimmering and blazing they began to crackle and then to roar, the sound swelling to crescendos that made us think the world might be approaching an end. Although we were awestruck it was too beautiful to be frightening. We stood in the center of this magnificent scene for nearly an hour forgetting the cold.

CHAPTER 3

The Blessed Arrival of Spring

WINTER WAS FINALLY fading, but that first year March arrived in a snarling rage of fang, claw, and bellowing winds.

Rain streamed horizontally before blowing gales that lasted for two days. Winter's snow disappeared in flooding torrents. Trees snapped and broken branches flew through the air. After the first spring storm, we couldn't get to work; it was a full day before Jim could clear the fallen trees from the road sufficiently for us to get to my parents' home to check on my father.

My mother loved to travel, but always combined it with employment at her destination. This particular winter she was working and living in California. There was a long-standing and agreeable arrangement between she and my father, who possessed no wanderlust, that when she wanted to spend a winter away she would leave for a few months while he stayed to cut the firewood they burned all year round, as even cooking for summer guests was done on the woodstove. My mother cooked and baked nearly everything that went on her table on that woodstove. Even after she bought an electric stove, she still considered the new one merely a "standby."

I walked up to my father who was standing on a high point outside the house. He was not tall, but was muscular and stalwart with a clean profile. His arms hung by his side as though he didn't know what to do with them. Wind whipped his hair and he stared at me as I queried, "How is it going, Daddy?"

"This is the fuckiest day I've ever had," he replied in a quiet desperation. I had heard him use that word once before in my life when he didn't know I was around and he was struggling with the plumbing. However, I had never heard anybody use this particular variation. His list of problems was long, and his reactions vivid. He was a placid plodder who could lift anything that needed to be lifted, grow anything that could be planted, and outwit any animal that could be trapped, but my diminutive mother was the creative problem solver, the optimist, the organizer, the dynamo, and without her he was clearly and literally loose in the winds.

The power was off, the food in the freezer had thawed, and the cellar (along with the freezer) was flooded. Shingles had blown off the roof, which now leaked. He just didn't know where to begin, so Jim and I pitched in and soon the chaos had subsided several degrees. When we finished mopping up the water, we went on down the road with an ax and cleared ourselves a path to work for the following day.

Later in the week I visited my dad again. Walking into the kitchen I faced a stench so vile it was a living presence clutching at my throat. I knew he liked experimenting with creative dishes when Mother was away, but no human being could remain in the same room with this. He was at the sink immersed to the elbows in a dreadful mélange from which he appeared to be extracting bits of meat.

He looked at me happily, gore dripping from his hands as he rested his elbows on the sink, and explained that he had rescued a

Great Blue Heron from a fox down at the shore, but the heron was so badly mangled it died soon afterward. Dad speculated that if the fox liked a heron dinner, he might prefer it cooked, and he was preparing tasty bait for a fox trap. The trapping (he was a great trapper) he did during the Great Depression helped measurably in winter income, and it was part of the hunting instinct he developed as a boy on his family's farm in Lithuania. As it turned out even the foxes turned up their noses at this foul-smelling concoction, but things were definitely back to normal with Dad.

As the March winds softened, so did the ground. The Shore Road became a morass of mud. In my school days this condition was a source of delight. None of the town roads were paved and transportation ground to a standstill. Schools were closed, and "Mud Vacation" could last days or even weeks. Winter sports of skating and sledding had passed, but nature was coming to life again. Even though we were essentially alone while growing up—our nearest neighbor was a mile away—I was never lonely as a child. There were newborn calves to hug, baby chicks and ducks being brooded, and clams to be dug between the shrinking ice cakes. I have always been mindlessly happy around saltwater. Exploring the shore and observing its unique inhabitants, reading stories about the origins of objects left above the tide line following the winter gales provided boundless fascination.

Now as an adult, attempting to drive on a dirt road in mud season is an irresistible challenge. There were no four-wheel drive vehicles to dull the sense of personal accomplishment if you made it through. It was thrilling to engage our little Ford in second gear and maneuver over that hilly, narrow, twisting road, attempting to stay between the previous ruts while avoiding the bottomless shoulders. Occasionally we roared through sloughs whose depths we never plumbed because

The Mayfair House on Greenland Cove as it looked in the 1950s.

we learned early on that constant speed is the only way to stay afloat. The trick is to remain on the road, yet never let up on the accelerator lest you sink on the spot.

Before the final hill to our cabin there was a flat stretch. Like the rest of the road it was a one-car track, but this part was cut into the side of a steep hill with a twenty-foot drop into the sea just off the running board, and there was no fence. This was the muddiest spot of all since overhanging pines didn't let the sun through. Faint hearts stopped here, or in an effort to avoid the precipice, they hugged the hillside too closely and skidded sideways into a semi-concealed narrow bog. When someone slipped into the bog, the vehicle remained mired until the end of mud season because not even a team of horses could rescue it.

We slewed along through flying gobs of mud, catching our breath when she started to bog down. We seldom got so stuck we couldn't dig ourselves out. Jim did the driving when we were together, but I had learned to drive on this road when I was twelve years old, and mud season was my favorite condition for the very challenge of it. I would still prefer it to big city traffic.

Spring eventually brought a softer wind, a tender blueness in the sea and the jubilant clamor of the gulls. There is no other time of year when a gull's cry is so piercing or so welcome.

Clams abounded in Greenland Cove's tidal flats, and as the ice drifted out to sea, we dug them eagerly and feasted on their sweet richness. Steamed and dipped in butter, we devoured them. We drank the liquor they were steamed in; we nibbled the connecting sweetmeats from the shells, we licked the dripping juices from our wrists. We ate bowls of them at a sitting. With little time lost between shore and cooking pot they lost none of their superb flavor. We didn't clutter these clam-eating orgies with bread, tea, or conversation. Silence was interrupted only by the clatter of shells into a bucket. We ate not with the hunger of starvation, but with a hunger for freshness of food that was not salted deer meat or root vegetables.

On one occasion just a few days after gorging on clams, Jim came into the cabin with a bucket of well water and said, "Tide's out, fog horn's sounding on Manana, and I can hear the bell buoy as the wind shifts. Probably we're in for several days of rain, how about going down to the cove for a few clams?"

Without hesitation I replied, "If you get more water for steaming them, I'll have the clam hods and hoes ready!"

Forgetting a recent oath to swear off clams for a while because we had eaten so many, we were soon immersed in the aromatic blue flats. The short-handled, tined hoes were sunk into the soft clay-like mud.

"Don't bother digging around that ledge," Jim called, "over here— they're big and fat, my hod is almost half full."

I slogged over through the sucking mud to join him in his find of the mother lode. In the spring of 1950, there were seemingly bound- less clams in Greenland Cove.

Spread-legged and bending, we exclaimed over the size of the clams and wiped our faces with muddy hands as they spit long streams of saltwater at us before we lifted them from the flats. Straightening up to rest for a moment, we took note of the increasing southeast wind, which was bending the spruce tops.

When our hods were full we put the clams into an old piece of fish net, tied it off with a long length of pot warp and secured it to an oak tree. Lying on a huge ledge, the bag of clams would soon be cov- ered and washed clean by the incoming tide. Then we would retrieve them and take them home for a satisfying banquet. It was only in spring that we celebrated food in this fashion, when the craving for fresh seafood and new greens from the mellowing earth is unmatched. Dandelion greens and fiddlehead ferns sent us into the same frenzy. Fresh produce was not available in local stores then as it is now, so by winter's end the inner soul and body as well as taste buds are des- perate for change.

CHAPTER 4

Gone Fishin'

MUDDY CONDITIONS IN the woods ended the sawmill operation where Jim was working. The owners, having more profitable options for the coming summer, would not restart the mill until fall. This worked out well as Jim had a number of lobster traps to repair and had purchased stock to build one hundred new ones.

Throughout the winter Jim knit potheads from rough green marlin twine. The base he worked from was a ten-penny nail driven into the framework of my sturdy old piano. The best light we had hung there, and it was companionable to watch him looping the twine as it unwound from the flat wooden needle, and pulling the knots tight over the smooth mesh board he had made. Lobster traps were known as "pots," and the net entrances to them as "heads," so we called them "potheads."

I played the piano between filling needles for Jim. I never could master the art of knitting heads, and the marlin twine took the skin from my fingers. In addition to those needing repairs, the hundred new traps all required three heads each, two for the "kitchen" end of the trap where the bait bags hung and the lobsters entered looking to eat, and one for the "parlor" end where the lobsters moved after

Jim with Mundy in the dory. Jim rowed this dory to fish before powering it with a five-horsepower Johnson outboard motor.

eating and could not escape. The plan was to have the traps ready for the spring "crawl," usually beginning in May.

The spring air was sweet with the scents of wet bark, melting snow, and the dark richness of newly uncovered earth. The pussy willows, downy and silvery velvet, burgeoned thickly on their smooth twigs. Evenings were filled with the lyrical whistle of the peep frogs, while loons spoke their nostalgic calls as they flew over the cabin between lake and sea.

In May, a crimson-coral mist flushed over the low-lying woods where the swamp maples were in flower, and soon the gold-green smoke of new poplar leaves rose in towers among the dark spruce. The small field at the shore where we were rigging our lobster traps was spattered with gold coins of dandelions, the spilled treasure of the season. Jim patiently showed me how to make the "walnut" knots necessary for tying the heads into the traps. He measured lengths of tarred pot warp and attached them in the form of a bridle to the end of the traps. The wooden buoys, painted our registered colors of red and white, were knotted to the other end then coiled neatly and placed inside the "parlor."

When our string of lobster traps was complete, the graying old ones, some speckled with bright new laths, and the golden oak of the new ones with their deep green heads, were stacked in tidy rows. They were ready to set except for adding the stone ballast necessary for extra weight to sink them until they became waterlogged. We collected these from the beach and put them in the boat when setting day came.

Using some of our winter savings we were able to buy stock for new traps and still had $175 left to buy a better boat. We bought a twenty-two-foot boat with an inboard engine to replace our small dory. The boat's age was unknown, but she would enlarge Jim's fishing range and the number of traps he could fish. We bought her from a lobsterman in New Harbor who had built himself a new one. The boat had an open cockpit with a canvas sprayhood. On the ride back from New Harbor, I sat on the engine box under the sprayhood looking out at the stinging blue of an early May sky. The cream-colored rocky coast supported dense spires of dark spruce, and gulls mewed overhead riding the wind like scraps of blowing white paper. My sheer joy was barely contained.

The boat's engine was a small Gray Marine in a Starr block. It rumbled quietly, sometimes bubbling on a louder note from its waterline exhaust as the ground swell lifted and dropped the hull.

We painted the boat and named her *Sea Foam*. At high tide, Jim brought her in to the sloping ledges of the shore, and we loaded on what traps she would hold, making a modest start to the season. By early July our entire string of one hundred or so traps would be set. In spring, lobsters are slowly beginning to come into the warmer protected waters to shed their shells.

Jim caught few lobsters at first, but did catch a lot of Maine's hard shell crabs. He didn't catch enough to sell, but to us they were another exquisite gift from the sea—we enjoyed them steamed and dipped in butter and lemon juice, or in a crab chowder with a touch of tarragon, or as a crabmeat salad. We dined in glee and glory.

Until lobsters became more plentiful in early summer, Jim joined a couple of local lobstermen and also went herring seining. Herring appeared sporadically, but schools of other fish often came into the calm waters and rich feeding ground of Greenland Cove. When they did, they were kept from leaving with the ebb tide by a huge stop seine the fishermen strung across the cove.

A stop seine is a long, deep length of netting capable of reaching a half mile, and in the 1940s and 1950s it was supported at its top on the water's surface by six- to eight-inch rounds of cork placed closely together and weighted at the bottom with lead weights. This type of seine was used to "shut off" a cove, bay, or river inlet. When large schools of fish were spotted heading into one of these areas on an incoming tide they were allowed to enter, then the seine was tied to several large trees, dropped out of the big seine dories length by length, and rowed to the opposite shore to be secured, effectively "stopping" the herring, sardines, menhaden, blue-backs, kiaks or whatever fish entered, from returning to the sea. While the fish pushed against the netting to try to escape on the ebbing tide, one end of the seine was released and pulled around to form a pocket. The fish were

Jim hauling a lobster trap. You can see the three mesh heads that Jim knitted in the winter: two leading into the trap, and one leading from the "kitchen" into the "parlor."

bailed by dip net into the empty dories, or into the hold of a fish carrier, known as a "smack."

In the spring of 1950, Jim and two other lobstermen made good catches, including some small fish then considered a "trash" fish and used for cat food and lobster bait. If the overall catch was not large enough to be picked up at the cove by the cannery "smack," it was hauled to Port Clyde in dories. Jim had the only power boat in the group. Many of the lobstermen who fished inshore but not in wintertime still used powerless dories while Jim's long-range plan was to go offshore so he could fish for lobsters year-round.

Port Clyde was some forty miles up the coast. Typical of these voyages is one I will always remember. The water at the edges of Greenland Cove was black in spruce shadow as the breaking dawn began to cast silver and rose on a flat calm sea. Three big dories had been arduously loaded with bluebacks the night before. They were tied end to end and anchored in the cove. Jim secured them by tow line to *Sea Foam*, which also had a fair load of fish on board. Ever will I see that little boat laboriously coaxing those laden dories into motion. Her effort and her own load pulled her down in the water to the washboards. In the early morning light, Jim appeared to be standing on the surface of the water itself with a steering wheel in his hands. There was no room for anyone to go with him.

Like any wife of a seafaring man, I didn't watch him out of sight. It took a greater power than avoidance of bad luck to bring him back safely from such trips.

Not every seining attempt went smoothly. We did not have a CB radio in those days, but word had still drifted along that large schools of fish were spotted about twenty miles up the coast and were heading toward an inlet that extended inland for about five miles. It was above what is known as Hockomock Channel, which flowed into a large broad cove, and then into a narrow river for several miles.

Two other fishermen, Leslie and Mac, and Jim agreed this could be a good catch to keep for lobster bait as well as selling to processors. The three of them took the nets, big dories, and *Sea Foam* up above Medomak, through the Hockomock and into the Medomak River. They got there late afternoon and stretched the seine across the river at the high tide mark, securing it to trees along the river bank. This took several hours and the timing was right for the ebbing tide to return the fish down river. Their escape was now shut off.

"As the fish began hitting we could tell by the bend in the twine that we had bitten off a mighty mouthful," Jim said. "The twine kept bellying and pulling at its ties."

Leslie estimated there to be a hundred ton or more, and they couldn't handle that many fish given that each dory was only capable of holding two to three ton. The trio decided to drop one side of the twine and let some of the fish out, until Leslie figured they could handle what was left and they tied the twine off again.

Jim said, "The tide runs about six hours and we were already three or four into the dropping tide. The fish continued to belly the seine and Leslie said, 'It's gonna be a long night!' What we hadn't reckoned on was that being so far up in the river so there was no water once the tide went out. It was ten o'clock and pitch dark. We were up on and surrounded by mudflats a ways up river and down. There were fish strung out on the flats for a mile or so. This situation is what fishermen call a 'dry twine.'"

"With no water left to float the fish, we were struggling around in the thick mud that sucked at our rubber boots every step, and with bushel baskets we were picking up fish and dumping them into the now grounded-out dories. Never having been in this mess before, we had no flashlights, and it was only by starlight and feel that we found the fish as we pulled our feet out of the mud step by heavy step. Our biggest hazard was the hundreds of horseshoe crabs also stranded on the mud. They kept lifting their long and razor-sharp spiked tails, causing agonizing pain if they pierced a hand or foot."

"We worked frantically all night. When the tide began coming in again there were still tons of fish everywhere. We tied the dories in a string to *Sea Foam* and I took off, returning by late morning. Leslie and Mac had the seines still tied off on the riverbank so the fish wouldn't float down river."

The fisherman worked around the clock for three days cleaning up all the fish by picking them up off the flats at low tides and out of the seine when there was water. None of the catch was wasted.

In the spring of 1950, Jim upgraded his lobster boat from the dory to Sea Foam, *which had an inboard motor and a center console.*

"We had barrels of salted down lobster bait, and after selling the rest for ground fish meal we had some money left for trap stock. The three of us were pretty tired but it all turned out to be worth it," Jim said.

In the early 1950s, and long before, most of the lobstering in the bays, rivers, and coves was still being done in fourteen- and fifteen-foot dories or the famous Peapod rowing boats. Lobstermen rowed these forward while standing up. This made sense as the lobster pot buoys could be easily seen, and there was no need to jump up from a seat every few minutes. These small but seaworthy boats allowed fishermen to get close to shore among the rocks and ledges where the shedding lobsters were. Jim had rowed his dory the same way until he bought his old, but reliable five-horsepower Johnson outboard.

Leslie, Mac, and Jim lobstered out of Greenland Cove. One elderly fellow, Seamore Simmons, came around the point from another cove and fished along these same shores. He was bent nearly double from so many years of rowing a dory forward. He always wore a battered fedora hat and yellow oilskin apron. A pipe was constantly in his mouth, and a bottle of home-brewed rum lay among his net bait bags. He was bright-eyed, quiet; high nose and chin met in his creased and weathered face.

Seamore had made a simple living with his dory and lobster pots. He had a small house on the shore and a barn that was home to a draft horse, cow, and a few hens.

Seamore planted a large garden each spring, and was especially fond of his turnip crop, which he referred to as his "turrups." The only vehicle he ever owned was a blue, four-door Model T Ford, and because of its limited use it was still going strong in the 1950s.

Every two weeks he took his wife, Hattie, to shop for groceries. It was a big occasion for both of them, but particularly for her, and she always wore her one black hat with a big pink rose on it.

Seamore's only self-indulgence was his homemade rum. But his lament was that he could never seem to let a batch age because it disappeared so quickly in the sampling.

Leslie told Jim that one year Seamore decided the cure for this was to make a big quantity of rum, set it on the floor of the hay mow and cover it with the hay he harvested in summer for the winter's feed. He believed this would guarantee the aging process. When Leslie asked Seamore the following spring how that plan had worked, he replied, "Well, say now, thet hoss an' cow et some good while the hay lasted, which weren't long."

Another day, Seamore and Leslie met in the cove as they were both coming in from hauling, Leslie came alongside Jim grinning and said, "Well, I jes took care of a problem."

When Jim asked how so, Leslie replied, "Started haulin' at daybreak yesterday an' when I got down along the shore to the Howland place, Bud Howland, he was standin' on his dock, and hollered to ask how things was going. I said, 'Well, can't understand it. I can haul from the cove clean down here and catch plenty of lobsters. From here on there ain't a counter in any of my pots.' "

"Well, Leslie," he says smiling, "I don't wonder, and I guess you won't be catching any neither so long as Seamore is hauling up the cove to where your trap strings meet!"

"So I said, 'that so?' "

"This morning when I met Seamore hauling down at the halfway point, I said to him, 'Seamore, guess ain't no use of me hauling any further to the southard, and I guess ain't no use of you hauling any further to the northard.' "

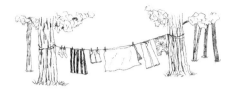

CHAPTER 5

Summertime

WINTER WAS GONE. Mud Season was over. And I was enjoying a warm and golden day. Tiny new leaves glistened like jewels against the sun. Bird song vibrated in the air. Two of Jim's army barracks bags lurked in a corner of the cabin stuffed beyond capacity with laundry. The rigors of existing on buckets of water from a dug well allowed only for cooking, dish washing, sponge baths and the lightest of laundry. Heavy clothing like blue jeans and shirts awaited springtime opportunity.

There were no automatic laundries in our area, and the expense of hand laundry was not to be considered. But I had a rugged old washboard, plenty of Fels-Naptha soap bars, the courage of a fool, and the lake was only about a mile away through a delightful woods path.

Jim was out hauling and setting new lobster traps, and the day was mine. Fels-Naphtha for the jeans, and a red cake of Lifebuoy for me found a crevice in a barracks bag. With this hefty burden plus the washboard I trudged through the woods. There was not a human for miles, and my spirit was singing in the soft breezes, almond-sweet fragrance of wild flowers and the comforting freedom and solitude of the forest.

The load was such that passage to the lake was not swift, and there were many diversions: A search for Lady Slippers, admiration of velvety purple violets, breaking off a knob of spruce gum pitch to chew on the way. The sun had climbed to warmth when I arrived at the lake. A small sandy-gravel beach was before me, and an island obscured any sign of civilization. It was my private shimmering lake on my planet.

The environmental impact of soap in a lake wasn't even thought of in the early 1950s, and I unloaded my laundry, wetting and soaping the jeans then weighing them down with several nearby rocks to give them a good long soak. Shucking my clothes, I unbraided my hair, worn below my waist in those days, took the Lifebuoy and dove in for a long, cool swim, a bath, and a shampoo. Lake water is soft, and no water I have experienced leaves such a clean feeling. I stretched out on a flat ledge to dry and to soak up the sun. I thought about how a few months ago the ice on this lake was roaring and thundering in its agonies of expansion in the subzero cold. Now the gilded heat of the sun belied those memories.

When the laundry was well soaked, I scrubbed it diligently on the brass ripples of the washboard sacrificing some knuckle skin in the effort, and wrung it out with all my strength. When all was stuffed back into the barracks bags, and the trail was before me, I quickly received the bad news that wet laundry is many times heavier than dry. I dragged and heaved the bags over roots and rocks, and after a few hundred yards decided the solution was two trips. Even for such an errand, I always welcome a walk in the forest, and before nightfall a clothesline among the trees at the cabin was flying a fresh-smelling wash.

As with all Maine summers, the summer of 1950 was passing swiftly. Lobstering was good, and the average price was twenty-five

cents per pound, gasoline about
twenty-eight cents per gallon.
We were making our mortgage
payments and even put away
enough money to pay for next
spring's trap repairs.

In a small pasture near the
dug well we spaded up a garden patch and managed to preserve what vegetables the deer
left for us, and harvested wild
blueberries. A few old Russet
apple trees lingered near the

May Davidson at age 18.

pasture verge, and those stored well in the always cold corner of the
cabin's living room.

Deer and moose were silent companions in our surroundings; we
would often hear the choking bark of a fox or occasional scream of a
bobcat on bright moonlight nights. One summer we heard a kind of
muted roar almost daily. It came from the direction of a large swamp
about a quarter mile away. In the fall we saw a black bear and her two
cubs traveling away from that area.

I enjoyed my job as a telephone operator with Nash Telephone
company in Damariscotta, and work days passed swiftly. There were
rewarding opportunities to be helpful, and the schedules changed often.
Even though newer head-sets were in vogue, we still used the ones with
the triangle chest piece and upward curving horn to speak into. Cum-
bersome, but they worked. The switchboard had only three positions
with twenty cord connections to each position. There was a toggle
switch in front of every connection, which we pulled back for the long

and short rings of the numbers used then, such as two long, ring three short, etc. Toll calls were recorded and timed by us on toll tickets— very confusing if there were several at once.

Thunderstorms were exciting. Occasionally actual blue flame darted around the switchboard, and once the whole thing tilted toward us then rocked back, at which point we scrambled for safety leaving the cords hanging in the jacks. The night operator managed the entire shift alone. There was a little cot in a nearby room for a rest when activity became quiet around midnight. When I was elected to replace her during her three-week vacation, Jim would sometimes come with me, and many nights he took half the positions and helped when every jack on the board was in use. It was a crazily woven tapestry.

CHAPTER 6

Browns Cove

OUR SECOND WINTER in the log cabin proved much like the first—relentless cold, constant battles with snow, and chopping an ever deeper hole through the ice for water. However, we had installed an oil-fired floor furnace to alleviate some of the cold issues and we found time to go ice skating and ice fishing for pleasure, not to mention the thrill of sometimes sledding to get in from and out to the main road.

Unfortunately, the lumber mill where Jim had worked the previous winter did not restart. As an army veteran under the GI Bill of Rights, Jim was eligible for education assistance and decided to learn the weaver's trade at Tenafly Weavers in Round Pond. Their materials were all wool and their designs were intricate and beautiful. Jim worked on a four harness, flying shuttle loom. He learned about heddles and treadles, winding a warp, and working his feet in the proper sequence according to the design pattern.

Learning quickly and well was vital. The weaving company was paid by the government for teaching the trade, and the company paid the weaving students by the yard. Weak points in the wool thread would break and had to be darned so delicately that the flaw was obliterated. Jim could always darn a sock better than I, when socks were actually

The house at Browns Cove in 1951.

darned, and he was of a mind to! He worked as a weaver for two winters and was frequently called back to repair looms when needed.

By spring, teaching was over and Tenafly Weavers opened their studio for the summer tourist trade. Like Jim, many of the weavers were veterans and lobstermen and ready to get back on the water.

During our second winter we met an out-of-state couple, a decade older than we, who had come into a modest inheritance and were looking for a reasonable shore property to buy so they could try their hand at lobstering. A favorite place we sometimes visited was the uninhabited old farm complex at Browns Cove in Bristol, which included many acres of land and several houses, all of which needed repair except for the main house, which was quite livable. The property was at the edge of a deep cove and offered breathtaking views over the islands of Muscongus Bay and on out to sea. The property had been willed to a Maine college, which listed it for sale at $7,500.

Our friends bought the Browns Cove property, which is about a mile off the main road and no other people lived there. They had not lived in this type of isolation, and when they purchased the property they offered to sell us an old, small, but reasonably priced and well-built house on a steep, rocky bank at the point of the cove. A narrow track was carved into the hillside approaching it, and the view of Monhegan Island, the sea, and other islands was incomparable. Beyond this lure, it offered a protected place to moor *Sea Foam*, and Jim could keep lobstering all winter. Greenland Cove froze solid, making lobster fishing impossible.

It was heart-wrenching to put our log cabin—our first dream house—up for sale, but in the spring of 1951 a family that owned Greenland Cove's Ram Island bought it as a summer guest cabin. It was our first home, and though primitive, it was built with our own hands, and helped us to prove our ability to withstand the elements.

Nearly three decades after we sold it, we saw an article in a newspaper in which a woman who rented the cabin wonderfully described the joy of our former home. She wrote:

"As I walked in, the first thing I noticed was the smell of old smoke, the lingering fragrance of the hundreds of fires that had burned there over the years. It was a natural, pungent smell, a Proustian evocation that brought back a flood of memories. The interior of the cabin and its surroundings were unchanged, remarkably unaffected by time. A couple of times we went to the lake where we swam and washed, sunbathed and fished. There was no sign of human life, a far cry from the madding crowd of New York. We feasted our eyes on the clean water, the clear air, the tall pines.

"At night we slept in the silence of pitch darkness with the fresh air blowing on our faces, and the only sound the occasional mournful cry of a loon, the loneliest and possibly the loveliest sound in the world. That cabin to me is the personification of Maine and Maine represents a state of mind. I love Maine because I love the way I feel when I am there. It is pure, rough and vital, wildly, gloriously beautiful, a heaven and a haven in one."

That spring, young and thirsting for new adventure, we tackled the project of making the Browns Cove house habitable. It had been vacant for many years, and squirrels had chewed on the window frames until the glass fell out, leaving the house exposed. There were three rooms downstairs and an open chamber, or attic, upstairs. An old wooden water tank outside caught rain and supplied the kitchen with gravity-fed water. The black iron sink was spacious and sported a drain to the outside, an improvement over the infernal catch bucket in our log cabin. An attached woodshed was a welcome addition, allowing us to keep our wood dry.

A roofed porch ran the length of the little house, and a dutch door from the bedroom opened on to it. From bedroom and porch we looked out to sea, spiked spruce islands, Monhegan's lighthouse, and the waters leading to Spain. Open ocean and cove were combined. *Sea Foam* lay where we could watch her in storms, and Jim could lobster year round. In ecstasy we plunged into washing, scrubbing, painting, and repairing with every hour we could spare.

In the lushness that is June we moved into this century-old home that now smelled of fresh cleaning and paint. A friend in Round Pond helped us move a couple of loads of furniture and belongings from the log cabin with his big dump truck. My upright piano was on the last load. The track to our Browns Cove house was hardly wider than the truck, the ledges of the hill on one side and steep precipice to the cove on the other.

There were dips and bumps. and the piano yawed and teetered, but our friend "griefed" the loads through and we grunted it all into place. We were content. The forest beauty that surrounded the cabin was exchanged for more forest coupled with views of open sea majesty. A better living from the sea was before us.

Even going to the outhouse was a delight. It was perched on a hillside at an angle behind the house that allowed a full view of islands and ocean. It had no door, and we never put one on. It wasn't possible for anyone to see us, and the seascape was too glorious to be obstructed.

A small chicken pen was attached to the outhouse. When we replaced the rusted wire on its open front, we bought a dozen white Leghorn roosters and made it their home. Though destined for the table by fall, they had an enviable life—an ocean scene to be coveted by the wealthy, fresh sea air, and fattening food. They summoned the dawn and mourned the sunset. They clucked companionably when we were using the outhouse, serenading us as we sat and looked out to sea.

The "road" to our house was not vehicle friendly, so we left the car at the main house belonging to our friends—only a five-minute walk through a clover-scented field, a delightful walk. One dark, moonless, starless night we were walking the path when we heard a thunderous crashing in the alder bushes. We had forgotten a flashlight, and the only way home was onward, so we continued foot-feeling our way, Jim chuckling and me with goose bumps as I clung to him tightly. The next day prints on the muddy patch on the path revealed tracks of a moose that decided to avoid us.

We spent an idyllic summer at the house. We ate suppers on the porch watching the boats, the weather patterns, and all that is the enchantment of the sea. Jim was out hauling at dawn. When I was not working at my phone operator job, I took dictation and typed for a prominent epidemiologist from Johns Hopkins who was summering nearby. Evenings were ours, and the sea's moon path to Monhegan Island seemed to belong to us alone.

When summer turned to flaming October and then somber, steely November, we kept warm by the wood fire and lit the rooms with kerosene lamps.

That fall, Jim set his lobster traps further and further out to sea as the lobsters kept crawling to deeper waters. Lobster was a steady food staple on our table and we prepared it in all conceivable ways: stuffed and steamed, and in chowders and stews. It was our cheapest meal and we never tired of it.

By late November, the weather proved fiercely savage for an old boat like *Sea Foam*. Her canvas sprayhood, basically a tent from bow to the engine box, provided the only protection from freezing spray and sudden snow squalls. When possible, I went out hauling with Jim. Even though I had thought it was cold in the log cabin, I soon discovered I had not yet felt the essence of cold. This cold at sea was not defined just by temperature; it included a beating by the elements of sea spray, wind, fog, and snow that laid ice over every surface and seemed to penetrate the arteries.

The engine exhaust vapors that curled under the sprayhood were nearly intolerable, but the frigidity beyond its edges was unendurable. Jim's buffalo plaid wool shirts, wool pants, oilskins and an extra pair of gloves always drying on the engine box offered him his only protection from the cold of dripping traps as he pulled them on board by hand, no hydraulic pot hauler in those days.

The handful of times I joined Jim in such conditions revealed to me the mortal dangers he and all lobstermen faced in winter seas. In that era, few lobstermen had a "stern man" with them, nor any radio to call for help if an engine quit and the anchor wouldn't hold or other emergency arose.

Lobsters not quickly placed in a bucket of seawater "shot their claws." The slender joint of the claw at the body would freeze and the claw would break off. This rendered the lobster a cull at a much lesser price. Not to be daunted, we wrapped such claws in aluminum foil, brought for the purpose, and placed them on the hot engine manifold to cook. They soon steamed to a luscious sea-richness, warm and satisfying to a body yearning for warmth and sustenance in this nearly arctic environment.

Sea Foam's old timbers and her faithful but mongrelized engine began to alert Jim that the heavy, brutal seas of approaching winter were going to be more than she could withstand. Jim had set his traps with the instinct of a good lobsterman and he was bringing in better catches than ever before, but it was obvious that year-round lobstering was going to require a bigger, high-bowed, broad-beamed, ruggedly built boat with the lines and endurance for the bigger seas and harsh conditions of a Maine winter. The boat also needed a more powerful and more reliable engine. *Sea Foam* had given us all she had to give, but we had to face reality—we needed a new boat. And the money to buy it.

As well as Jim had done that fall, the money for a new boat was not in the bank, and at this point we were still operating based on the old ethic of not adding debt if at all possible. We had paid the remaining mortgage on our log cabin when we sold it, while the balance of money for the sale had gone in to making the Browns Cove house habitable.

To see what might be possible, a visit with Jim's fatherly lobstering friend, Leslie Collamore of Greenland Cove, was in order. Leslie was also a boat builder and built handsome, able lobster boats that could rival any on the Maine coast. A Collamore hull was a proud thing to own. He built one every winter from his own special design, and each one was meant to be his. He was tired, he said, of pushing a dory around all summer. But come every spring someone always wanted to buy his work of sea-going art, and Leslie couldn't refuse them. In all his long life he never kept one of his own boats.

We visited Leslie to discuss dimensions, materials, and prices. Over the winter, Leslie said he could build a twenty-six foot hull for $1,200. Jim would then have to supply the cabin, and other items to finish the boat.

Leslie's wife, Jenny, worked at the clam factory or anything available, and Leslie lobstered. Each kept their own money. Jenny confided to me that she hated their outhouse, and wanted a real indoor bathroom in the house, but Leslie said he was content with the outhouse. If she wanted a bathroom she could pay for it herself, but she said, "Well, I ain't paying for no bathroom he's going to use, too!"

By the end of our visit, Jim and Leslie had agreed on a price and a plan. Next spring, we would take possession of a new lobster boat hull.

Now we needed to spend the winter trying to find a way to pay for it.

CHAPTER 7

New York, New York

WE WERE LOOKING at a minimum of $2,500 to build and finish off a new boat, a small fortune to us. *Sea Foam* couldn't provide it for us that winter even if she survived it for she could not go far enough out to sea for the lobster catches needed. My telephone operator's job was enjoyable, but offered meager money, barely paying enough to buy our groceries. The question was: Where could we make enough money for a new boat by spring? We quickly realized that, like many others, we needed to go out of state and find jobs for the winter. Unfortunately, New York City seemed like the best destination to accomplish what we needed.

The Browns Cove owners had never gotten around to signing papers on our house purchase, but all the money and labor we had put into the house was more than adequate rent to that point. We better understood the reason for their procrastination when they mentioned renovating the other buildings for summer tourist rental, and that ours sat in a prime spot for high summer income.

We liked the little house and we were energized by the view and proximity to the sea, but we also knew that it wasn't really a lifetime home for us. There was no land with it, and the steep cliffs were unsafe

May Davidson and The Blue Canary, the only convertible the Davidsons ever owned. They bought it when they went to New York for work.

for children. By sheer providence we drove by an old farm in nearby Chamberlain, part of which is known as Long Cove. We had admired it for years, and had recently seen a realtor's sign on it. Inquiring swiftly we learned that it had been in the same family for two hundred years, then some city people bought it. They wired it for power, installed plumbing and a drilled well, but then decided rural life was not for them after all and they headed back to the city.

The house featured seven rooms, two open chambers upstairs and a real bathroom! Low ceilings and wide pine boards added comforting charm to the old Cape Cod. To our joyful surprise it also included one hundred acres of fields and pine and spruce forest. Since Jim is a World War II veteran, we were eligible for VA financing after we paid a five hundred dollar down payment. The owners agreed to hold for a spring purchase agreement but would wait no longer.

Long Cove, with a town shore access, was only half a mile away and our new boat could be moored there. We were euphoric. We now had a new boat under construction and a house waiting for us come spring. Now we just needed jobs.

Our 1941 Ford Coupe had no more miles to give us so we traded it for the first, and last, convertible we would ever own. It was a snappy robin's egg blue, nicknamed The Blue Canary. It never ran true and eventually we learned it had been in a collision that damaged its frame. But it was dashingly pretty! We packed a couple of old suitcases into the car, and with silent tears I watched the coast, the fields, and my beloved pine trees disappear as we headed for New York City. I knew what it was like. I had been trapped (as I viewed it) in the city several times during my childhood when my parents went there to work during the winter. Those stays convinced me that I could never get far enough away from it. But now, if such a sacrifice as a winter in New York City would secure our future in Maine, then we would face it together.

We rented a room at the top of a five-flight walk-up in the Bronx to be our home for the winter. The elevated train screamed a few blocks away, and the general landscape consisted of dark, ugly buildings that seemingly stretched into infinity. You couldn't escape the constant roar of traffic. After living in the heaven of clean and unsurpassed beauty, I saw this as a world from Hell.

Again, Jim's army experiences served us well, as he quickly found work driving a truck that fueled aircraft for American Airlines at LaGuardia Airport. The job's particular appeal was that it allowed him to work as many overtime hours as he could stand. The drawback for many applicants were the long night hours in freezing temperatures, but Jim didn't mind the cold, so he regularly worked fourteen- to sixteen-hour stretches on the night shift.

The little three-position switchboard in Maine stood me no stead when I applied to Bell Telephone for work as an operator. It would have taken six months of training for me to be hired by Bell. We didn't know how long we would be in New York, but we prayed to be breathing Maine air again in no more than six months.

An employment agency had job openings for typist pools at what was then named National City Bank at 55 Wall Street. I had done some manuscript typing at home on my old dinosaur Royal Portable, and although I hadn't used shorthand in three years, I had enjoyed it in school. After passing the typing test at the bank, I found myself in a pool of fifty typists copying bank communications from around the world. The age of computers had not yet arrived, and the fifty typewriters clattered away. The work was stultifying and offered no challenge, but it paid the rent so that we could bank Jim's income for our lobster boat and farm.

After a month, I was offered the opportunity to work as a secretary for two financial analysts in the statistics department. It paid more money and sounded more interesting. My new bosses were two fine men. Mr. Kadri was humorous and jolly, while Mr. Wheaton was soberly serious. Both men read and analyzed daily reports on grains, hogs, and cattle markets. I never pretended to understand it.

I filed heaps of papers that had been waiting for someone like me and took their limited dictation. The office was tiny and cramped.

No windows. There hadn't been any in the typing pool either. Our three desks were so close to the wall that we nearly had to climb over them to be seated. Most of the space was occupied by filing cabinets.

When I had been there a week, Mr. Wheaton, the deadly serious one, was leaning back as far as his chair would allow, deep in thought, and tapping his teeth with a pen when his chair suddenly fell over on its back and slid part way under his desk. The chair had arm rests so Mr. Wheaton couldn't slide out sideways, and he was too jammed in to help himself upward. He was trapped like a seal in a stop seine. His face was fiery red, he was puffing and struggling, but he never smiled even though his situation was wildly comical. Mr. Kadri, with some help from me, managed to haul him out. I have never been able to control laughter, especially when I know I should, but I felt my job depended on a powerful effort to stifle, which I did until lunchtime.

After I had worked with the two men for a month, I was approached to work as a private secretary for a man who wrote the monthly newsletter for National City Bank. His secretary was leaving to be married. His office was posh, and my large desk area outside it had a window. Bricks were the only view, but at least it was a window. Another slight raise went with this promotion. I was reluctant to leave Mr. Kadri and Mr. Wheaton; we had gotten along very well together and eventually Mr. Kadri and his family visited us in Maine.

Norris O. Johnson, my new boss, had been the Treasurer General of Iran for thirteen years. He was tall and slender with hair and eyes the color of steel. His mind and manner had the cold sharpness of that same metal. He wore a grim and sardonic expression that was almost cruel in its severity. He was the most intimidating person I ever met. I was terrified of him and felt certain he would cast me out when he learned I was just a little know nothing from the woods of Maine with only a high school education.

If I had gone to college for ten years I could not have understood the complexities of what he wrote. The first day Mr. Johnson called me into his office for dictation my heart pounded, and my fingers were so cold with fright I didn't think I could hold a pencil. My steno pad was balanced on shaking knees and I yearned to flee. I forced a quick picture in my mind of Leslie building our new boat (which we had decided to name *Spindrift*); I could do this.

Fortunately, Mr. Johnson chose his words after long thought. No shorthand could be devised for most of them, and I was able to write them in long hand praying they were in the dictionary for proper spelling. Mercy was with me, for he did not complain, and told me I was to correct the galley proofs when they came in. The words may as well have been printed in Hindu, but I could recognize typographical errors. What saved me was that Mr. Johnson took long and frequent trips leaving me with literally nothing to do. I was overcome with guilt, but Miss McKeegan, an elderly secretary to one of the many vice presidents, told me to read a book, or write letters home if I wished, it was perfectly fine.

Miss McKeegan spent her summers on Monhegan Island, and I had a photo of it on my desk; another picture of our future farm was in a desk drawer. My typewriter pulled out from my desk, and Miss McKeegan called it my dory. Her kindness and her tales of summer people on Monhegan endeared her to me.

Working in a bank of this caliber was a valuable life experience. Miss McKeegan's boss's chauffeur came in from Long Island every afternoon to take the gentleman home. His uniform was sharply military: leather banded cap, jodhpur breeches, and highly polished leather leggings reached to his knees. He all but carried a whip.

Leaving this atmosphere, I descended into the filth and insanity of the subway system each night. At five o'clock, it appeared that a greater part of the city's population wanted to board the train from Wall Street to the Bronx. It was an hour of torture every day, starting with a pack of humanity that leaned forward as one unit when the trains pulled in. More than once I was herded aboard without my feet touching the ground.

A vice president who often passed my desk noted my photograph of Monhegan Island's majestic headlands and asked me where it was. I told him it was an island off the coast of Maine. He asked if people lived there, and I told him it was home to about twenty-five fishing and lobstering families. He looked incredulous and asked, "Do they have a police force?"

Surprised at his question, I answered, "Oh, no!"

"Aren't they afraid?," he asked, unconsciously taking a step backward.

"They depend on each other," I told him. "All they have to fear are the elements of the sea and weather, and they battle those together."

He walked away shaking his head at the thought of such frightful conditions.

My lunch was usually a red apple from the newsstand and often a walk among the cement canyons of Wall Street to the nearby East River. I could wander into a ship chandlery and look at a 14-9 wheel (propeller) such as Jim planned for *Spindrift*, run my fingers over the dock lines, and picture where Jim would be placing chocks and cleats.

Sometimes I ventured onto a balcony of the Stock Exchange and viewed the pandemonium of paper waving, shouting, screaming, and bell ringing. It was a scene of bedlam.

Jim worked nights and I worked days so our schedules did not allow us any time together. We sometimes passed in the hallway and we always left daily notes for each other. We did have one special day together. Jim had put in so many hours for American Airlines that he earned a free flight for two for one day to Washington, D.C. We had never flown, nor had we seen Washington. There had just been a violent American Airlines crash two weeks previously, but our noses had been steadily applied to the grindstone, and we craved a break. Having breakfast above the clouds was amazing. On the ground, it was cherry blossom time, which also assured spring was coming. We had only a few hours, but we walked the forty-four flights of the Washington Monument both ways. It was a memorable day and made us proud of our country.

By April our bank account had reached our savings goal. Leslie wrote that *Spindrift* was ready for her engine, and by this time Jim was literally collapsing to the floor in exhaustion because of his long working hours and lack of sleep. I gave the bank generous notice, and it was soon time to go home. It is true that happiness lifts the heart, I could feel mine rising in my chest and joy pouring from it. My entire time in New York I felt this dark fear that we wouldn't make enough money to return home to Maine. It was a fear I could not shake. Now, finally, the freedom, adventure, and glory of Maine was before us, while the miasma, clamor, and squalor of the city would soon fade further with every mile traveled and every bridge crossed. My soul howled for this return to what I consider the true country of God. I couldn't wait to cross the bridge at Kittery, open the windows, and inhale the Maine air.

And I knew it wouldn't be long. We left our apartment, packed The Blue Canary and drove under the train track heading toward Route 1 North—toward Maine! On our route out of New York City, we stopped at a red light and both leaned across the seat for a kiss.

Then Jim smiled at me and said, "Well, here we go. A new chapter!"

CHAPTER 8
Life on the Farm

It was late May before we could move to the farm. As we waited, we rented a shore camp from Leslie for a couple of weeks. Our wait was a little longer because the former owners forgot to turn off the water when they left. Water flowed out to meet us along with many kitchen floor tiles. Mops and buckets took care of it, and our spirits were still high. It was worth all this to have running water and a real bathroom. The well water was icy cold and still, the sweetest and purest I've ever tasted.

The house had endured for more than two centuries and we believed it would last a few more. The foundation consisted of granite rocks lined with brick. The central support was a double stone arch capped with a huge flat rock.

As we waited for our furniture, we didn't know what to look at first. We wandered outside to touch and feel, and to see and plan, and to absorb the fact that we now owned one hundred acres of field, spruce, and pine trees. We inhaled the scent of balsam fir, creamy-rose apple blossoms, the spicy sweet fragrance of the Balm-of-Gilead trees, and, of course, the nearby sea. The horse chestnut's blossoms vibrated with the humming of bees, and the old lilac tree was laden with budding purple plumes soon to add their glory to the air.

Suddenly, we became like two exuberant children released from months of confinement, and we said, "Let's play hide and seek!"

And we did!

We discovered great hiding places in the huge old cattle barn, carriage house, and woodshed. Mountains of work stretched before us, but we had a lifetime for it—without question we had found our "forever" home.

Walter Watts, who gave us fine tips while we were building our log cabin, and Lulu, his charming wife, were now our nearest neighbors. They were both small and in their seventies, but still so spry, vibrant, and so eager for adventure that even though there was a half century difference in our ages, we formed a joyful friendship that lasted until their deaths years later.

When we moved to the farm, Lulu and Walter welcomed us warmly with kind words and Lulu's melting apple pie. They turned a little sober though as they quietly told us they felt badly because they thought we had paid too much for the farm.

"Them city people you bought it from only paid seventeen hundred dollars." Walter announced, continuing "and the seven thousand, five hundred you've paid for it is pretty stiff."

Lulu shook her tight and perfect curls in agreement.

We knew they intended to be helpful, but they had lived a lifetime in their small home, and none of the houses in our immediate area had changed hands in many years. Lulu and Walter didn't realize the property values near the sea were rising and that the farm's previous owners had wired the house for electricity, drilled a well, and installed modern plumbing. The houses nearby had very little acreage compared to ours. Our mortgage payment was $53.43 per month. It did seem a little overwhelming given my weekly take-home pay for working six days was just $29.17. But my wages were supplemental; our main income came from lobster fishing.

Lulu still used kerosene lamps, and a black iron sink with a hand pump on one side of it, which supplied water from a shallow dug well. There was an outhouse attached by a hallway so it wasn't necessary to go outdoors. The pails of "otts" or garbage were stored in the hallway waiting for Walter to dig a hole in the woods to bury it all. In those days, most people took care of their garbage this way. Their baths were once a week in a galvanized tub in front of the kitchen wood stove.

Our biggest field was separated from the farm by Route 32. A smaller one, with several lovely old apple trees, sat alongside the house and was bordered on two sides by spruce forest. The tar road formed the fourth side. Our small field was badly overgrown with several years' growth of field grasses and was impossible to mow—even if we had had the equipment. The simplest method to clear the field was to burn the dead grass on a calm evening. I had a deep fear of this method for my father used to burn his field, wooded on three sides, and he torched it in several places at once. My mother and I begged him to do a stretch at a time.

"It won't go anywhere," he always said disdainfully. Somehow a wind always came up and soon we all ran like mad idiots to fill buckets at the shore and rushed to dose the flames. On every occasion we managed to subdue the fire, but the trauma and exhaustion took its toll.

Jim and I armed ourselves with water buckets and brooms and waited for a still evening. When it arrived we followed a careful plan, and the small flames slowly devoured the dry grass in a most civil manner. Suddenly a gust of wind burst upon us, followed by several more, and we soon saw two fires rapidly heading for the woods. We each took a front and only because we were young and strong did we stop it just as it was tickling the lower spruce branches at the beginning of the woods.

We were black soot from head to toe and our brooms were now only handles. I started with sneakers and socks and now I stood completely barefoot, my shoes scattered about the field, but I hadn't remembered losing them. A good, solid stream of profanities can be satisfying at moments of intense fear and emotion.

With what breath I could muster I looked at the blackened ground under the spruces and exclaimed, "I don't give a goddam if this whole field becomes a forest, no more fires!"

"Christ almighty that was close!" Jim whistled softly.

We were exhausted, haggard, and frightened at what could have happened. We vowed there would be no more grass burning. Jim came up with a solution that ultimately effected our lives profoundly. We have Scottish blood on both sides and have always loved lamb, so Jim suggested we buy a couple of spring lambs. They would keep the pasture growth down until fall, then they would grace the table throughout the winter. I agreed it was a great idea and we hunted up a sheep farm to buy two pretty lambs.

The lambs dutifully kept the pasture neat all summer. By October they were in prime condition to be processed. But we kept putting it off and finally admitted to each other that their presence and charm didn't allow such an end. Besides, they were ewes and could be bred to produce more of their kind that we would avoid falling in love with. We considered it a fine plan.

Later, we brought home a black-faced Hampshire ram. This is a well-known meat breed. He was very friendly with the ewes, which was the whole point. And so our sheep business was born.

———

Jim was also working hard on *Spindrift*. When we first saw the boat in Leslie's shop, we stood in silent reverence at what we viewed as the epitome of a Maine lobster boat. The lift of her knife-edge bow, the sweet sweep of her shear line, her long deep keel, and her broad-beamed stern sang of her powers to engage any sea and her yearning to be upon it. We were spellbound. However, Jim still had weeks of work to perform on her yet. He had to find and install an engine, shafts, couplings, stuffing box, keel pipes for engine cooling, a cabin, wind shield, engine box, and steering wheel. This list was long and the time short before Jim had to set his traps. He, of course, started immediately.

In relatively short order, Jim found a six-cylinder Chevrolet engine in a local junkyard and patiently rebuilt and installed it in *Spindrift*. There was no transmission, so he rigged one from a Model A Ford. It was a straight shaft with no clutch; it had to be snapped into forward, neutral, and reverse. There was some crunching, but it worked fine. (Two years later, Jim changed to a Warner-Velvet transmission.) By working every available daylight hour, he had *Spindrift* ready to launch shortly after we moved to the farm.

Spindrift slid into the water eagerly and did a couple of gentle rolls as if to say, "This is my destiny, and now my life begins." Her sea trials were exhilarating. She and the Chevrolet engine performed together with speed, power, and agility. She was all we had wished her to be, although at this point her real potential had not yet been realized. Leslie remarked with quiet pride, "She's able."

With his larger trawler, a fine New Harbor fisherman, Sam Morton, brought our granite mooring rock from Browns Cove to Long Cove and *Spindrift* was home. She now lay in sight of the New Harbor

Jim hauling traps in Spindrift.

bell buoy that we had been hearing faintly in the right winds in the log cabin days and more closely from Browns Cove. We could also hear its haunting sound at the farm and, between that and the thick sob of Manana Island's foghorn, we could quite well forecast a storm from its changing tone as the seas rose.

From these open waters Jim lobstered year round. His only navigational equipment was a compass, nautical chart, personal knowledge of the waters, and natural instincts. During the winter he was alone offshore in snow squalls and the flesh-searing chill and obscurity of sea smoke on bitterly cold days. Sea smoke is a strange phenomenon created when "steam" rises from water warmer than the sub-zero air temperature. The steam wind-blown spray froze and glazed the decks

The old cattle barn in the 1940s.

and washboards with ice. He had no radio communication. It seems like a winter didn't pass that a lobsterman didn't slide off an icy deck trying to clear his windshield. There was no returning from this event. Thinking back on it now makes me shudder. But, as has been said, the young feel invincible.

It was a tough way to earn a living, but he loved the sea, coming from a line of British sea captains and ships' masters. It was a challenge of skill and endurance: the beauty of winter's cobalt sea and snowy white shores austere, and the glory of summer's foggy dawns of honey and smoke inspiration.

A short time after we began living on the farm, now in our mid-twenties, we felt it was time to begin a family, which meant a change in lifestyle.

Jim hauled lobster traps from dawn until early afternoon and then tended to our sheep, not to mention taking care of old buildings and acreage. Jim rightly believed that if we could establish a business at home that we could both work at, it would prevent all our eggs from being in the same basket. He was a skilled lobsterman, but no one can control the vicious storms and loss of gear. Fall and winter gales took their toll each year.

Our huge barn, which once presented a looming problem, now seemed to offer a solution. It had been built—as writings on its walls attested—in 1902 from lumber that had come into Long Cove, half a mile away, by lumber schooner and barge, and brought up the road to the farm by ox-cart. The barn was thirty-six feet wide, forty-five feet long, very tall and nobly built in the post- and beam-style with joints secured by wooden pegs. While structurally sound, its roof was leaking copiously and badly in need of repair.

Our flock of sheep now numbered around twenty and were comfortably dwelling in an old carriage shed. The big barn was an expensive upkeep we couldn't afford and didn't need.

But that soon changed. The contract chicken broiler business was coming to Maine. And we were joining the flock.

CHAPTER 9
Here Come the Chickens

JIM AND I decided the chicken broiler business, which had been rapidly growing in Maine, was a good one for us and a way to generate income from the buildings we had on our property while allowing me to work from home.

The Maine broiler industry had started in the late 1920s and early 1930s, mostly shipping live poultry to Boston and New York. During World War II two things happened. With tires, trucks, and gasoline rationed, several live poultry buyers established poultry dressing plants in Maine and the overall demand for poultry increased because it was one of the few meats not rationed. The existing supply of live poultry in the state was inadequate, so chicken growers began to increase rapidly. The development was encouraged because many people were looking for work and a lot of former dairy and cattle barns now sat empty because of the changing times.

By the middle 1950s, the industry was well established in Maine. There were nearly eighty farms statewide that could grow an average of eleven-thousand or so birds.

We would be a contract grower, meaning, the chicken processing companies would provide us with baby chicks, grain, and heating fuel for brooding and pay us one cent per bird per week. We, the contract grower or chicken farmer, would provide the barn for housing the chicks and raise them for ten to twelve weeks, also providing the heating, feeders, watering equipment, and labor.

Jim loved to build, so he set about exploring this new possibility and soon drafted a business plan, which considered the cost of propane gas brooders, equipment, and building materials. Our old cattle barn could be expanded to four floors and he could wire it for electricity and handle the carpentry work himself.

Still, we needed start-up capital, so our next step was visiting the local bank for a loan and then contacting a chicken processing company for a growing contract. After renovations, our barn would accommodate five thousand chickens, which at one cent per bird per week would generate a weekly income of fifty dollars. We estimated the labor required to feed the chickens and clean the watering equipment should only take on average three hours a day, maybe less. I could easily take care of a baby (I was already pregnant), and with these *simple* chores, stay home and still earn nearly twice what I did working a forty-eight hour week as a secretary at Saltwater Farm in Damariscotta.

As we talked through the plan, our hearts soared with hope and zeal. We found T&T, a Waterville-based chicken processing company that was as eager to find contract growers as we were to have a contract. The bank, on the other hand, was not so excited. However, since our credit was solid, they loaned us a small amount to supplement our meager savings. The key to the plan's success was Jim's ability to expand the barn without having to pay for outside labor.

He tackled the old barn whenever he wasn't lobster fishing and within six months, by early March 1954, the barn was ready and our first chickens arrived. I missed the grand event as our new baby

The Davidsons' farmhouse was built in 1777, while the cattle barn was built in 1903 with lumber brought by a schooner. The cattle barn was converted to a chicken barn that could hold eight thousand chickens.

daughter, Connie, arrived within one and one-half hours of the first indication she wished to do so. It was March 7—a gloriously brilliant Sunday that vibrated with promises including a possible early spring. Blue-edged ice floes were melting and drifting with the tide in the Damariscotta River. It was a time of birth and renewal in all things, especially our lives. We wept tears of joy together over the magic of this wondrous gift of a healthy, sweet-natured, beautiful child.

At the same time, our barn was suddenly full of five thousand yeeping tiny gold puff balls. Even better, our fifty dollar payment arrived in the mailbox each week as promised.

During the winter of 1954–1955, prolonged spells of bad weather prevented Jim from getting out to haul his lobster traps. During his time off, he studied how to enlarge the barn so it could accommodate even more chickens. While building a structural addition was too expensive, using the area underneath the barn seemed a promising idea. An area equal to about one quarter of the total barn size had already been excavated to create an area that was once used as a drop-through manure pit for cattle.

Jim believed he could dig out the remaining three quarters of the area under the barn, pour a new cement floor and thus add capacity for three thousand more chickens, bringing us to an eight thousand chicken capacity in total.

It seemed to me a monumental task, much like trying to dig a tunnel all the way to New Hampshire. But, Jim was not one to worry about perceived impossibility, so he studied the mechanics of how to accomplish the task. He decided that using a wheelbarrow to carry away the excavated material was too slow, so he built a small trailer with an old set of car wheels and, through a friend, found a Model T Ford that had been modified into something the owner called a "tractor." He was willing to be rid of it for two dollars. It was a temperamental beast, but Jim learned its ways.

Jim set a goal of finishing the project by spring, regularly disappearing under the barn with pick, shovel, and mattock. It was slow, grinding, and backbreaking work, but every shovelful he removed meant one less to go from the thirty feet by thirty-six feet by twelve-foot depth of dirt and rock that needed to be removed.

By mid-January of 1955, Jim faced a new obstacle as frost settled three feet into the ground thus requiring Jim to chip away at the frozen gravel rather than shovel it. I marveled at his determination and endurance.

I remember one day my father came to check on the progress. It was a sub-zero day in February and Jim was about halfway through the job, and painstakingly pick-axing his way through frozen earth around one of the many large boulders that kept cropping up. My father always prided himself, not unjustly, on his ability to perform hard physical tasks. On this day he stood there in his Sunday-just-came-from-church clothes and said: "Jim, it's too much of a job. You'll never make it."

Jim's smiling reply was, "Anyhow, I plan to keep trying!"

One day in early March, it had snowed, rained, frozen, thawed, snowed some more, and then started sleeting. There was two feet of a coverage whose bottom foot was wet, freezing slush. The Model T tractor, nicknamed "The Bug" was having one of her really bad days suffering all the breakdowns she could manage.

While Jim was replacing a coil and buzzer in the ignition system, the pieces slipped from his freezing fingers and vanished into the slush and snow. Since Model T parts were literally antique—even then—it just had to be found. I helped him hunt for a while by pawing through the stiffening slop to no avail. Eventually Jim found it and, after reviving his half-frozen hands under cool water in the house, put "The Bug" back together.

Finally, his perseverance paid off and by May he finished the floor, complete with drains under the barn. We had managed to buy an old but fairly sound dump truck at this point, and when we cleaned out the manure from the last flock by shoveling it through floor hatches to the waiting truck below, we would prepare for a new flock of eight thousand chickens instead of five thousand.

That spring of 1955, I cared for Connie, chickens, and sheep, while Jim hauled lobster traps, and, although I had enjoyed my previous work as a secretary, I loved being free from an eight-hour-a-day office job.

The chicken processing company sent an inspector once a week to check on the care and conditions of our chickens. We took pride in the good reports. We also learned the company was offering a bonus for producing a high conversion flock. "Conversion" was a term measuring the efficiency of pounds of weight gains per pounds of grain consumed. Eager to earn the bonus, we visited a local dairy each day for the last few weeks our flock was in and bought big milk cans of skim milk to mix with the chicken feed to provide extra protein. The chickens loved it, and although it was toilsome and messy, we weighed a sampling of birds regularly and knew we were making real progress. When the company crew came with crates to pick up our chickens, they remarked at the unusually heavy weight of the birds for their age.

Chickens in the old cattle barn.

Mysteriously, the company scales and conversion figures didn't seem to reflect any of this, and our total "bonus" for those weeks of mixing milk into the feed was twenty-nine cents—*twenty-nine cents!*

The disappointment was a harbinger of things to come.

In our disbelief we asked the inspector for verification of this figure. He assured us that although he didn't know just how the figure had been arrived at, it was indeed correct. We gave up on conversion bonuses and continued the routine of caring for chickens, sheep, and hauling lobster traps. We also sold a few sheep from each flock to meat market each year and the sheep sales were increasing. Our three-part plan to earn a living—lobster fishing as well as raising chickens and sheep—seemed to be developing nicely when we were hit by a blow in January of 1957. T&T informed us that while we were doing a fine job, they couldn't efficiently service a "small" flock of eight thousand birds with chickens, grain, and fuel so far away from Waterville. They said we needed to increase our flock to twenty thousand chickens within a year or they wouldn't send us any more birds.

We had already waded into the Forbidden Swamp of Debt to grow eight thousand chickens, but it appeared the best way out was to push in even deeper. The money we earned from lobster fishing and selling a few market lambs could not pay the debt on our present chicken barn. The building had to generate its own income or we were at risk of losing our dream farm.

We decided to look around for a different contract and soon visited another broiler company, Penobscot Poultry, in Belfast. We explained our situation to them, but they told us they would require us to increase our capacity to twenty thousand birds before agreeing to a contract, although they would really like to have us on board. They went on to describe their expansion and bonus plans for the future.

Penobscot Poultry would require us to use hanging metal feeders rather than our existing wooden floor feeders and add long metal trough waterers that filled automatically. Since Penobscot Poultry just happened to be a distributor of these items they would be *happy* to sell all this to us and would simply deduct money from each flock to pay for it. They painted a glowing picture, and it sounded like we would make so much money we would soon afford regular vacations to Europe, if we just joined with them.

Of course, we weren't interested in riches, we simply wanted to pay the debt we already owed. While the business arrangement was referred to as a "contract" there was actually no written contract or even a handshake to seal the deal. It was all trust on our part that they would pay us what they promised. All the chicken processing companies appeared solid and reliable. In addition, we believed that if the United States Government, through the Farmers Home Administration, saw fit to loan large sums of money all over Maine based on the words and promises of these processing companies, then they must indeed be stable and trustworthy.

We decided that spending the money to increase our chicken capacity to twenty thousand was the best move we could make. We believed that Penobscot Poultry seemed like a more honest company than T&T and had better future plans. Jim hit the drawing board once again and calculated the cost of building an addition that could handle twelve thousand more chickens. I worked on financial statements and projected debt repayment and living expenses. It certainly looked feasible and we were excited at the prospects. Installing better feeders and automatic waterers would make labor easier and, despite the additional birds, would still allow Jim time to go lobster fishing and tend our small flock of sheep.

Armed with our plans we approached the one and only local bank. The answer was a speedy, "No! We are not commercial and do not grant loans to farmers and fishermen." We were now both.

Other banks believed if our local bank didn't want us, they didn't either. Discouraged and worried, we pursued other avenues and visited the Farmers Home Administration. They agreed to look over our figures and, unlike the banks, said our loan request did not pose any problem. Congress was apparently concerned at the time with keeping us all "down on the farm" and away from the already crowded city labor markets. So FHA was making fairly low-interest forty-year loans to prospective "contract" broiler growers. Forty years to repay seemed quite

When the cattle barn proved to be too small, the Davidsons built an addition to increase their chicken capacity to twenty thousand.

safe, and at one cent per bird per week, now equaling $200 a week, we figured we could probably repay the debt in half that time.

Since we expected this to be our only big mortgage ever, we looked to resolve other looming issues by using the loan to buy other necessary equipment: farm tractor, a small bulldozer, and a manure spreader. With a manure spreader we could more easily spread manure on our fields to increase pasture yield for our growing sheep flock. We also needed a mower, baler, rake, and tedder to harvest our own sheep hay. It was such a neat package. None of our equipment would be new, of course, but Jim enjoyed the challenge of welding and repair. FHA was cooperative and we borrowed sixty thousand dollars. We were now well and deeply into the Forbidden Swamp, but the way out certainly seemed clear and promising.

Jim lobstered that summer while also building a four-story barn addition. He worked on the barn each afternoon after he came home from lobstering, and I, once I had finished feeding the chickens and sheep, helped him by passing up the boards that he sawed and nailed. We expected to receive our first twenty-thousand bird flock in mid-November of 1957. Our barn addition was proceeding right on schedule. On time, that is, until unseen forces gave us a smack upside the head.

One night Jim couldn't sleep because of severe abdominal pain, which prompted an emergency trip to the hospital. Three doctors said he exhibited symptoms of appendicitis, but the pain was on the wrong side. Their conclusion: He should remain in the hospital under observation. By the third day, his high fever and continued pain, despite medication, prompted the doctors to begin exploratory surgery. He had suffered a burst appendix.

We, of course, had no health insurance.

The resulting infection required three more weeks in the hospital and heavy doses of antibiotics. Jim came home weak and as thin as a stick, but in less than three weeks, he was back nailing and sawing. There was still one more story and the roof to go and the mid-November deadline was looming less than a month away.

A good friend helped us out by taking Jim's lobster traps out of the water for him, but we realized that we also needed to hire help to finish the barn on time. Three excellent carpenters, also neighbors, took the job and pounded the last roofing nail in place just as the twenty thousand birds arrived.

By this time, we were using oil-fired hot water heating pipes along the wall rather than the infernally temperamental gas brooders we started with. We had spread fresh sawdust on all the floors and laid layers of newspapers under the brooding pipes. The golden peepers had a warm and comfortable welcome. A busy two weeks went by and we were eagerly, actually desperately, looking forward to the broiler company's first check for two hundred dollars.

It never arrived.

Penobscot Poultry called us in to attend a very important meeting. We were not alone and were now among a large group of chicken growers, all financed by the FHA, at the meeting. The message was this: Costs have been high, and market prices low. The company beseeched us to understand that it could only pay us half a cent per bird per week instead of the one cent base originally promised. We were led to believe that this reduction was for this flock only. Starting with the next flock, we would all receive one cent per bird per week.

The next three months receiving half the expected pay was scary, especially given our unexpected costs of hiring labor and paying hospital bills.

We made the construction deadline, but there was still a lot of finish work to do on the building, including installing feeders and waterers. For the first couple of weeks, the chicks were fed out of the boxes they arrived in. Since they were too small to reach the automatic waterers, hundreds of one gallon glass water jugs had to be washed and filled daily.

It was now too late and Jim was too busy to set out lobster traps for winter, so *Spindrift* was floated onto a wooden cradle and hauled out onto the banks of Long Cove where she would rest until spring.

Scraping along on half pay greatly altered our scheduled debt repayment plan. The company still took full payment for the equipment we bought from them, even though our paycheck was cut in half. They did inform us all by letter that we should feel free to enjoy chicken on our tables. And we certainly did. I learned to kill, pluck, clean, cut, and cook chicken in every conceivable way—even in orange juice and winter-picked juniper berries.

In the contract growing business, chicken processing companies only paid growers while the birds were in the barn. Meaning, we cleaned out the barn and prepared it for a new flock on our own time with no pay. It was a filthy, dusty, grueling procedure, but we always pounded to get it done in less than a week so we could bring new birds in quickly. However, the company sent the chickens as it suited them, playing market forecasts perhaps, and we sometimes waited anxiously for three weeks or more to refill our barn.

As we waited for our next flock (not to mention a return to full pay), we were called by the chicken processing company to another meeting. This time we were told that all chicken processing companies in Maine were suffering from the same problems and that while they *hoped* to pay us the penny per bird base originally promised, it would have to be paid out as a bonus, not weekly. They said we would receive the half cent pay in our weekly check, but the other half cent as a special "settlement" after the chickens were marketed. There might also be extra bonus money if markets were especially good.

However, when it came time to sell the next flock we were told that oil and feed prices had risen and the wholesale market was terrible because grocery chains were featuring broilers as "loss leaders." Essentially that all meant: "No settlement check this time, fellas, your half cent was it. Better luck next time!"

Meanwhile, the FHA was still taking our full mortgage payment out of our weekly check on "assignment," meaning it was paid directly to them by the poultry company. So basically our weekly check remained small—but the FHA and Penobscot Poultry were taking their full payments out of our check, so our ability to pay other bills and living expenses depended on the settlement check. Over time, the settlement checks usually equaled anywhere from ten to fifty percent of what they should have been, but we were always told: "Bad markets, high costs."

The pattern and policy was crystal clear. The processing companies knew they had us all with our heads firmly stuck through the noose of heavy debt. There was no way out except to hope markets improved. In later years, we learned that many of the chicken processing companies, although differently named, were essentially owned by the same families through blood or marriage, so competing for growers through improved offerings was not necessary for them. We also learned they held meetings to regulate their payment systems and to hold a united front toward all growers. Of course, none of us knew all that at the time. We just kept struggling along and hoped.

During this time, I was pregnant again, but I stayed busy with all the normal chores on the farm and felt fine—I just didn't bend over as easily by the end! On July 1, 1958, we were blessed once again with a second beautiful and sweet-natured baby girl, Deborah Jo, who we always called Debby Jo. A violent thunderstorm accompanied our race to the hospital—a ride that normally takes fifteen minutes but that Jim made in ten. His speed was a good thing, because we arrived just in time. Debby Jo took only forty-five minutes to arrive into the world after she made that decision. Jim and I believed she hurried knowing there were sheep and lambs to love. After Debby Jo arrived, we looked out the window of Miles Memorial Hospital in Damariscotta and the storms had cleared. Taking its place was a most beautiful rainbow, a glorious symbol of a joyous event. Once again, we held a precious child with our tears of love and joy. .

The clean-outs between flocks were extremely dusty work and made everyone very thirsty. Buying bottled soft drinks were too expensive, so to provide an alternative to water, we made sure home-made root beer was on hand. Our root beer was a refreshing drink and, of course, non-alcoholic. We had made it often through the years and our only problem had been that the bottles we used sometimes blew their corks when the yeast began to work in the mix. The root beer was lost and mop-up was needed behind the stove where we let the mix "work" in a warm spot.

We knew that finding bottles with screw tops would solve this problem, but such used bottles were hard to find. A kindly summer neighbor helped us by saving the empty screw-top bottles from the PM Whiskey he brought with him to drink during long summer evenings. Luckily for us, he drank a lot. The root beer worked to a splendid carbonation and not a bottle was lost.

During one hot summer the clean-out crew had consumed all our root beer and there were about forty empty PM Whiskey bottles sitting on the sink that I planned to wash for reuse. While Jim and I were in the kitchen eating lunch before we went out to continue shoveling, a well-dressed gentlemen knocked at the door. We were in no condition to receive visitors having just spent five hours in clouds of chicken litter dust. Feathers clung to our clothes and hair and we looked like we had just climbed out of a flour bin, given all the chicken litter dust. Of course, we were also wearing the most ragged clothes we owned—the only sensible outfits for such filthy work. We looked like a pair of bums, but there was no sense in cleaning up until the end of the day. We greeted our visitor and asked him to come in.

It turned out the man was the new minister at a local church and he stopped by to find out why we were not yet members. His inquiry soon turned to a lengthy lecture on the sins of alcohol, and he got more stern by the moment. We took it in rather numbly wondering where this concern was coming from. We had nothing against alcohol, we simply couldn't afford it and seldom had any in the house. We didn't have time to inform him of this before he plopped his black hat back on his head and, after a few final words, left in a flounce of outrage.

We looked askance at each other, and then the light dawned—he saw all those whiskey bottles on the sink. We had used them over and over again so many times for the root beer that they were just part of our kitchen equipment and their origin had no meaning for us—they were just the "root beer bottles."

We laughed until the tears rolled. We weren't concerned about meeting him again because while we were both very strong believers in the Good Lord, our "church" was the glorious one He created Himself of land, forest, seas, and the love and goodness in the hearts of people.

With our chicken growing pay cut in half and the unexpected expenses of hospital bills and hired labor, we faced serious trouble. Lobster catches were down in winter and gasoline prices increased, but we kept at it. We needed to earn money from somewhere else to help pay the bills. Jim used our farm equipment, bulldozer, and dump truck for town roadwork and continued lobstering during the summer. We still were not at breakeven. I could and did handle the daily care of the chickens for the most part, so I couldn't leave to bring in any other money. On top of it all, another problem was rearing its demanding head.

Our well, with its wonderful crystal water, was only thirty feet deep and twenty thousand chickens required a great deal of water. Weather conditions were very dry that first summer of the increased chicken flock, and the well couldn't keep up. We rented a five hundred gallon tank and bought a fire pump. Jim arranged it all on the dump truck and went to a nearby river at least daily. He hooked the tank up to a special pump he had rigged to carry it through to the chicken waterers.

From my parents' experience, and many others we were aware of, we knew the expense of drilling a well and that there was no guarantee of good results. A local well driller suggested drilling our existing well deeper. We agreed and while even at 280 feet there was little increase in the flow, we hoped that the larger reservoir would suffice. We were wrong. Before long it was obvious the increased depth still wasn't adequate, so we drilled to four hundred feet. At that point, the well driller believed he had entered some sort of cave as the drill swung loosely. There was no increase in the flow, however, and at six dollars per foot we had to quit.

The only way to effectively solve our water problem was to dig a farm pond. A short distance into the woods behind the house Jim discovered a large, boggy area. It was low-lying and seemed like a logical place for a pond. He cut many cords of spruce and we burned the brush. With our bulldozer and a large one we hired, we dug a satisfactory pond. It was about twelve feet at its greatest depth. The ledge bottom had seams for spring water to trickle in and that, combined with rains, helped fill the cavity to around 200,000 gallons. It was good, clean water and Jim piped it up to the barn using a pump.

This solution only lasted a couple of years until another dry summer forced us to enlarge the pond to hold more than a million and one-half gallons. In addition to its economic value, our pond proved a source of pleasure as well as beauty. We swam there and skated there, and it became an ecological wonder supporting a myriad of wildlife as well as our farm animals.

Digging the pond solved our water problems, but it didn't add any money to our income. We once again studied our options and tried to figure out just how we could make more money.

As it turned out, the best answer was grazing right in our backyard.

CHAPTER 10

North Country Cheviots

IN OUR CASTING about for additional farm income we took a closer look at our small flock of about twenty sheep. We had been raising sheep since 1952 and kept strict cost figures on all projects. The woollies were always well in the black, although the profit we made was just a drop in the great bucket compared to our bills and debt.

We had grown to love our sheep, and we reasoned that if we could increase their numbers we could generate needed extra income in a pleasant way. We already had the land, the haying equipment, and a bulldozer. Jim could easily clear more land to increase our pasture. We had limited the flock to slow growth by keeping just selected ewe lambs each year.

Market lambs were always in good demand, and wool paid well. Jim had long since learned to shear and could remove a sheep's fleece with his electric shears so that it lay in a whole piece as if it were still on the hide itself. This was important to a good wool price as the wool classers at the mill could lay it out and easily select the desirable sections of shoulder and back wool. I learned how to carefully remove the dung tags, roll the fleece sheared side out and tie it properly with the paper twine that had to be used so it would dissolve in the mill's scouring process. We managed to keep up a fairly smooth rhythm, Jim catching the next sheep and shearing it while I handled the fleece he had just removed. Then we stuffed the fleeces into a burlap bag, about fifteen feet long.

After shearing, our hands were always supple with lanolin, also called wool wax or wool grease, which is secreted by wool-bearing animals. It is used to protect wool and skin, but Jim's farm boots were also soft and richly shined from the sheep sitting rump down on his feet as they were held in place by his knees and ankles in a grip that left his hands free to shear. Since their feet couldn't touch the ground, the sheep had no way to get a purchase and go rocketing off in the distance, which is exactly what they wished to do.

Our black-faced Hampshire ram, a breed that dates back to 1829 in the United Kingdom, produced nice meat lambs, but the breed has a large head, which sometimes caused lambing problems and losses of both ewes and lambs. We tried to be on hand whenever lambs were being born and had learned many ways to assist, including reaching in and turning a breech lamb (coming out backwards) around, or arranging twins—one coming forward and one backward and sorting out their feet so they could arrive properly.

We sold our wool to the Knox Woolen Mill in Camden and prices were good. Selling the wool came close to paying for the flock's winter feed, while selling the lambs for meat provided us with a little profit.

The mill paid a better price for wool with no black fibers since black fibers will not take dye for lighter colors, so we decided to change rams, and I wasn't sorry. Our black-faced ram had become possessive of his ewes, and while he didn't bother Jim, I would sometimes be standing at the hay crib breaking a bale to make it easier to eat, when I would suddenly find myself literally sailing over the hay crib. I would never see the ram coming; he would just back off, get a running start, lower his head and send me flying right over the top. He never really hurt me, but it was an ugly surprise.

We knew a white-faced ram would give us better fleeces, but we didn't know what breed to look for. We needed a breed that offered a combination of meat and wool sales. Typically, the finer-wooled white-faced sheep provide good quantities of wool, but their lamb carcass quality is on the lighter side and doesn't provide as much income.

After reading a lot about sheep breeds, we learned that an old breed of white-faced sheep had been recently imported from Scotland into Canada, and the three-year quarantine period before they were allowed into the United States had just ended. The breed was reportedly extremely rugged, living with no shelter on the highlands of Scotland year-round. It was also claimed they were excellent mothers and milkers, easy lambers because of their neat, smooth heads, and produced mostly twins with an ideal blending of wool and meat. In Scotland, their fleeces were almost exclusively used in the weaving of the famous Harris Tweed. They were called North Country Cheviots, a large breed of sheep not to be confused with the small Border Cheviot.

The North Country Cheviot breed can be traced back to 1791 in Scotland. It is considered a large breed of sheep that is deep, broad, and long throughout the body. Their heads and legs are covered with white, short hair. They are a hardy, strong-willed, independent breed of sheep that does well in harsh climates and on rough pastures. They lamb easy, have good mothering instincts with offspring that are vigorous at birth and have high survival rates.

The more we read about these sheep, the more they seemed ideally suited for our climate and requirements. We contacted the Canadian Sheep Producers Council and located a North Country Cheviot

North Country Cheviots at North Country Farm.

flock just below James Bay in Ontario. We contacted the owners of the flock and made arrangements to get a ram. We also needed an import permit and blood tests of the ram, provided by the Canadian Department of Agriculture to bring him into Maine and the United States. The ram was purebred and registered and bore ear tattoos that corresponded with his papers.

The price of the ram was steep, although not unreasonable. However, the trip from Maine to James Bay would be costly and as always, we had little extra money. While we knew it would be a long time before the new breed could help us measurably, they did offer a future avenue out of our financial quagmire that we couldn't ignore.

We shuffled figures around and by "borrowing from Peter to pay Paul" managed to gather the money together. My parents were delighted to have Connie, five, and Debby Jo, one, with them for a few days, and Jim rigged up our dump truck with a canvas top. The old dump truck was the only vehicle we had fit for such a long trip, although its fitness was questionable.

It was a cool, green-scented dawn in early July 1959. The air was filled with jeweled bird song and ducks were sailing across the farm pond in a lattice work of Vs, barn swallows darted over it in an intricately swooping ballet as they collected breakfast insects for their young. We were filled with the excitement of adventure and the glowing inner flame of hope that seemed to abide with us. With a small suitcase and a pillow we climbed into the dump truck, which we hoped would survive the long trip, and headed the roughly 1,500 miles toward James Bay, Canada, located just below Hudson Bay. We took turns driving so we could keep rolling as long as possible and avoid the expense of overnight stays.

By the end of our third day, we reached our destination and found the Canadian sheep farmers warm-hearted and jolly. Their North Country Cheviots were truly impressive: large and snowy white, noble roman-nosed heads with intelligent dark eyes and long upright ears. Their fleeces were lustrous and lofty, and their spring lamb crop was vigorous and showed excellent growth. The ram we were to have was huge, but gentle and friendly.

After traveling the last few hundred miles through lake and forest wilderness, it was incredible to emerge into the fertile farming land that now surrounded us in what was known as The Little Clay Belt.

Mr. and Mrs. Pettman, from whom we purchased the ram, raised Black Angus cattle along with the North Country Cheviots. Mr. Pettman was tall and lean, almost a double of Gary Cooper. He was a gentle man with a keen, dry humor. Mrs. Pettman was a petite and jolly woman who wore her silvery hair in a neat chignon. The farm consisted of six hundred acres of flat, rich land. The sheep and cattle wallowed in lush depths of alfalfa. This forage was so abundant and nourishing that grain was never needed. The alfalfa was also harvested as hay for winter feed.

We spent a delightful day and night with the Pettmans. They were pioneers in the sense that they lived in a relative wilderness under very harsh conditions for most of the year. Winters in James Bay averaged fifty degrees below zero. They were supremely contented people, old enough to nearly be our grandparents. Their lives were rich and full, and they wished for nothing beyond the realm of their farm. In addition to their extraordinary farm animals, Mrs. Pettman raised Keeshond dogs. Their hair was soft as angora wool and she combed it from them then carded it into roving and spun it into yarn with which she knitted wondrous clothing. She had a charming assortment of barn and house kitties, which she called her "pooty, ooty cats."

We were intrigued with all we saw at this farm, but we were so powerfully drawn to the North Country Cheviots that we could think of nothing else. All through the night we pondered how we could possibly find money to also take along some ewes. We had driven a long way to get here and the dump truck could easily take a nice load of ewes. But the money, oh God, the money! We had seemingly stretched every option to its screeching limit just to get this far for the ram.

The following morning over a breakfast of eggs that Mrs. Pettman gathered from the henhouse and some of their own Canadian bacon, we poked at the question of prices and availability of their ewes. They were interested in having us establish a flock in the northeastern United States, as they knew it could generate additional sales for them as well. The Canadian government was very generous with its farmers in outlying areas and paid them handsome subsidies for their sheep sales. The effect of this for us was that the Pettmans were willing to take a price for their purebred ewes so bewitching in its fairness that we had no choice but to fall into the foaming pit of temptation.

There were ten yearling ewes ready to be bred in the fall that could go along with the ram and that were not related to him. They were brought into the barn for us to look over, and we were left alone to do so. Measuring their long, wide loins, the depth of their britch, (hindquarters), their fleece quality and their sound, solid conformation, our minds whirled at what such a flock could do for us—purebred animals that could be sold for purebred prices. And then Jim hit on an idea that could make it possible. When we got home, we would sell most of our "grade" flock or unregistered sheep. Sheep of any kind were in good demand, and it was quite likely we could get enough for them to pay for this North Country Cheviot flock.

Trembling, but determined, we made the deal with the Pettmans. Obtaining blood tests and proper paperwork was not a problem as Canada required the whole flock to be tested before even one animal could leave. The sale turned out to be a news item in this farming area and we were photographed and interviewed by local newspapers. In our minds, despite the fears, this had been a day of triumph.

By sunrise of the following day, our Chevy dump truck was thickly bedded with golden straw, several bales of alfalfa hay, and eleven sheep and we were bound for Maine. Back at home, we unloaded the North Country Cheviots, and that summer they helped create a beautiful scene. For several years we had been casting about for a proper name for our farm. It had been known as the Old Russell Place (named after Lem and Webb Russell and built in 1777) when we bought it, but, with all due respect, we wanted a name based on something meaningful to us. We were talking about this as we watched the lovely scene before us. After a quiet moment Jim said, "How about North Country Farm?"

The name entered my heart, swift and glowing. As a girl I read all of James Oliver Curwood's wonderful stories of the North Country, of the Canadian northwest. They were so special to me for I felt, and still do, that Maine is that kind of country also. It fell into place as if we had been waiting for this name. These beautiful sheep had come from the North Country of Scotland to the North Country of Canada and now to the North Country of the United States. Between their breed name and our location, our farm now had its destined identity.

CHAPTER 11
Sheep Over Our Shoulders

IN THE WEEKS after our North Country Cheviots arrived in the summer of 1959, the University of Maine and many sheep farmers came to see them as they were the first of the breed in Maine. We took orders for both rams and ewes to deliver the following year and were thankful we decided to bring this nucleus of a flock back from Canada. One visitor insisted that we must take the ram and some ewes to the agricultural fair in Union the following month—such exposure would be valuable, especially if they were judged to be the worthy animals we all believed they were.

As a child I had been to the Lincoln County Fair in Damariscotta and never forgot the joys of the merry-go-round. Jim and I had only ever attended one fair together and it happened to have been the Union Fair.

It was early in our marriage, long before the farm and children, and one of our most memorable days. Even though we arrived early in the morning, the only parking place was beside a grassy field, under some trees at the edge of the river. We spent the day like two children wildly happy at being freed from school. We inhaled the wonderful aromas of trampled grass, frying onions and peppers, hot dogs, and the satisfying smells of the cattle barns—so rich in their natural, primitive appeal. We listened to the calliope music of the merry-go-round, and Rosemary Clooney's "Come On-A My House" that played regularly over a loudspeaker. We rode every ride and saw every show, even the not-quite-naughty "girlie" show. We ate hot dogs and sausage and onion rolls, french fries, and popcorn. We stayed for the vaudeville show at the grandstand on the racetrack.

When we started across the field toward the car munching on cotton candy, a snickering voice called to us, "The grass is pretty wet back there!" We just smiled knowing he wouldn't believe we were only headed for our car. We drove the hilly, winding, pine-flanked roads home in brilliant moonlight completely fulfilled and jubilant.

And now here we were heading back again, only this time with work to do. The sheep were only required to be at the Union Fair for one day. With all our chicken chores done by daylight, we loaded the North Country ram and five ewes, as well as hay and water buckets into the good old dump truck and headed for Union some thirty-five miles away. Actually appearing at a fair and bringing our sheep before a judge for awards began to seem like an act of ignorance. We even debated turning around and going home, but we sucked it up and soldiered on.

On arriving at the fairgrounds, we unloaded our sheep into an empty pen in the sheep barn. Many varieties were already penned and some of them were being carded (a form of fluffing out the wool) and trimmed. We had no tools for this and knew nothing about it. But our sheep were clean and looked as presentable as most. Other sheep breeders showed an encouraging interest in our North Country Cheviots.

When the show began we watched how the animals were presented and what the judge appeared to be looking for. Screwing up our courage, we trotted ours out when the time came. To our gape-jawed amazement every single one of our sheep received a blue ribbon and some fine comments from the judge. To our further rapture, a tidy little sum of money prizes came with the ribbons.

Fair fever was now squarely upon us.

With some inquiry we learned that a county fair was always held on Labor Day weekend in Blue Hill, a small coastal town reached by a long side road that ran down off Route 1. Luckily, our current chicken flock would have just been taken to market and a new one wouldn't be in yet, so we could sneak in a few days at the Blue Hill Fair, which dates back to the 1800s, before cleaning out the barn.

The fair promised to be high adventure. We would spend three nights at the fair, so Connie and Debby Jo would stay with my parents, and we would bring food in a cooler and some bedding. We unearthed a couple of old sleeping bags that zipped together and invested in two of the cheapest plastic inflatable mats we could find.

Early on the Friday of Labor Day weekend we once more loaded six of the sheep, hay, bedding, and water buckets into the big Chevy and struck out for Blue Hill. Route 15 runs along a high ridge through beautiful blueberry fields, and evergreen woods, with long views of bays, lakes and mountains. This whole idea was getting better by the minute.

The fairgrounds were located at the foot of Blue Hill Mountain. It loomed over the fairgrounds like a stately, tender sentinel. It was an impressive backdrop for the fair's big Ferris wheel.

After unloading the sheep, we found a place to sweep out the soiled bedding, then parked the truck near the shed with its back end facing the mountain. Jim had been hauling big stones for a summer resident who wanted to build a stone wall, and the steel bed of the

THE BLUE HILL FAIR - LABOR DAY - 1964

The Blue Hill Fair as it looked on a postcard in 1964.

truck was deeply pocked with large dents made by the heavy rocks. Since we had to sleep on this we were glad we bought inflatable plastic mattresses.

By nighttime, the sheep were settled comfortably, and after a quick trip around the fairgrounds we were also ready for bed. The sleeping bags were invitingly laid over the mattresses and the truck canvas was stretched above us, while the mountain rose before us in dark splendor.

Around midnight we awoke to great discomfort. Our cheap air mattresses couldn't take the grief of the undulated steel of the truck bed and the seams had let go. We tossed and turned until we found the dents that seemed to accommodate us the most. We had barely fallen asleep when we awoke to howling winds and lashing rain. Although it held, the truck canvas whipped and snapped. Before long the wind shifted and was now blowing down from the mountain and bringing the rain in sideways under the canvas. We were soaked. We huddled together hoping it might just be a passing shower. We were not so lucky. The wind picked up and the rain came raging in under the canvas in torrents. Wet, cold, and thoroughly miserable, we crawled out of the sopping bags and into the truck cab to spend the rest of the night sitting up, watching nature's fierce spectacle.

We eventually dozed off again and awoke to dazzling sunshine and soft drying winds. My most urgent wish now was to find a bathroom. I came upon a wooden edifice that bore the sign LADIES. After opening the door I stood in stupefaction not knowing where to look. I had expected an outhouse, but large as it was I also expected it to have stalls. It didn't. There was just a huge bench with the usual carved holes and it was arranged in a semi-circle. A number of pleasant and chubby older ladies were attending to their business companionably conversing across the semi-circle and passing the necessary paper around. It all seemed very clubby, but it was not for me. Blushing and stammering my apologies I backed out the door.

Regardless, my issue still had to be addressed. I spied a big pine woods at the edge of the fairgrounds and headed for it. In the early part of our log cabin days, the woods had been our "big potty in the sky" so I was comfortable with the arrangement. This woodsy place, not a communal semi-circle, was my refuge for the next few days.

After feeding the sheep we treated ourselves to a hot breakfast at one of the hot dog stands. We spread the sleeping bags over a fence to dry and threw away the air mattresses, which hadn't a hope of being repaired. The weather forecast was fine for the rest of the weekend, and that evening, when the truck bed was dry, we planned to spread hay in it to sleep upon.

The sheep show was not until the following day and the mountain called us to climb and explore. A rough trail was carved out of the blueberry clearings for blueberry rakers. They had already been there since this was September and harvesting was done in late July or August. There was a fire tower, at the top of the big hill.

Even halfway up the mountain, the view was spectacular. At the top of the fire tower it seemed that most of coastal Maine lay at our feet in endless panorama. Blue Hill Bay, spruce-covered islands, and Cadillac Mountain all shimmered in the blue distance.

The fairground below seemed only a small scrap of activity with a tiny oval racetrack at its center. The fairgrounds were surrounded on three sides by thick evergreen forest that extended for many miles. It appeared to be in a wilderness except for the lovely little coastal town of Blue Hill off to one side.

On our way back down the trail, we found clumps of blueberry bushes among the fern-lined boulders and ledges that hadn't been raked because they were accessible only by hand. The blueberries were powdery blue, sweetly juicy, and warmed by the sun. We ate them until we could hold no more while gazing at the scenic glory below and around us. Spicy fragrances of sweet fern, bayberry, and the blueberries themselves rose around us.

We couldn't remember a time when we felt such peace and so removed from real-world stress. We loved the farm and all that we were doing there, but always—and each day—was the lurking specter of the clutching claws of debt and lack of funds. We had no control over and no protection from the shifting programs of the chicken companies. We knew that soon after returning home we would hear about our "settlement" check for the flock that just went out—if there even was a check. But for now we savored this moment, filled a bandanna with blueberries and returned to the fairgrounds.

There were many good sheep at the fair, including a breeder of Border Cheviots that other breeders said frequently won and was famous throughout the Northeast. His name was Denny Bascom and he was an irascible fellow. His sheep were trimmed and groomed to perfection. We had yet to learn this art, but at least ours were snowy white and clean. Bascom remarked to Jim, "Those are big sheep."

Jim gave him a pleased smile and said, "Thanks, yes they are good sheep."

Bascom replied, "I didn't say they were good sheep, I said they were big sheep."

We began to get a feel for what the word "competition" might mean.

The sheep show took most of the next day. The sheep were shown singly and in groups according to age. We were learning by the minute. In the groups, we helped others to show, and they helped us. Once again every one of our animals received a blue ribbon, and our ram was awarded a purple rosette for Grand Champion Ram. We could have slept on the cold, lumpy steel of the truck and been rained on every night for this!

For the finale, the judge selected ten rams to compete for "Best in Show." This didn't happen at the Union Fair and was new to us. To our delight our ram was selected as one of the ten. The judge looked carefully at each one, checking all points of conformation and soundness and one by one eliminated them until only two were left, Bascom's and ours.

The judge took a long time, measuring loins, examining fleeces; tension was climbing. Bascom and the judge knew one another, and Bascom said to the judge with a smirk, as he pointed at Jim holding the ram,

"Alpheus, I've got a double-barreled shotgun, and if that North Country wins, he's gonna get one barrel and you're gonna get the other!"

The judge grinned back and said, "Well, Denny, you better go get your gun because I'm giving it to the North Country Cheviot."

A shining trophy came with this honor, and warm glory caught in our throats. We took the ram back to his pen, where he checked on each of his ewes and settled down to chew his cud. It had just occurred to us that he and his ladies earned us a nice little bunch of money on this day.

No question now, we were irretrievably hooked on sheep showing. Of course, the magic of winning so early in our career helped, and the significance to all this came to light as we talked with the other sheep and cattle breeders. They were all serious farmers who spent their summers traveling to the ten or so agricultural fairs held throughout the State of Maine each year. Their reason for attending was two-fold: there was no better way to advertise and sell breeding stock than committing it to impartial judging in competitions, and winning offered good prize money. The original and ongoing concept of these competitions was to encourage the production of excellence in farm animals, and to further promote this ideal, only purebred registered cattle or sheep were allowed to compete.

We filed all this information away in our minds. There were still several more fairs left in the current season, but we knew we couldn't take the time to attend them—prize money or not. We had a big barn cleaning job waiting for us at home, our two girls, and twenty thousand chickens on their way. The summer lobster crawl was about over and instead of risking the lobstering gear in the uncertainties of winter storms, we planned to bring the traps and *Spindrift* ashore for the winter. Also, Jim had the opportunity to use the truck to plow snow along a section of the Bristol roads, a winter job that could offer an income at least equal to lobster fishing.

During our first Blue Hill Fair, a new sheep dog trial competition was introduced. Since it would be the first one held in the Northeast, it was being called the Northeast United States Sheep Dog Trials. It was a brave and impressive title and did eventually come to live up to it. But that first year, there wasn't anybody connected to it that had a clue on how to run it, except the county agent who was a most willing soul but also not experienced.

A flock of grade sheep for the dogs to work with had been brought in from a local farm. About half a dozen sheep dog handlers and their border collies came in from around New England. They worked their dogs on their own farms and in field trial competitions. While their dogs could work under conditions found around a farm or the average enclosure, none of them had seen anything quite like what awaited them at the Blue Hill Fair. A couple of small holding pens and posts to be walked between had been set up in the middle of the racetrack infield. It was completely surrounded by parked cars, but nary a square inch of fence. The dogs were to drive a group of sheep into a holding pen after herding them between the fence posts. The course was well explained, the handlers were to run their dogs one at a time, the spectators were ready and the sheep were released.

Pandemonium was also released—to the tenth power. These sheep had never been off the farm and were wound to a fever pitch after a long, bumpy ride in a truck. And now they faced a crowd of people, loud fairground music, and—of all horrors—their worst enemy, a dog, coming after them. A sheep dog pretty much has to count on the flocking instinct of sheep to keep them in a group. In their panic, these sheep forgot all about their instinct to stick together, so it was every sheep for himself. They split in all directions at top speed and the best of dogs could not have rounded them up. They headed for the circle of parked cars, went between them, under them and some even tried to go over them.

The dog handlers sent out all their dogs to try to save the situation, but it happened too fast to retrieve any but just a few into one of the holding pens. One sheep headed for the county agent, and in his anxiety to keep the animal from running away he committed the cardinal sin that every shepherd learns quickly and painfully not ever to try again: He put himself squarely in front of the oncoming sheep with arms and legs outspread. The thinking is that the sheep will be intimidated by the obstacle and will come to a stop. Never. A sheep in terror will attempt to run through a brick wall. The hapless county agent got hit in the midriff and took a ride for a few feet until he pitched off to the side and hit his head on an outcropping of ledge. A fast trip to Blue Hill Memorial Hospital proved him to have a light concussion. He would have a headache for a couple of days, but would soon be fine.

The disastrous sheep dog trial ended before it really began, but a lot had been learned. The dog handlers had come a long distance and had planned to stay overnight. When the fairgrounds shut down at midnight, the cars in the infield were gone, and all was quiet; most of the sheep came back out of the woods and the dog handlers assisted in getting them penned. Two of the sheep remained hidden, but we heard later that a few days after the fair they were also caught.

We were the youngest, by quite a bit, of the sheep exhibitors and did a lot of running to help get the trial sheep back together. We were keenly interested in what we had just seen of a working dog's ability and brains. The following day when fair officials were wondering what to do about continuing this program, we joined the dog handlers in encouraging them to offer it again the next year. For even though it had been a fiasco, we had all seen the interest of the initial gathering of spectators and believed it would be a valuable addition to the fair's livestock shows. The problems encountered could be solved by using a fenced-in area, and the dog handlers offered many other practical ideas from their experience.

It is a truism that if you show interest in a project you will either end up on a committee or be asked to take some kind of responsibility. The fair officials had divided their duties to the maximum each one could handle, and none were willing to take on a sheep dog trial as well. So they asked Jim to work as superintendent of this program. It would only take a few days and included a paycheck. Jim would run the trial, see to course set-up, take entries, hire a judge, contact the dog handlers, and I would do the judge's score keeping for each dog. Not that we knew anything about such competitions, but we were willing to learn and the dog owners were happy to help our education. They knew the prize money was excellent. And with that the Blue Hill Fair was over.

As we pulled up over the steep road at the base of Blue Hill Mountain headed for home with our load of sheep, we looked back at them. They were gazing over our shoulders through the rear window of the truck cab with their soft, dark eyes seeming to watch the road ahead. We were finding that riding along with a flock of sheep over our shoulders was getting to be a fine experience.

Chapter 12
Back to Reality

THE DAY AFTER we returned from our Blue Hill Fair adventure—our blue ribbons, rosette, and trophy already in a place of honor—we returned to the chicken barn. We donned our worst clothes, rounded up a crew, and started cleaning the barn. When it was done and swept spotlessly clean for our next flock, the chicken company called us to meet with them. Usually, that was a bad sign, but this time we sat across the desk from the business manager and to our grateful surprise, he told us that markets had been good and we were paid a settlement equal to nearly a half cent per bird per week.

Yes!

It was great to pay our bills and also put something toward a new dump truck. We hated to say goodbye to our faithful old Chevy, but Jim was going to work snow-plowing town roads and needed a bigger and more reliable truck. He found a used GMC with a dump body; she was long-legged (long wheel base) and had the power to handle the huge and heavy plow and wing required. The truck could also carry bigger loads of chicken litter out of the barn and handle more hay bales. We never had trouble finding ways to spend money; there was always something screaming for it.

As another winter loomed, lobster traps came ashore and *Spindrift* was nestled in her wooden cradle on the bank of Long Cove. We battened down for winter and banked the house with spruce boughs to help keep icy winds from prying their way in. The chickens were warm and cozy and the sheep almost seemed to welcome the cold. We actually wished for it to snow so Jim and the truck could start earning $4.01 per hour plowing snow. The pay covered Jim's driving, the fuel, and the truck. The town provided Jim with the plow, wing, and a wingman. A wingman rides with the plow driver to watch the wing as it rides off to the side of the truck and at the edge of the road, to be sure it doesn't get hung up on a stump, ledge, or other obstacle. If the snow is not winged back well off the road while plowing there won't be room for snow from the next storm.

During one storm, Jim's wingman was an older fellow named Mac. Mac didn't have a great attention span for most things, but keeping an eye on the wing didn't require much thought. The storm lasted for three days and Jim barely had time to catch an hour or two nap before working again. Jim would stretch out on the bed, and Mac slept on the living room couch. We owned an enormous black cat named Blackie who was a splendid fellow, affectionate and a great mouser, but he did have one annoying habit—if he wanted to go out at night he wouldn't jump on the bed to ask, instead he headed for my piano in the living room and walked up and down the keyboard until someone got up to grant his wish.

On one stormy night when Jim and Mac were grabbing a quick nap, I heard Blackie banging away on the piano, so I got up to let him out, but found Mac already shoving him out the kitchen door muttering disgustedly, "Black bitch!" I guess he couldn't get back to sleep because when I got up a short while later to make a pot of coffee for their thermoses, he was sitting reading the telephone directory. It was upside down. That was when I realized he couldn't read. He struck up a conversation while I fixed the coffee and began talking about cars he had once owned. He said his favorite was a "tombstone" car. He mentioned it a couple of times and I listened intently hoping to pick up a clue as to what this might be.

Finally, I had to ask him what he meant by a "tombstone car."

"Well," he said, "you know, one o' them cars with two colors."

He also had a saying that remains one of my favorites. If he was talking about somebody who took an extremely long time to accomplish a task, he said, "He's slower than death chained to a stump."

⸺⸺

Winter and life in general was not all hard, tiring, grubby work and days filled with money worries. We are happy people by nature, and always loved a challenge and the feeling of accomplishment that goes with a good day's work. We also love to laugh and have fun.

Sure, as we waded through the Forbidden Swamp of Debt unseen monsters whispered gleefully in our ears, "No fun for you! No meals out, no movies, no luxuries. You're here now, and that's not allowed!"

We knew all that, but also, fortunately, realized that good mental health requires some recreation—however simple—along the way. We sneaked off to Moody's Diner a couple of times each month for the primitive pleasure of a hamburger and fries, or to Damariscotta to watch a movie at Lincoln Theater.

Our finest times were getting together with other couples who were also working to make some sort of business succeed. We played cards occasionally, organized potluck suppers, and sometimes attended dances at Bristol High School a couple of miles away. We also attended dances or gathered to play whist or attend potluck suppers at the lovely little community building, Laurel Hall, just beyond the farm.

One New Year's Eve we joined our friends at a dance held at Bristol High School. It was our first one since we had been married. The gym floor was smooth, the local saxophone and piano player in great form, and a neighbor had brought his special blend of homemade hard cider and a triple sec chaser. It was nearly lethal. We were accustomed to none of this, but it was an evening of fun and release never to be forgotten. I think one of the town official's wives—she was in her early seventies—summed it up best. Marion was a big-boned, handsome woman who tried to hold back the years with brightened auburn hair and deeply rouged cheeks. She was a hard worker and had raised nine fine sons. This night she wore a dazzling crimson dress that foamed around her in flounces and frothy lace.

She and I were catching our breath on the bleachers and she turned to me with a jolly, conspiratorial chuckle and said almost reverently, "Ain't this a shittin' mess!"

—oⲟⲟo—

There was enough snow that winter to keep Jim busy, and the GMC did a fine job. She did have a disconcerting propensity toward breaking rear axles, which was costly, but she was paying her way. On one snowstorm that turned to ice, Jim had a young wingman named Richard with him. They had crossed a narrow, curving bridge quite high over a river and were climbing the very steep winding hill that came immediately after it. The ice was such that the wheels, even with their double-linked chains, couldn't move ahead and the truck began to slide backwards and sideways. Brakes were of no use. They weren't moving at great speed, but there was no stopping. Jim said to his wingman, "Jump now, Richard, because if I can't stop her that's what I'm going to do before we land in the river."

Richard jumped, but Jim didn't want to lose the truck if he could help it, and somehow, he fought her to a halt with rear wheels just inches from the bridge's edge.

That winter was so stormy that the town needed to put on more equipment to handle the snow and ice. The Selectmen told Jim that if he had an extra truck they would like to put it to work spreading sand on the roads. We wanted to "make hay while the sun shone," or in this case as the snow fell, so we hunted up an old dump truck that was priced right and seemed like it might last the winter. I went with Jim when he first brought it home. I got in my side and shut the door while Jim paid for the truck. When he got in and shut his driver's door, mine flew open. So I gave it a good slam to be sure it was tight, and Jim's door flew open. This happened a couple of times until Jim suggested we slam the doors in unison. We did after a count of three and the hood popped open to its full height. The truck did its work for the winter, and the sanding crew named it The Whale for she looked like one with its mouth open every time somebody shut the doors at the same time.

Sanding in those days was hard work. The truck was backed up to the town sand pile so Jim and his crew could shovel the heavy, half-frozen stuff into the bed by hand. Then as Jim drove the icy roads, the crew shoveled it off. It was severely laborious, but at least we had some money coming in when the chicken barn was empty between flocks. The old Whale did her job for the winter, but she didn't have another mile to give come spring and she went to a junkyard to provide parts for others of her breed.

One of the winter's storms was neither snow nor ice but rain that wouldn't cease. The ground was frozen so the rain was not absorbed, but instead just flowed all over and into everything. At the end of several days we faced an approaching problem that quickly bordered on catastrophe.

The basement in the old barn that Jim had dug out was flooding. Rented sump pumps couldn't handle it, as the chicken litter kept jamming them up, and the natural drains he had built into the floor were overwhelmed by such volume.

It was soon obvious the chickens in the basement would drown if we didn't get them out of it. The basement flock consisted of a new experiment by the chicken company. The birds were capons, castrated roosters. By this point, they were big, heavy birds and even though neutered still had the aggressive temperament of roosters. They would soon be going to market, but the only thing we could do with the basement birds now was get them up and onto the first floor of the adjoining addition to keep them from drowning.

The addition had no basement, and because of the lay of the land there was a two-foot aperture near the ceiling of the old barn basement and the first-floor of the new barn. It was the full width of the pen, thirty-six feet. This allowed for good air circulation and so was left open.

The only way we could move the chickens out was to lift them up over our heads and fling them through this opening so they could join the first floor birds in a dry pen. Well, picture this: There were more than fifteen hundred chickens to move and they didn't want to be caught, picked up, or flung through the overhead space. It would have been a difficult task even if they and we had been dry, but we were standing knee-deep in a thick, gooey, mixture of sawdust, water, chicken manure, and feathers. The birds, originally white, were now big blobs of dung-covered muck flopping around. We could only deal with one bird at a time because as soon as we caught one they squawked and flapped their wings wildly, spraying this awful mixture all over us. Since we had to lift each one above our heads, the goo ran down over our heads, faces, arms, and bodies. This went on for hours, and we couldn't stop because the water kept rising. It was without question the most filthy, fatiguing mess we had ever been in. If we didn't know who we were we could never have recognized each other, we were completely drenched in this manure concoction. And we stunk. The water enhanced every bit of odor in the manure, and a wet chicken has a most unpleasant odor anyway.

By the time we finished we were utterly vile. We couldn't possibly go into the house they way we were—just two dripping pillars of manure. Our only solution was to go behind the house, hook up the hose, take off every stitch of clothing and hose each other down, even though the rain was lashing down in icy torrents. Finally, cleaner, but blue with cold, we tore naked into the house through the back door, and since we were too chilled for one to wait, we crowded together under a hot shower with a big bottle of shampoo and plenty of soap. We stayed there until we looked and felt like human beings again.

The rainstorm washed away the snow and when sub-freezing temperatures quickly followed, the farm pond became a wondrous, gleaming sheet of glass that begged for skaters.

There had been so much snow that winter that this provided the first good skating of the season, so we organized a skating party with our Round Pond friends. About thirty of them and their children arrived that evening. We built a bonfire at the edge of the pond, made hot chocolate, and played a game of Prisoner's Base. In this game, two leaders alternate in choosing their team always aiming for the best skaters. A line is drawn in the ice across the pond and the object is for each team to tag anyone who crosses it. To obtain prisoners one must cross the line daring to tag a prospective prisoner without being touched in return. Once tagged you are a prisoner of the opposite team, and having the most prisoners constitutes victory. It is fast, challenging, and exhilarating.

A full moon lit the pond in blue brilliance; there were dark shadows of spruce on its eastern edge, deep silent forest beyond, but around all of us was excited laughter and shouting at tagging and near misses. The temperature was cold, but our strenuous activity kept us comfortably warm. There is a magic about skating at night that makes you feel you aren't even connected to the ice but floating almost effortlessly above it in a mysterious exultation.

Even as physically active as we were each day, we used muscles that night that apparently had been dormant. The next morning we hobbled through our chores as our thigh and calf muscles shrieked with pain and stiffness. After supper, Jim helped me stretch out on my couch, and he eased himself onto his and we turned on our small black-and-white television vowing we wouldn't skate like that again for a long while.

After settling in for about ten minutes, we heard pounding feet and clanking skate blades in the kitchen. Our gang came bursting into the living room yelling at us to come skating. We stared at them in pained disbelief, and told them we could barely walk. They replied they felt the same way, but the weather would soon change and good skating would be gone. True. They pulled us off the couches, and we were soon back on the pond. We were younger than many of the group so we didn't have age as an excuse. Our legs quickly loosened up and we played Prisoner's Base into the night, skate blades flashing in the moonlight.

We were sure we would need wheelchairs the next day, but amazingly, we awoke and dove into our chores with not an ache or twinge. The resiliency of youth perhaps.

Winter makes everything one must do outdoors fraught with hazards. It also brings profound beauty. When a snowstorm has ceased it is like being inside a pearl, a white world except for the rich and eternal warmth of green pine and spruce. Early evening horizons are sometimes the color of smoke and tender opal, but most often the dusky blue of a purple grape blending upward into soft violet and rose. The stars of January put on an astounding display, probably because of the clear, cold atmosphere. They hang in the sky like jewels of ice and fire. On windless, silent nights fairy crystals of frost float in the air. There is always a reason to take a last inspiring look out the door before going to bed.

One early February morning I was driving around the shore returning from an errand. The ocean scene was so compelling I had to stop. The tide was low, each frond of seaweed was crystallized and the rocks wore custom-fitted ice caps, making the shore look like a primordial scene from an approaching ice age. Through the clouds, a ray of sun shone on the islands blazing their snow covers white against a blackened sky. Scattered wraithlike spirals of vapor rose like ancient smoke signals. Although winter-dark and moving stiffly in the frigid wind, green of pine and spruce attested to enduring life in this otherwise dormant world of winter.

The sounds of shell ice breaking as the tide receded: combined with by the deep, soft boomings of the tidal surge drifted inland on air filled with the rich smell of kelp and seaweed. Handsome black-and-white Eider ducks rode the swells close to shore. Experiences like these are what make living on the Maine Coast worth whatever it requires to be here. The seasons, like the tides, flow in their certain and infinite pattern. Maine winters are long, but well worth it when spring's enchantment arrives.

Late February has a special light that foretells it's coming dawn. The side of the pond reached by the sun has melted into a melon slice of ice. The fall cry of the seagull is shrill and desolate, silent in winter, but in March the gulls sail the sky with joyful calls that clearly declare their exuberance at the coming of the soft and gentle times.

There are other harbingers of an early spring, which rise from their dormancy to look out upon a more kindly world. One of these caused a problem in the chicken barn. The new broiler flock was about six weeks old, and each morning on the first floor of the old section of the barn we were finding chicken parts. Strangely, these consisted of only tiny gizzards and lower legs and feet of the birds. There were dozens of them. We couldn't imagine what would discard just those. We knew Blackie, the cat, was fond of the baby chicks if he had a chance, but like his mice, he would have devoured them totally.

Jim began checking the barn after dark, and one night came hurrying in and told me to get the big flashlight. He grabbed his shotgun. He had surprised a skunk in the first floor chicken pen. He reasoned that using the barn's electric lights would cause too much confusion with startled chicks running everywhere to shoot the skunk, but chickens don't move in the dark.

The pen was approached by an entryway, and a wooden door with hook and eye latch led into it; there was a spring to keep the door closed when we were working inside. Jim flashed the light, located the skunk and gave me the light to hold on him as he gazed at us, then Jim shot him. Taking the light he made a sweep and found another one. Within a few minutes he had shot four skunks in the pen and we were sure that was it. But no, a further look revealed a fifth one, and for some reason he was running straight at us. Jim was frantically searching for another shell, but had grabbed only four, thinking there was but one skunk.

As they were shot, each skunk released their perfume making it barely possible to breathe. We didn't want this one spraying us directly. Jim said, "Douse the light, we'll get out of here and I'll get more shells." We knew the door was directly behind us, but when we reached it, it wouldn't open. When we had entered the pen the spring brought it shut with enough force to make the hook vibrate and fall into its eyebolt. We were securely locked in from the outside. Another flash of the light showed the skunk still coming. He was purposeful with a nasty expression on his face. With a couple of good shoulder heaves and kicks, Jim freed the door and we skipped out quickly. We did manage to do in the fifth skunk. We don't like to upset nature's balance, but the numbers of chicken deaths were increasing nightly, and it was likely that the kingdom of skunks were being notified about this wonderful free lunch program.

The next day we put up screening and opened the sliding front doors to air out the barn. A neighbor half a mile down the road said he could smell the skunks.

CHAPTER 13
And Then There Were Pheasants

So much comes to life and activity in spring it was hard to decide what we looked forward to the most. No question, getting *Spindrift* scraped, painted, and back in the water, not to mention preparing two hundred lobster traps, was highest on our list. But that was followed close by lambing season. This was our first year producing a purebred lamb crop and we waited eagerly all winter to see what our North Country Cheviot ram and his ewes would produce. We had some nice orders for breeding stock to fill and still wished for enough ewe lambs to keep for building our flock. One aspect of purebreds that appealed greatly to us was that most of the lambs would be registered and reproduce their kind rather than the whole crop going to market for meat as in the past.

In mid-March the lambs began arriving. Old black-faced Sheba was first, as always, with a pair of brockle-face lambs, their faces and legs splotched black and white.

Before long the North Country Cheviot ewes were popping them out daily. They were just yearlings when they were bred, but they bore the lambs with ease. The ten ewes presented us with eighteen lambs, almost evenly divided between rams and ewes. We were jubilant! Beyond the numbers were the excellent breed characteristics. They were alert, vigorous lambs and on their feet and nursing in less than half the time to which we were accustomed. The ewes were great milkers and avid mothers. Sometimes ewes view the whole process of bearing a lamb as a dull bore and don't want any part of raising it. This meant we had to feed some lambs on a bottle. And while it may seem charming, it becomes just another chore when you already have too many. These North Country Cheviots were the only sheep we had ever seen that actually wanted to steal each other's lambs.

The crop was looking great, and the future of our purebred sheep operation showed glowing promise. Also dancing in our minds was building a new barn for the sheep. The old carriage shed now serving this purpose was decades-old and required more repair than it was worth—and it was too small. We planned to add to the brood flock and hold over yearling stock for sale, so we needed more room for hay storage. One thing always led to another.

Jim had plans for a good pole barn that could be reasonably built. It would be ideal for sheep as it would have a dirt floor for absorption and easy cleanout, and a low roof. The center part of the barn would be for hay storage and the sides for sheep pens. It would have a separate cement-floored grain room for dry and protected storage of grain bags. It would be a good, efficient building, but financially we were reaching for every dollar we could find just to hold what we had.

Still, we put together another proposal and paid a visit to the Farmers Home Administration. We needed twenty-five hundred dollars to build the barn. FHA had little or no experience with purebred or commercial sheep operations and weren't sure they wanted to. They were getting their debt repayment through assignments from the chicken company—even though our labor and investment in that business was paid for by lobstering, town work, and hopefully sheep. On that basis they had no complaint and after committee meetings and tedious delays they loaned us money for the sheep barn.

Finding time to build it was another issue. Jim needed to work it in between lobstering, taking care of the chickens, and cleaning out the barn. We also needed to cut and harvest the winter's hay.

We had little time to read anything but the weekly paper, and one night Jim noted an article detailing the State of Maine's intent to rebuild the wild pheasant population by raising day-old hatchlings and releasing them into the wild when ready. The state was looking for brooding facilities and would pay reasonably well. Since we were always scrambling for ways to earn money, we gave it some thought.

We certainly couldn't put them in the already full chicken barn, but Jim did some "ciphering," as he liked to call it, and reasoned that the square footage of the planned sheep barn would hold eight thousand pheasants. We still had the propane gas brooders from our original broiler flock, and the barn wouldn't be needed for hay until the pheasants were ready to leave. And the sheep wouldn't be moving into the barn until fall as they pastured all summer.

The only hitch to this neat idea—we needed to build the sheep barn immediately. So here we went again. Once we launched *Spindrift* and set out the lobster traps, Jim started on the new barn. We had met with Maine game officials, and they were pleased to have us brood the pheasants. They knew we had extensive experience with brooding young birds by this time, but there was a tight time frame. The young pheasants had to be released into the wild by mid-summer while adequate food remained available for them to learn how to survive on their own. Our new barn had to go up, now!

My contribution to the effort was to care for the twenty thousand broilers. It may be hard to believe, but Jim built the new barn in just nine days. During the last three days a neighbor helped us by running a small crane to lift rafters in place that Jim had built on the ground. The roof was aluminum, and the sheets, alternated with green plastic panels for light, went on quickly. We spread the sawdust and Jim set up the gas brooders, which were big metal hovers that look like flying saucers. The heating elements are in the center and provide a gentle heat and still plenty of air. Setting them to maintain a proper flame is a science in itself and one Jim learned through pain and patience. Each brooder is surrounded by a small, wire fence so that the appropriate number of birds have room to keep warm until their feathers begin to grow.

The gallon water jugs not used in the chicken barn were filled and ready for these little creatures of the wild. They arrived in a truck, packed one hundred to a four-sectioned cardboard box. The pheasants were much smaller than broiler chicks, and not bright yellow but instead a sort of gray-and-white mottle cleverly designed by nature to camouflage them in the woods.

We placed the pheasants inside each brooder area and they took a lively interest in the feed and water. Grain was supplied by the state. Poultry of any type is not strong on brain power, and even though these were creatures of the wild that one might think should be a little smarter, they didn't seek out heat and shelter; it took a loving mother to tuck them under her wings come nightfall. We provided the mothering in this case, which consisted of gently shoving them a handful at a time under the brooders. It was time consuming and we were extremely quiet for even a slight noise caused them all to rush out from underneath their hover and forced us to start all over again.

The first night it took several hours to get all the pheasants under cover and just as we were tiptoeing out of the barn, a wrench in Jim's back pocket accidentally hit a water pipe with a slight clang, and every last little pheasant rushed out from the brooders to huddle against the surrounding fence. There was little time left for sleep that night. We repeated this procedure for a couple of weeks. But as the weather grew warmer and they feathered out, this nightly chore wasn't so critical.

Eventually the brooders and surrounding small fences were no longer needed and the birds could have the entire dirt floor of the barn. As they grew we found that they were great little diggers. Instinct taught them, as is true with most poultry, to scratch in search of feed. Most of their scratching was along the outer walls of the barn and before long they were burrowing out under the barn wall and into the big world. We were kept busy shooing them back in and trying to plug the holes.

When it was nearly time for state game officials to come and get them, they were already escaping on a regular basis and we couldn't plug the holes fast enough. We got them back by being on hand almost constantly. At least they didn't escape at night.

A couple of days before their scheduled departure a group from the state came to inspect the pheasants and ascertain their readiness to leave. It was a day we'll never forget. It seemed the birds must have planned their escape starting at dawn, for even as early as we arose, we found about five thousand of them already outside, wandering the pastures, bouncing along the banks of the pond, all just happily scratching and pecking. Those who had suddenly learned to fly were roosting in the apple trees and atop the barn's ridgepole enjoying the early morning sun. The state visitors were due in just three hours and we faced a challenge equal to sweeping back the tide with a broom.

Regardless of the challenge, the pheasants absolutely had to be back inside the barn before the state team arrived.

Our first move was to entice them with rattling grain buckets and spreading feed in the barn feeders. This eventually took care of the greater number and once we had them inside, we frantically worked to plug up the ditches they had dug around the walls to escape. We were sweating physically as we mentally and nervously watching the road for the state officials.

There was so little time left when we got back outside that we quickly realized we could not possibly get the last few hundred birds back into the barn in time. We decided our best strategy was to drive them into the woods and hope they would return to the pasture by nightfall. Taking brooms we swished them out of the apple trees, threw pebbles on the metal barn roof to scare them down, and followed them with brooms to the woods edge. Finally, we had driven them all out of sight or so we thought.

So, now back to state inspection day. Luckily, the state group arrived just after we had swept the last pheasant into the woods. After greetings and small talk were exchanged we headed for the barn to view the pheasants. To our heart-clutching horror we could see that many of those that we had driven into the woods were already back in the pasture wanting to return to the barn. We couldn't sweep them away either from it or into it; we just had to hope no one would notice. Worst of all, our cats were all outside stalking the returnees. Baby and her daughter, Shag Mop, were running madly for the same poor pheasant. Blackie had cornered two by the stone wall. Esmeralda was climbing an apple tree to pursue a few who had flown into its branches. Sandy already successful in his hunt, was hauling one away, his head high like a proud lion trying to keep his kill from dragging on the ground.

Jim and I didn't dare look at each other. We babbled to our visitors trying to keep them distracted and we hustled them into the barn where the large flock was scratching and digging away no doubt planning their next escape. To our relief they never noticed the big hunt going on outside. They were impressed with our pheasants and planned to pick up within the next two days. We hustled them back to the car, none the wiser.

Whew!

We successfully rescued the rest of the birds that night—with the exception of those the cats enjoyed for dinner. When the state crew came for them a few days later about three dozen pheasants escaped and flew into the woods. For the rest of the summer they came back in through the open south side of the barn and spent their nights roosting on the barn rafters. By fall they were beautiful examples of bright copper-colored males and sleek hens and eventually made their own way to the field and forest life.

CHAPTER 14
Haying

OUR FIELDS WERE ripe for haying, the timothy was heavy and high among the red-top, the yellow blossoms of the buttercups and flaming orange of devil's paint brush and purple blossomed cow-vetch were overlaid with the heady scent of white clover. It was all wild hay but full of rich nourishment. When the hay crop is ready and the weather is right for drying it, nothing else comes first. Jim would mow it one day, and with sunny, hot weather be able to ted (fluff it up) and bale it the next day. We lost our share of good hay to extended rainy spells but somehow never failed to get the crop in.

Our own fields didn't yield enough hay to support our farm, but many area people owned old farms no longer operating and didn't want to see their fields return to forest. Paying to cut them was expensive so they were glad to exchange the hay for free mowing.

Once baled, all hay must come into the barn even if it means working late nights, which it often did. My job was rounding up a crew of teenage boys, transporting them to the fields, and then driving our GMC truck around behind the tractor as Jim baled so the boys could stack it on the truck. The GMC would hold about two hundred bales. This job was a highlight of my summer; the fields

Jim working the fields on his tractor.

smelled so herbal and fresh and were in beautiful places near lakes, rivers, forests, or the sea.

Driving flat pastures is the easiest, but there aren't many of those in Maine. If the truck is half-loaded going up a hill it must stop wherever the bales are, because the loaders can't run up the hill after the truck. The driver must stop and start slowly and smoothly, because if the clutch grabs too quickly and the truck jerks ahead, the delicate load as well as the teenage stacker may spill onto the ground. When restarting from a full stop mid-hill, it is essential to know the "release-the-emergency-and-engage-the-clutch-move." Reloading the same load is not fun. Riding the clutch so a complete stop isn't necessary is not good for the clutch, although it does provide a nice, smooth operation for loading. The GMC was a very forgiving truck and she let me ride her clutch for many a load of hay without a breakdown.

When the truck was loaded, Jim tied it down with rope and secured the load tightly. The boys would climb on top of the load for a cooling, breezy ride home. By the time the hay was neatly stacked in the barn, I had sandwiches and cold drinks ready for hungry and thirsty workers.

Before going to bed at night Jim and I always made one last visit to the barn just to admire the growing haypile, breathe its sweet smell, and know the comfort of a good harvest that would feed our sheep for the winter.

With the right weather, haying should end by mid-July or even earlier for the best nutritive value, but that doesn't often happen near the shore. The sun may be out, but fog slows the drying process. Hay must be dry for two reasons: If the bales are too damp, they will mold internally and be unusable, or even worse, will generate heat from the retained moisture and spontaneously combust, in which case the barn and everything in it quickly goes up in flames.

Chapter 15
Hurricane!

IN THE SUMMER of 1960, the North Country Cheviot lambs were growing rapidly. After we got the pheasant litter cleaned out of the sheep barn, the flock moved into its new quarters. The sheep could come and go from their pasture, and although they were rugged and didn't need shelter, especially in summer, they looked upon the barn as home. They settled in at night looking out its open south side, peacefully chewing their cuds, eyes closed in bliss and long white ears shaking with the chewing motions. We imagined that they also inhaled the fragrance of the new hay knowing it assured them of being well fed for the winter.

Lobster fishing had been excellent, and our present broiler flock would leave in time for us to show our sheep again at the Union and Blue Hill fairs. Jim had boned up on techniques for trimming sheep and we had bought wool cards (hook-toothed flat paddles with handles) to bring all the fibers straight and to full length and hand shears for clipping.

It was early August and much of the garden had been harvested and was in the freezer; tomatoes and squash continued to grow. My parents had recently sold The Mayfair House, which they had renamed Snug Harbor Inn, and bought a new inn, which they called Ocean Reefs Inn, that was closer to us in Chamberlain. Connie, six, and Debby Jo, two, were both delightful and delighted with life. It was a richly rewarding season and everything was going well.

Until Mother Nature hammered us with the Big One.

We always knew she could, but had also hoped she wouldn't. We had survived summer blows, fall line gales, Nor'easters, and winter's worst. Each time there was always some loss of lobster gear, but nothing we couldn't replace.

Jim came back from lobstering one day in September and said he believed something bad was probably rolling up the coast. He had spent so much time on the sea that, like many who worked on the waters, he had a sense of portent when observing sky and winds. We had radio weather forecasts then, of course, but no satellites or sophisticated forecast systems. Hurricanes brewing far in the south had been mentioned, but opinions varied whether they would come this far north.

As a precaution, Jim moved most of his traps further off shore. The following day he felt things looked even more threatening, so he checked his anchor rodes and made a thorough investigation of the mooring chain and shackles. The pawl post in *Spindrift*'s central bow deck was solid oak, and if the mooring chain could break that in a bad wind, all would be lost anyway.

The next morning seas were churning and swells were rolling into Long Cove. In addition to the anchor always aboard the boat, we had an old but sound one hundred pound anchor that we had never used. Jim rigged it up and took it down to the shore. We had a little punt, square at both ends, named *Egad*, because that was what everybody said who got into it. It was more seaworthy than it felt, but was used only as a means to get back and forth to the mooring.

Egad was well loaded when Jim put the big anchor aboard and headed into the heaving waves, which seemingly increased in size and height with every passing moment. Anxiously, I watched him battle the wind and the rollers that tried pushing him back to shore. He would disappear in a deep trough for so long I thought surely he swamped.

Eventually he made his tortuous way to the bow of *Spindrift*. He stood up in the punt despite the seas and managed to secure the bitter end of the anchor rode to the pawl post on the bow. Then he continued fighting his way to a point about one hundred yards off *Spindrift's* bow. This location allowed adequate scope for the anchor rode. As Jim shoved the heavy anchor over *Egad's* side, a huge comber slopped in and swamped him.

In cold and helpless fear, I saw him standing in the nearly submerged skiff. Grabbing the anchor rode, he labored his way back to *Spindrift* pulling himself and *Egad* hand over hand until he reached her gunwales. With the punt's painter in hand, he pulled himself along the boat's side to a point near her stem. She was now rising and dropping at a great rate. So was Jim and the half-sunken punt, but because of their difference in size the two boats were not doing so in unison. Jim could only board *Spindrift* by reaching over her washboards and hauling himself chest first over the side. A mighty sea lifted her just as he caught hold putting such a strain on his body that he cracked three ribs. But he did get aboard and managed to haul *Egad*, mostly full of water, over the side and turn it to dump the water out.

He had installed an automatic bilge pump under the floorboards. It worked off the battery and was designed to handle rainfall and water that came in over the sides in rough seas. He did everything for our boat that could be done; she was now at the mercy of wind and wave. *Spindrift* was committed to the mooring for better or worse.

As time passed, we watched from shore as conditions grew wilder; strong winds whipped the water to a frenzy, and the booming surf didn't diminish even with the ebbing tide. The air was filled with the deeply rich marine smell that comes from the sea's churned up depths. That night we made several trips to Long Cove and used our headlights to see our boat. Most of the time it was impossible to see her as lashing rain and shrieking winds combined to create a nearly solid wall of water. Occasionally, we would get a glimpse of her as her bow dove down into the swells and, once reaching the bottom, soared skyward again. She looked good on the waterline, so we knew the bilge pump must be working. Her position against the shore background showed that the mooring wasn't dragging, and the anchor rode was taut. It was a prayerful and sleepless night. And it wasn't the last one.

The next day the cove was a boiling mass of foam and white-crested rollers. A few smaller boats had broken loose of their mooring and gone ashore. It wasn't possible to reach *Spindrift* in this weather, but it looked as if she was holding well. We could only wait for the storm to pass. Unfortunately, that didn't happen quickly. The storm continued in full force and we suffered another day and night of the same anguish.

Finally, the storm backed off a bit and the rains stopped as the sunlight streamed between clouds. *Spindrift* remained right where she was supposed to be. However, she was the only boat left in the cove. All other boats had been pleasure boats, and if they hadn't been taken ashore by their owners, they were sent there by the storm. One lovely sailboat lay on the rocks upside down with her mast driven right up through her hull. It was all a sickening sight. Despite the sunshine, the seas were still too rough for us to reach *Spindrift*.

The following morning we could no longer stand the anxiety of not knowing whether we had any lobstering gear left. Leaving Connie and Debby Jo with my mother, we headed for the shore. The breakers were no longer white-topped, just rolling swells. We shoved off in *Egad* and took a wild ride out to *Spindrift*. It took some time to get aboard, but the relief was great to see that all was safe.

She had been well washed in both salt and fresh water, and some of her windshield glass had been broken by the power of the wind. The anchor rode had chafed but not dangerously. Luckily, the bilge pump and the battery had done their jobs.

The engine was damp, but soon started and settled to a steady beat as if it was the boat's heart. Jim pulled up the anchor, hooked *Egad* to the mooring and cast the mooring chain. Its clanking rattle was comforting because we knew it and the anchor had kept *Spindrift* safe.

When we moved beyond Long Cove Point we didn't seem to be looking at water, rather at individual mountains rolling toward us. They came slowly and majestically with long valleys between them. We engaged each one. The boat rose and kept rising, I expected her to come down pounding, but this was not a choppy sea, this was a moving alpine range and *Spindrift* continued to lift until her stem was flush with the frothing wake, and it seemed as if the water must pour over it and into the cockpit.

Then she slid down a gleaming hill of water into the valley's depths, and once more began to rise for long moments until it seemed as if all of her twenty-six feet stood on end. Anyone watching from shore would have seen her entire washboards from stem to stern outlined against the great heaving sea that rose up under her. Jim kept his hand on the throttle because a steady power could drive the boat's bow so deep into a rising peak that she would be swamped. Even at the slowest speed she descended in a rush into the next trough throwing spray outward from her high bows in a distance nearly equal to her length. *Spindrift* was young and strong, but these were killer seas.

It probably was not wise to be out in such weather regardless of Jim's skill or the boat's ability, but these storms were making the ultimate decision on the future of our lobstering, and we had to know the answer. We made our heaving, plunging way offshore and as near the islands as we dared, seeing nothing but floating logs, whole trees, and pieces of boats and docks occasionally.

Stretching to look upward at the top of a sea mountain above us we saw a huge snarl of lobster buoys of every color. A couple of them were ours, but there was no way to retrieve them in these conditions. It was all we saw of any of our gear. Soon, we headed home. Now we were in following seas; coming at our stern they drove us ahead as if we were on a high-speed roller coaster. This was far more dangerous than taking them head on, because if Jim didn't keep his speed and steering under perfect control in the tremendous forward rushes, the boat would swing, then broach, and either roll over completely or fill and swamp. These swells were now coming from the ocean's heart and not from the wind. The Pemaquid gong buoy and New Harbor bell buoy were sounding strong and deeply in response to the tortured sea.

To me it was one of the most exciting and challenging adventures I had ever been on, and after *Spindrift's* performance in it, I would have ridden in her to England with Jim as captain if he said we had to. The promise *Spindrift* had made to us of her sea-going capabilities when we first looked at the beautiful lines she presented in Leslie's boat shop had been kept. Indeed, she was able.

But it was a heartbreaking day.

We sat in silence and both knew without saying a word that our lobster fishing days were over. There was no insurance for lobster gear. Even the price to insure *Spindrift* was prohibitive so she was not covered either. We had no money to buy the stock to build the two hundred new traps necessary. And with the debt load we now carried, it was certain no bank would loan us more money.

A few days later we returned to the sea in calmer weather and located maybe a dozen lobster traps, all badly smashed. We were not alone. Lobstermen up and down the coast suffered tremendous gear losses, not to mention some lost their boats.

We had no choice but to move forward. This began with "counting our blessings," as my mother used to say. We were both now in our thirties, we had two sweet and precious daughters to protect and provide for, and while the farm was deeply in debt, we were determined to make it work.

If we lived long enough to get it all paid for it would be worth all efforts—*Spindrift* was a beautiful boat that was ours free and clear and could provide some family pleasure in the future. At the time, we didn't even once consider selling it, no matter how much we needed money. No, *Spindrift* had a soul and was created especially for us. We loved her so.

Connie and two lambs in 1961.

CHAPTER 16

Traveling the State Fair Circuit

WITH OUR LOBSTER fishing days over, and with it income we desperately needed to pay on our top-heavy chicken business debts, we needed to find another source of money. And fast. The dump truck and farm equipment were providing all they could in roadwork, but it was still just a temporary patch over the "hole in the dike." We searched our minds frantically trying to think of ways to supplement our income before we faced the horror of losing the farm.

Our minds continually returned to the sheep. Our breeding stock sales were encouraging, but advertising was expensive and we were often told it was not productive. Sheep farmers wanted to examine sheep firsthand before buying them and usually wanted to see how they fared in competition. Showing our sheep at Maine agricultural fairs might be a stopgap answer until we became more established and could take the sheep further afield to regional shows. We had become dedicated to our sheep and were eager to learn every aspect and ways to improve our breed quality. We read as much as we could and attended University of Maine seminars whenever possible. If our sheep were as strong as we thought, we could earn good prize money at the fairs, even if we didn't always win first place, while the business was building.

Connie, May, and Debby Jo in Blue Hill in the early 1960s.

In the early 1960s, there were essentially ten significant agricultural fairs in Maine, and most of them were also attended by out-of-state exhibitors. Most fairs lasted a week and, through state rules and common sense, the fairs didn't overlap each other. You could leave one fair on the last Saturday afternoon and arrive at the next one that night or the following morning.

We had the sheep, equipment, motivation, and enthusiasm and, now that we didn't need to haul our traps, we could spend most of the ten weeks from late July through early October showing our sheep. Of course, it wasn't all that simple. Attending fairs and showing sheep would require both of us, and we would need to take Connie and

Debby Jo along with us. There were also the chickens to consider. We still needed to feed twenty thousand chickens daily, and returning each day from the fairs, some more than two hundred miles away, was impossible.

However, since each broiler flock was in the barn for ten to twelve weeks, with careful planning we felt we could get a flock in the barn and established before we hit the road for fair season. While clean-out and setup had to be done by us, once the birds were established in the barn, the feeders and automatic waterers reduced the daily time commitment to just four or five hours. To make this work, we needed to find someone willing to take care of the chickens for ten weeks. Our tentative projections showed that if we won at least average prize money, we could pay someone to work and still earn enough between the chickens and breeding stock sales to earn a good profit. We wouldn't get rich, but this arrangement would help replace some of our lost lobstering income.

At the time we made this decision, we had nearly a year to plan for the timely arrival of broiler flocks to make it all possible. We found a willing neighbor, retired but strong and eager for something different to occupy his time, to take the chicken feeding job.

We passed the winter in usual fashion and as spring turned to summer we had finished the spring roadwork, we had filled the barn with hay, and we had scraped, painted, and launched *Spindrift*. We even managed to slip away on her for a few evenings and fill our freezer with fresh mackerel caught out on Muscongus Bay.

By early summer, the premium books from each fair began arriving and our excitement grew. We both agreed that beyond our primary goal of earning extra money we were excited to start a new adventure, enjoy new experiences, and live a kind of "gypsy life." In anticipation, we began to assemble buckets, feeders, and trimming tools. The four of us living in the back of a dump truck for ten weeks was not appealing or practical so we bought a tent, camp stove, lantern, and air mattresses. Jim built a tall wooden body on the dump truck with steel bows and heavy canvas cover. It had a second deck to carry hay, grain, and equipment. The sheep would ride on the floor of the truck body. We considered it our covered wagon.

We planned to return home weekly, when possible, to check on the chickens and the farm. And in case of emergency, we could always be reached by telephone by calling the fair's livestock office.

Our first fair was the Bangor State Fair in late July. Bangor, one of Maine's largest cities and once considered the lumber capital of the world, is located in Penobscot County at the headwaters of the Penobscot River. The drive to the Queen City would take us more than two hours, so by 4 a.m. the day before the fair opened we loaded the sheep into the truck and packed our station wagon with camping equipment, clothing, and food. We hit the road before daylight. Debby Jo and I rode in the car following Jim and Connie who were in the truck. We were on the road, our hearts singing in anticipation. We felt like we were running away to join the circus.

By sunrise, we were enjoying coffee and doughnuts at Lights Motel and Restaurant in Searsport. When we reached Bangor a short time later, the fairgrounds were humming with activity as the grease-covered midway crews assembled the Ferris wheel and thrill rides. At the livestock area, which was well removed from the carnival, huge farm trucks lumbered up to the cattle sheds. The cattle, neatly tied in rows to the inside of the tall, wooden truck bodies, hung their heads

over the truck sides. Their soft eyes gazed in mild curiosity at the commotion as other cattle were unloaded.

Each farm brought their own breed so the uniformity of the faces
in each truck was striking—the black-and-white Holsteins, honey-
colored Jerseys with dark-ringed eyes, deep ebony Black Angus, and
the almond-and-peach Brown Swiss. Each cattle exhibitor brought
in truckloads of sawdust or shavings and mounded it in their stalls in
the long cattle barns. A clean resin scent filled the air.

It was exciting and there was so much to see, but first we had to
unload our own animals. Finding our pens clearly marked for us in
the nearby sheep sheds, we spread fresh straw in each pen then backed
up the truck to them. We sorted the sheep by age and sex and fun-
neled them into the proper pens. After providing them with water
and feed, we proceeded to find a high and grassy spot near the barns
to pitch our tent. It had a canvas floor, but we spread a sheet of plastic under it to cut down the potential dampness.

The sheep show didn't start for a few days so we had time to wash
the sheep with hoses and special soap and set up the blocking stand. The
stand was a low table-like device that the sheep could stand on while
being trimmed. There is an upright rod at one end with a neck-piece
that the sheep's neck and head rests on. A piece of rope holds the sheep's
head in place and it feels secure, but until the animal becomes used to it,
the sheep will often swing itself from side to side stepping partway off
the stand and causing difficulty for all concerned. We have seen unruly
sheep running around the livestock area with this piece of equipment,
which weighs almost as much they do, flopping along with them. They
never seemed to get hurt, but they can be hazardous to catch.

Our sheep were not wild, but they always required some training
at the first fair. Later in the season, the sheep would climb up on the

stand, close their eyes and chew their cuds while we carded out their wool and Jim trimmed their fleeces, literally sculpting them in wool to their best and proper body form. I never mastered the trimming shears, but I was a master at washing out the dung tags that sometimes collected under and around their "docks"—or tail areas. Meanwhile, the testicles of young rams are nearly always wool-covered and sport a tangle of "grease locks" caused by the wealth of lanolin produced in wool. Since male sheep have the ability to breed many ewes within a short time, they are well endowed in this particular area. Washing and combing out these locks was also one of my specialties. So much so, I was known as the "Bag Lady."

To each his own, I guess, but those not skilled at trimming get the lesser jobs that also must be done. I truly never minded. Any task that involved animals never offended my senses. Even though, this particular job did feature a lot of messy manure and lanolin dripping off my elbows, it was all necessary—you just can't show an elegantly coiffed sheep with a dirty rear-end and scruffy testicles.

Each sheep must be trimmed more than once, as the carding process does not bring out every tuft of fleece during the first few rounds. As we finished each sheep we covered them with a blanket—light canvas covers that I custom made (it was too expensive to buy them) by first measuring the yearlings and lambs with an old sheet to establish a pattern. The public always thought these covers were to keep sheep warm, but keeping them clean was the real purpose.

Soon, the sheep pens were full and other exhibitors were trimming, near their pens just as we were. Most of the exhibitors had growing children, many of them in 4-H, so there were other children for Connie and Debby Jo to play with. The kids invented wonderful creations using mud and wool trimmings and they spent naptimes on

May and Jim finishing a shearing job.

cozy beds of straw in an empty sheep pen. Through the daily hours of working on our sheep near the other exhibitors we soon established friendships, some that continued for decades. Since we were rookies, we learned a lot from older exhibitors and general observation.

Denny Bascom was there and did his trimming apart from the rest of us. He guarded his grooming secrets and did not share them with anyone. Although none of us could afford to think of sheep showing as a sport—we all needed the prize money and sheep sales—we all believed in friendly competition.

Connie and Debby Jo holding a trophy won at an agricultural fair in the 1960s.

It was at the Bangor State Fair during our first full season of show-ing sheep that we met Frank Gilbert, an old gentleman who forever remained in our memories. Frank owned a farm in the mountain country near Starks. He didn't appear to weigh even one hundred pounds, but his strength was wiry and his spirit fiery. He had wispy white hair, a warm smile dotted with a few teeth, a long drooping white mustache that naturally bent upward at the ends and china-blue eyes merry as morning sunshine. Frank was already in his eighties when we met him, but we never knew Frank's age until he died some years later. He had been showing sheep at Maine fairs since 1905.

During evenings around the sheep barn, he told us how in the old days the State of Maine provided transportation by rail to some of the major livestock fairs such as Bangor. The railroad cars of sheep, dairy cattle, draft horses, and oxen were unloaded at the train station and driven by their owners through the streets of Bangor and up the hill to the fairgrounds. It was a long route and fraught with sights and sounds most strange to these animals who had been living a peaceful rural life at their home farms. This "cattle drive" was a popular annual event and drew many spectators. There were minor mishaps, but Frank said he never forgot one day of terror when a long-horned bull went berserk due to the commotion and gored his owner to death.

Frank loved his sheep and his two little cocker spaniels, named Brownie and Blackie for their colors. When Frank spoke, or told a story, he closed the fingers on his big, gnarled hands, but left his thumbs sticking upward and flung them about to emphasize the points he was making. He matter-of-factly told all of us that each year he went to his local bank and borrowed money to buy feed and fuel for the show circuit and then paid it back in the fall using his prize money. Apparently, he kept his word through the years, because the bank always came through for him each spring.

At the start of the season, Frank's sheep were not unhealthy but definitely thin. Winter feed was hard to come by on his sparse income. He had about six breeds and typically entered more than thirty sheep in competition (which afforded him more chances to win individual breed prize money). Frank's remark about his sheep at the season's start was: "Them poor slab-sided bastids wouldn't make a pot o' soup!"

There were too many sheep and too many individual breeds at the Bangor State Fair to complete judging in less than four days, which included one day for the 4-H sheep. The 4-H show was an inspiring display of youth at its best, for those 4-H'ers with purebred flocks tended to their projects year round. They performed the daily chores of feed and care then handled special times such as lambing and grooming to show their sheep. Responsibility to a living being and good sportsmanship in the show ring were a must, and these young people from nine to nineteen (4-H required ages) were heartwarming examples of clean-cut American youth.

This was true, of course, of everyone in 4-H. Those with goats, dairy, and beef cattle wore snow-white uniforms in the show ring. Little children with pulling cattle got out into the rings with their teams hitched to a stone drag and could "Gee" and "Haw" with the best of them. Little as they were, Connie and Debby Jo watched all of this with awe and would eventually become very active in 4-H.

Because of the North Country Cheviot's rugged health and excellent results in cross-breeding with other sheep breeds, the University of Maine was encouraging sheep farmers to purchase them. Some farmers bought them from us, while others bought from breeders in Canada. Although we were the first to establish this breed in the Eastern United States, we were pleased to see other flocks come in, as this was necessary to promote the growth of the breed and to provide new bloodlines.

It was exciting to compete within our breed, and although we didn't win every class we won enough to be satisfied and earn good prize money. There were typically ten to twelve classes in sheep showing based on individual ages and sexes as well as combinations of groups. At the first fair of the season, sheep haven't the slightest idea what is expected of them and don't care to cooperate. There were many runaways and breathless chases to keep the spectators entertained.

Only registered, purebred sheep can be shown at the fairs, as promoting excellence in breed type is the object of competition. Each breed has its own registry and pedigree papers and ear tags to match are sent to the sheep breeders upon filling out forms indicating the sires and dams of the animals to be registered. The agricultural fairs were very strict about inspecting registration papers and ear tags on all livestock before they could be permitted to show.

Debby Jo dressed as little Bo Peep in the 1960s.

During our first year at Bangor, Frank was having a problem. Although he had applied for his registration papers they had not yet arrived, and the state inspector would not let him enter the sheep show without them. If he couldn't show his sheep, he couldn't earn the prize money he desperately needed. However, the inspector was not without heart. Knowing that Frank had shown sheep most of his life, the inspector agreed to accept a telephone confirmation that Frank's sheep papers were indeed being processed.

An agitated Frank was throwing his thumbs about and his mustache was fluttering as he breathlessly explained to the inspector that his failing eyes and ears didn't permit him to make proper use of a telephone. Since my end, literally, of the sheep prep was done, I was just watching Jim trimming. The inspector, who had many other animals to check, asked me if I would accompany Frank to a telephone and help him verify his sheep papers.

Frank was a charming soul and I was happy to comply. Making sure he had the telephone number (the registry was in Pennsylvania), we headed for the nearest public telephone. It was nearly show time so we had to make this call speedily or Frank would miss his classes. He was woefully deaf and as we climbed the hill to make the call he briefed me on the information needed from the breed secretary.

The phone booth stood next to the ox-pulling ring and there were ox teams crowded hard by the booth waiting their turns to pull. The air was filled with noise from the cheering crowds, the lowing of the cattle, and the hysterical shrieks of the ox-drivers urging their animals on to victory as they leaned on the rumps of the oxen screaming, "H I I I I I K E!" I couldn't shut out even a little of the din with the booth door because Frank hadn't finished giving me instructions.

He continued while I placed the call. He brought forth an antique leather purse containing change. At the moment I needed coins to complete the call, an ox swung against Frank knocking the open purse from his hand. While I tried to shout to the operator above the uproar, Frank, who was extremely nearsighted, was on his hands and knees crawling among the feet of the waiting oxen. He was laying an eyeball nearly to the ground here and there and groping frantically in the dust and fresh oxen droppings to find the scattered change.

There wasn't time to describe the total scene to the operator, so while she was demanding money for the call, I begged her to wait and let the phone dangle while I hastily helped Frank search underneath the oxen. When we found enough coins fit to deposit, we crawled out and somehow made ourselves understood enough to verify his sheep. With manure-stained knees and fingers, but happily victorious, we hurried back to the show ring with barely minutes to spare.

Since Frank had so many breeds of sheep to show, it was hard to find anyone free to help him who wasn't already involved with their own sheep of that breed. Our breed was done so we helped. As he pushed his sheep through the pen gates he whispered that we should pick off any ticks we might see because if the the officials saw them he would be disqualified and probably sent home. He said he would get all the sheep treated and cleaned up when he got to the next fair at Presque Isle, but until he won some prize money, he couldn't afford the tick powder.

A sheep tick, properly called Ked, is blood sucking, but not a source of disease and has no interest in human blood. If a tick lands on a person it is anxious to leave in search of sheep. A large infestation can eventually weaken a sheep, but it is a problem easily prevented by dipping (which we did annually after shearing even though we did not have ticks in the flock).

Frank's sheep were feisty and didn't want any part of the show, but we were young and supple so we could handle them. Frank was right about the ticks. In the warm sunshine they began to appear quite profusely and we held them in our hands as we caught them, surreptitiously mashing them underfoot when there was an opportunity, and trying hard not to look like we were catching them. Between classes we tried to remove all we could before taking them to the ring. We had stuck with Frank this far and couldn't let him down now. At the end of the show we disappeared behind a barn and searched each other for any ticks that might have crawled onto us in fear of taking them back to our own sheep, for we could not afford to be sent home. It was all worth it to see Frank's broad tooth-spattered grin as he calculated his earnings, which for anyone with enough good sheep might range from two hundred to four hundred dollars or more per week.

—◦◦◦—

On the last day of Bangor State Fair, we refueled the truck and car and struck our tent. We had enjoyed a pretty spot looking out over the hills beyond the mighty Penobscot River and the distant sparkling Ferris wheel. What is now the Bangor International Airport was then an Air Force Base, and the planes boomed overhead night and day. We were not accustomed to this type of noise on our farm, but those planes will always remain a nostalgic memory of the Bangor Fair.

All livestock were allowed to leave the fairgrounds on Saturday afternoon, and there was an orderly approach of trucks to the various barns. When this first fair began we had all arrived separately from many parts of Maine and other states. Now we were all heading out together for the Northern Maine Fair in Presque Isle. We had never visited The County, as Aroostook County is almost universally known, but we knew it was so big in area that both Connecticut and Rhode Island would fit within its borders.

We headed up Route 1 together in a long convoy of trucks and camping trailers. We didn't organize as a group; we were just simply headed to the same place at the same time. From then on, all through the summer and fall we traveled together from fair to fair and it was a fine way to go for we watched out for one another. The journey to Presque Isle, located on Route 1 between Houlton and Caribou, took several hours and was the longest of the year. It was especially long before Interstate 95 was built to Houlton. We pounded the long, seemingly endless road through miles of wilderness and the Haynesville Woods made famous by Maine country singer Dick Curless in his national hit song "Tombstone Every Mile." The refrain went:

It's a stretch of road up north in Maine
That's never ever ever seen a smile
If they'd buried all them truckers lost in them woods
There'd be a tombstone every mile
It's a stretch of road up north in Maine

That song came to symbolize the beginning of the fair season as did Roger Miller's "King Of The Road" which mentioned Bangor.

Third boxcar, midnight train, destination, Bangor, Maine
Old worn out clothes and shoes,
I don't pay no union dues,
I smoke old stogies I have found, short, but not too big around
I'm a man of means by no means, king of the road.

There was a lot of a sentimentality in those songs because for us they reflected some very special and happy times in our lives.

The going was slow on the first long night, and at about 2 a.m. we all pulled in to a lonely all-night diner frequented by potato trucks traveling south. Coffee was a must to keep going. Connie and Debby Jo were sleeping in the car seat beside me, but woke happily to have a glass of milk. Connie's little face looked tired and one of the sheep exhibitors, a jolly fellow named Clem, also a 4-H parent, smiled at her and said, "Your eyes look like two cane holes poked in a cow turd." Connie smiled back although she had no idea what he meant.

It was near dawn when we arrived at the Presque Isle Fairgrounds. Like most fairs the livestock barns and sheds were well removed from the carnival. The cyclone perimeter fence ran behind and alongside the sheds and the camping area, but we didn't become aware of our surroundings until the sheep were settled just as a pearly dawn was breaking.

The morning sun was pleasantly warm, and the surrounding grass released a spicy mint-like fragrance from blue flowers and thick ground ivy. Even the sheep were tired from the long journey and didn't rise to bleat for food until they saw the first person moving about.

The fair's livestock superintendent, Floyd C. Cunningham, had graciously stayed up most of the night to spread oat straw in sheep pens and to greet everyone with a warm welcome. Floyd, a farmer and a native of Caribou, became an unforgettable part of our life. He was in his mid-forties, had heavy dark eyebrows, mischief-merry eyes, a sort of three-cornered smile seemingly always in evidence for he constantly found or created a rich reason to laugh. He spoke in the quick, crisply northern accent of The County that has a touch of Canadian inflection and features rolling "r"s not heard Downstate, as any part of Maine below Aroostook County is referred to in the region.

Tired as we were, he kept us chuckling as we unloaded and sorted sheep, feeders, and water buckets. Floyd had undergone surgery that spring and described some of his experiences. He said he was a little concerned for the outcome because he overheard his wife checking the funeral homes to see which ones were giving green stamps. When he arrived at the hospital, he said, "They wheeled me down two miles o' cobblestone corridors then dumped me int' a little bed felt like it was made o' two by fours—unplaned. Hospital's a good place though when ya need one. Rushed me there once an' I thought I'd died and gone t' heaven for sure. There were women in white standing around my bed, an' nothin' but breasts hangin' over me in a complete circle. I thought, 'There! I've died and made it!'"

—∞—

The first week of fair season is the most exhausting for all animals. Sheep and cattle are fresh from pasture and must be cleaned and trimmed from scratch. Even cattle are clipped with electric shears to smooth around necks, briskets, heads, and rumps. The Bangor State Fair had been hectic and was followed by the long, arduous drive to Presque Isle, so this more laid-back agricultural fair was a welcome rest for us and the sheep—which needed only touch-up and daily care. Meanwhile, we were free to explore the countryside, which was covered by rolling squares of golden oats, an alternate crop for the potatoes, and the deep green of potato plants. Presque Isle is the largest city in Aroostook County, which was founded in 1839. As recently as the 1940s, Maine was the top potato producer in the nation because of Aroostock. Only a few years before we visited, the famed author John Steinbeck traveled into what he called the rooftop of Maine and wrote in his book, *Travels with Charley*: "I saw mountains of potatoes—oceans—more potatoes than you would think the world's population could consume in a hundred years."

Aroostook was nearly synonymous with potatoes and it was worth the trip just to see the beautiful display of potato blossoms. I always thought potato blooms were only white, but the fields in Aroostook were filled with lovely soft yellow and pink blossoms as well. However, we didn't find the flat lands expected of crop country, rather undulating land with narrow seams of spruce forest stitched around the edges of fields. The air bears a rich and loamy essence and the skies were crystalline; mountains, lakes, and rivers abounded. The potato houses—barns buried in the ground with only gambrel roofs show-ing—provided frost-free winter storage so farmers could store pota-toes in hopes of better market prices.

We also found large crops of green peas that were harvested with gargantuan machines. Floyd, anxious for us to enjoy the offerings of The County, gave us directions to the Bird's Eye packing and freezer plant. We followed Floyd's directions to the plant and found those in charge very hospitable and agreeable to an informal tour. The peas were harvested complete with the vines, meaning the whole plant was ripped from the ground. Machines then separated the pods and vines and extracted the peas, sorting them by size before packaging.

As we were leaving we asked our guide if we might buy a few fresh peas because they looked and smelled so good. "Sure," he said, and told us to wait in the car. In a few minutes a tractor with a great pile of pea vines clamped in the jaws of its bucket approached us. We thought we were in the way so Jim asked the driver if he wanted us to move our station wagon. "No," he said, "just open the rear door."

To our slack-jawed surprise he stuffed the contents of his tractor bucket into our car until peas and vines nearly reached the front seat. The driver smiled and said, "There, now you got a shellin' job ahead of ya!" Stammering, we asked him what we owed him. He laughed and waved us off.

The pungent pea vines were tightly packed in the interior of the car and were adorned with masses of deep green pods. Back at our own little corner of the fairgrounds we found a clean, grassy spot, backed up the car and pulled the mass of vines out of the car. Then we gath-ered the sheep and cow people to join us in a pea-shelling fest. We sat around as a large and happy group with pots and basins shelling peas and swapping stories throughout the afternoon and into the evening.

We shelled so many peas and they were so sweet, tender, and delicious that we all ate peas for several days, devising several ways to serve them. One way, based on a fine old Aroostook County recipe, called for them to swim in sweet cream. Rich Jersey milk was supplied by the dairy exhibitors. They milked their cows daily but typically disposed of the milk because it couldn't be sold given the state's rules.

The next day, after sheep chores and some light carding and trimming, we again ventured out into the countryside. The four of us found a wonderful quiet lake, went swimming, and enjoyed a refreshing bath and shampoo. The roads were long and narrow, and we followed one dirt road for several miles just to "see where it would go." It led to a stark and deeply weathered shell of an old house whose once-farmed fields were now returning to evergreen and poplar trees. Tree branches reached into the house through glassless windows. In addition to trees, the old fields now included great patches of lushly foliaged wild raspberries bushes just drooping with deep maroon berries featuring a silvery-dust sheen of ripe perfection. The berries were sweet and luscious.

We grabbed a couple of clean buckets from the car and began harvesting: one berry for the mouth and two for the bucket. Even at that rate the buckets filled rapidly. As we picked, we noted that this must be a popular spot even though it was miles away from the nearest house, for we could see clear and trampled trails through the bushy growth. Jim said, "Well, whoever comes here they must bring some pretty big dogs!" and he pointed out large piles of what appeared to be dog droppings.

When the buckets were full, we placed Connie and Debby Jo in the back seat of the car for naps while we stretched out in the grass nearby. Wild flowers grew all around us and we watched cottonball-like clouds sail over the spiked spruce skyline and listened to the soft, whispering click of long stemmed poplar leaves—appropriately called quaking aspen for their unique leaf action.

Once again we met the approval of the other livestock exhibitors when we returned to the fair and shared our flavorful harvest, once again enhanced by the rich milk of the Jersey cows. That evening when Floyd came to visit, we asked him about the abandoned farm where we had picked raspberries.

"Jeezus!" he shouted, "That ol' place is right run-over with Christless black bears in summertime. They just love them raspberries!"

Black Bears! That certainly resolved any mystery about the trampled paths and big piles of what we thought was dog doo. The raspberries tasted even sweeter after learning we had apparently snatched them from the jaws of big black bears. I've since wondered if while we were picking berries the bears were lounging in the woods sleeping off a raspberry binge, or if perhaps they sat back and watched us from the trees.

As we were all discussing bears and raspberries, Denny Bascom came limping by, complaining about a bone injury to his leg. Denny was a loner, but he enjoyed sympathy when he could get it and continued to make dark predictions about what might happen if his leg didn't heal.

Floyd finally shook his head and said, "You're comin' to it, Denny. You're comin' to it."

Denny asked, "What am I comin' to?"

"I knew a fella with almost the same trouble you got," Floyd said. "His broken leg wouldn't heal, and it wouldn't heal. So finally his doctor transplanted a bone to replace it and it healed up quick and good as new. Only trouble though wuz it wuz a dog's bone, and that fella had awful trouble gettin' past a fire hydrant!"

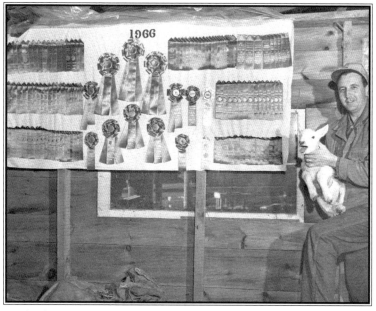

Jim holding a lamb and showing off some of the ribbons won at fairs in 1966.

Denny's face turned red enough to ignite and he huffed and mut-tered as he shuffled off to his truck—he was no longer limping. Floyd said, "When I'm in argument with somebody and their face turns red like that, I say to myself, 'Floydy-Boy, it's all comin' your way now.'"

The livestock exhibitors camped together, and we were so near the sheep and cattle barns we could view the animals from our living quarters. The sheep sheds had not quite collapsed, but they were try-ing to. The roof leaked in many places, and we had to replace old and rotting boards in the pens with other old and rotting boards almost daily because it didn't take the rams long to learn that rubbing their big heads on certain boards created an easy pathway to the great out-doors. The sheds had no walls, which was fine, as sheep need plenty of air both summer and winter. Meanwhile, Frank had taken some of his prize money from Bangor and managed to get his sheep all tick-powdered and cleaned up before unloading them in Presque Isle. During this fair we got to get to know him a little better and observe his daily life and the resourceful way he lived it.

Frank's home at the fairs was his truck. It was an old Coca-Cola truck and still bore the bright yellow paint and curving red letters of the Coca-Cola insignia. Frank called it his ten cent truck because "that's all she's worth," he'd say.

It seemed that at every other fair the old yellow truck had a tripod of logs mounted over her front end so relatives from back home could haul out the suddenly non-working old engine and replace it with a temporarily working old engine.

One day I managed to bake a batch of brownies using an oven I'd improvised over the camp stove. I wrapped up a bunch for Frank and found him snuggled in an old patchwork quilt on the seat of his truck. Not wanting to wake him, I thought I could quietly open the passenger side door and slip the brownies onto the seat. But when I turned the handle and pulled gently, the entire door landed on the ground with a horrible clatter. Frank shot upright in his seat.

"Oh, Frank! What have I done to your truck?" I was horrified, for I knew it was his transportation and his home.

"Don't worry," he grinned, "the old bitch always does that!"

Frank's early morning routine was fun to watch. He fed his sheep before anyone else, and while we would all be "feeding up" (as it was called) Frank proceeded with washing up and shaving. He had an old electric frying pan that he plugged into one of the barn outlets. It had lost one of its four legs and he had squashed a Campbell's Soup can to the proper height as a substitute. He filled the pan with water, and when it was hot enough had his morning shave aided by looking into the side mirror of his truck. His suds-covered razor was dipped into the pan frequently.

When this was done, he rinsed out the pan and heated more water for coffee, then cooked his breakfast in it, which often consisted of bacon, eggs, and fried bread. The pan was also his plate. The spaniels performed the pan washing chore when he was done. Some mornings he poured himself a bowl of dry cereal and went off to the cow sheds, and squatting next to a selected cow, would milk what he wanted directly into the bowl. Every morning without fail he brought a bucket of milk from the cow sheds over to his sheep pens, dipped out two baby bottles of milk and fed them to a couple of lambs whose mothers weren't giving adequate milk. Meanwhile he called Blackie and Brownie over and they stuck their heads into the milk bucket and drank their fill. When they were all finished, Frank dipped his little chipped enamel cup into the pail and had his share. In all the years of showing sheep with Frank we never knew him to have a sick day. Concerned for the health of his sheep, he never fed them grain without tasting it first.

Since the sheep barns were located at a quiet corner of the fairgrounds it was a great spot for young and daring locals to sneak into the fair without paying admission. They usually prepared the day before the fair by cutting a slit in the cyclone fence in a bushy area behind the barns thinking they wouldn't be noticed. But Floyd was an old fair hand and skilled at finding these little entrances. To reduce chances of discovery, the fence was never cut high enough to walk through, rather the slit was small and low to the ground requiring people to crawl through on their bellies.

As I have said, Floyd came to visit us each evening at the barns. In addition to his duty as an official to not let people sneak into the fair without paying, his love of comedy inspired him to devise ways to discourage the youths while also entertaining himself and the rest of us.

He and some members of our group would borrow a wheelbarrow and fill it with cow manure from the end of each barn. The cattle people brought lawn chairs and sat beside their cattle all day removing what they called "tickets" dropped frequently by the cattle. If the tickets were not picked up quickly, the cows would lie down in them, thus needing another hosing down at the washstands. Constant vigilance kept the cattle and barns clean, but piles of manure accumulated rapidly at the ends of the barns and had to be removed daily by fair maintenance crews.

Returning from the barn with a full wheelbarrow of manure, Floyd and his eager young crew spread the fresh cow pies all along the ground right at the opening cut in the fence. Since attempts to sneak in were never made until after dark, the cow pies were nearly invisible. Each night as we sat around the sheep barns listening to Floyd, he simultaneously kept an ear tuned to rustlings and whisperings at the fence hole. When he quietly signaled that a victim was about to sneak in, we would continue talking but would watch for them to appear. We were rarely disappointed. Those youths trying to wriggle through seldom noticed the cow manure not only because they couldn't see it in the dark, but because Floyd cleverly sprinkled it with shavings to further obscure it and to keep the smell down. After the youths had snuck in and were rounding the corner of the barn, Floyd would switch on a barn light to reveal them standing there with their entire fronts plastered and smelly.

Once they realized they had been caught and understood what they had crawled through, they generally sprinted toward the midway, although some in their confusion raced back toward the fence hole. Floyd usually let them all go figuring they would not stay on the midway long looking and smelling so awful.

Since many out-of-state exhibitors did not travel the long distance to Presque Isle, the sheep and cattle show days were shortened considerably from Bangor. The Canadian judge placed us all about where we had been at Bangor, and the highlight of the show was a special presentation recognizing old Frank Gilbert. The fair president gave him a shiny trophy inscribed with a message of appreciation for fifty years of showing sheep. Frank's cheeks crinkled, his bright blue eyes gleamed, and his mustache swooped upward with the force of his delighted smile. He clasped the trophy to his narrow chest and walked back to his Coca-Cola truck, careful to use the driver's door as he placed his prize on the dashboard.

The last couple of days of the fair were also relaxed. The camping field was a good size, and one late afternoon we all set up whatever we had for chairs and found something that could serve for tables—including sheep-blocking stands with a clean towel over them. Then we brought forth what we had prepared earlier in the day for a pot-luck supper. There were casseroles and salads, small new Aroostook potatoes, and wonderful chowders.

At the fairs, if anyone received a message from home, we were notified via loudspeakers at the fairgrounds. None of us wanted to hear our names called out, because, unless we were expecting a message, it was typically unpleasant news. When the messenger announced "urgent" or "emergency" along with a name, everyone was concerned.

One such message featuring both these words came for a Massa-chusetts beef cattle exhibitor. He was well liked and when he returned from the livestock office telephone with a haggard expression on his face, he shared the bad news. At his farm, which bordered a turnpike, three pigs had broken through the fence, rooted up his entire garden and then headed for the turnpike where they were run over and killed.

Meanwhile, many of his cattle found the hole and wandered over to visit a neighbor where they ate most of his large garden, destroyed much of his young orchard, and trampled his newly seeded lawn to soft mud. Of such stuff nightmares are made. He loaded his cattle and headed home.

We were not far behind him. Northern Maine Fair officials under-stood we all faced a long journey to the Skowhegan State Fair and let us all leave by mid-morning so we could travel in daylight. As we drove along, all the scenery we missed seeing traveling to Presque Isle during the night was now revealed to us at every turn—and it was spectacular. We rose and dropped through hills and valleys and passed wondrous croplands until we worked our way through the narrow, interminable wooded roads of the Haynesville Woods.

Along the way, we saw Mount Katahdin rising majestically against the sky. We saw mysterious bogs dotted with feathery hackmatack trees, an occasional moose, and acres of soft mosses. And we chuck-led while trying to pronounce such names as Mattawamkeag, Macwa-hoc, Wytopitlock, Passadumkeag, Mattamiscontis, and (my favorite) Molunkus as they appeared on small road signs.

Skowhegan, located in Somerset County on the Kennebec River, was a good five-hour drive from Presque Isle. When we reached the

Skowhegan State Fair, we bedded and fed the sheep, then we drove another one hundred and five miles home through the darkness to check the mail and to see how our neighbor was handling the broiler flock. He was cheerful and his inspection reports were fine, so we headed back to Skowhegan early the next morning.

The fairgrounds were surrounded by the town and thus did not offer the wealth of open space available at Presque Isle. This didn't present a big problem, but everything was closer together and the camping area was just a narrow strip of grass next to a fence, and bounded by a quiet road and tall pines. The area was so small you had to squeeze in amongst trailers and trucks, and on the first day of the fair, chaos reigned supreme as everyone tried to make the space work.

Competition was serious in all livestock categories at Skowhegan, because it attracted many exhibitors from out of state. Sheep shows at Skowhegan are long, intense, and always seem to come during a hot spell, but we always held our own and made good sales of sheep. Helping Frank with his variety of breeds was a given, and others helped too when they could. One year, we went over to Frank's pens to begin helping him with a black-faced breed that was due in the ring. As we approached we were amazed at Frank's actions. He was a gentle little man, but now he was literally hopping mad. He was rapidly jumping up and down, his closed fingers and raised thumbs were slashing the air, his white hair and long mustache rose and fell with each hop and his blue eyes were snapping.

He shook a raised fist at Denny Bascom on the other side of the sheep barn and yelled, "Come over here, ya Jeezly bastid, so I c'n pound the skillety shit outta ya! Ya cheatin' lyin', preachin', rot-in-hell, sunuvabitch!"

Denny looked at Frank with a sly smirk and turned his back on him.

Frank was starting to climb the pens to get over to Denny. Since Frank was then in his early eighties he was at least thirty years older than Denny and nearly half his size. Jim put an arm around Frank and asked him what the trouble was.

In addition to his Border Cheviots, Denny also showed the same black-faced breed of sheep that Frank did, and he always had the winning animals. Partly because he could afford better sheep than Frank, and partly because Denny knew and used every unfair trick there was, such as filing teeth to put a bigger, older sheep in a younger class, or changing the animals' natural head color. When Frank had received his Presque Isle premium money, he invested some of it in a black-faced ram he bought from Denny believing that it would help him improve his own black-faced sheep.

With a pious air, Denny would remind us all occasionally that he was a part-time minister, though he never declared the denomination.

Frank had been getting his new ram ready for show and part of this was to wash its head and face free of dust to bring out the shining appearance of its natural black, an important breed characteristic. As Frank washed, the black disappeared and the ram's face was mostly white. This was a serious breed defect and the ram would have been disqualified had he been shown. It should have been sent to market and never registered, and certainly never sold at a purebred price. Frank couldn't afford to be cheated this way and Denny refused to refund his money. But that was Denny. We got Frank calmed down though he was close to tears.

He said, "Someday that Denny is gonna get his comeuppance! It's all right, everything will be better at the next one." That was always

Frank's philosophy: "Everything will be better at the next fair if I can just make enough money at this one to get to it."

We had left Presque Isle elated with several good orders for rams and ewes, and it was imperative that trend continue. To earn prize money we needed our sheep to look their best, so we spent days washing and grooming them before the showing began. As much as we were enjoying our gypsy life, we knew we weren't on the road just for fun and games.

Our sheep blankets helped keep the sheep clean, but the dust of travel and the ongoing production of manure and lanolin forced us to perform the same jobs over and over again. When I finished my part of the sheep washing, I loaded the car with soiled sheep blankets (I had made two sets, and in later years carried three) and Connie, Debby Jo, and I found a local laundromat. While not filthy, the sheep covers were heavily barn-scented and I couldn't seem to approach the washing machines with the innocent nonchalance of someone bringing in their household laundry. But when I saw the bigger and well-stained cow blankets, and the grease-encrusted jeans and shirts of the "Carnies" getting sorted and thrown in without guilt, I jauntily threw my loads in as well.

Skowhegan always featured a large horse show, and when the show moved out each year, plenty of good grassy space opened up next to our tent. This was not always a blessing as we soon learned. On the third night of the fair in 1963, the four of us went wearily to bed in our cozy sleeping bags, taking one last look at the glory of a full, golden moon before zipping the tent flap. Mid-August is deep summer and it was announced by the soothing song of the crickets, which accompanied the soft, hushing murmur of the pines overhead helping lull us to restful sleep. Until that is, about 2 a.m. in the morning when Jim gave me an awakening pat, and said, "Listen to this."

Outside the tent we heard heavy, rushing breath, quickly followed by a sound of ripping, as if plants were being torn from the ground by their roots. That was followed by a slow methodical crunching. Ocassionally, the ground seemed to rumble as if heavy objects were being lifted and set down again. We also heard the rattle of chains. I was certain my hair was rising as Jim slipped over to the tent flap and unzipped it. Smiling, he motioned me over to look. Just a few feet from our tent stood three massive elephants. Each had a heavy chain around one of their front feet and was tethered to a stake in the ground. They were wrapping their trunks around big bunches of the grass and clover, pulling them from the ground, and munching them down. Snuggling the girls between us we returned to uneasy rest, knowing there was only a thin curtain of canvas between us and tons of elephant. To our relief they moved on to new territory the next day.

Unfortunately, theirs was a sad story. That summer the Fleurus, a circus boat, had sailed from St. Petersburg, Florida on its way to Yarmouth, Nova Scotia. During the voyage, the ship suffered a series of mishaps, including a loss of refrigeration resulting in the loss of the animals' meat supply. The ship, severely listing, limped into Yarmouth, the first stop of a highly publicized tour of Atlantic Canada. The circus included fifty-one performers, as well as exotic animals such as lions, tigers, leopards, ponies, zebras, elephants, and a llama. All were in poor conditions when they arrived. They were taken off the boat and moved to a circus tent, which offered better conditions, and the show went on. After the final performance in Yarmouth, with most animals back on the still-listing ship, a fuel line burst, sprayed on hot engines, and the thirty-seven-year-old circus ship burned and sank. Most of the animals survived the fire but had to be transported back to Florida. It was some of these animals that showed up as our neighbors for a night or two at the Skowhegan Fair. We were told that to earn enough money to help pay for food and transportation, some of the animals were stopping at fairs along the way where people might pay to see and feed them. One of the elephants, Shirley, lived to be more than seventy years old and eventually lived on a sanctuary in Tennessee.

The next night, while the elephants were gone, in their place were a couple of bright yellow, red, and blue, very old, wooden wagons. Frail-looking wooden bars covered each side of them, and curled inside were large, very thin, wolves; their feral yellow eyes bore a hungry and malevolent look. There was nothing neighborly about this group. We slept with one eye open.

During the night, the wolves began howling in long and mournful calls. The cattle, whose serenity was seldom ruffled, responded to an instinctive fear of this natural enemy and roared and mooed. The cattle were soon joined by bleating sheep and neighing draft horses. We threw on our clothes, put Connie and Debby Jo in the car and flashed a light on the wagon cages. Some of the bars of the cages were starting to slip sideways and it appeared only a matter of time before the wolves escaped. Given all the commotion, other livestock people were now on the scene, and fair officials were soon summoned to make sure the circus folks removed this hazard before disaster struck. The wolves were hungry and could smell an abundance of prey so near.

For a number of years we also took our sheep to the Piscataquis Valley Fair in Dover-Foxcroft until its dates eventually conflicted with the Union Fair and, since Union was our "hometown fair," we opted for that one. Dover was a small fair, but the premium money was excellent and it was always well attended. The fairgrounds, nestled on a slope with a blue mountain ridge in the distance, were like a large and well-kept lawn. The buildings, although old, were always freshly painted red and white. In later years, after we traded our tent for a trailer, our spot was only a few feet away from the sheep pens and they were the view from the side windows. Our front looked out over the midway and the dreamily remote hills. While the inside of the trailer never changed, it always appeared to be different to us at each fair, I suppose because of the new directions that light comes in and the variety of view changes from the windows. Perhaps this proves that redecorating at home wouldn't be necessary if one could simply shift the house around for varied exposures to the sun.

Being a late August fair, the days were usually warm and sunny at Dover-Foxcroft while nights sometimes gave us a preview of the September crispness to come. When sheep judging was over, and if the day was warm, we would swim at nearby Peaks-Kenny Park. This beautiful place alone was worth a trip to Dover-Foxcroft. Its setting is a classic cove on Sebec Lake banked by spruce, birch, and pine. There was a generous beach with glacier-smoothed boulders at each end; dark reflecting waters and majestic mountains dominated the scene.

At the Piscataquis Valley Fair, as at the other fairs, the exhibition halls overflowed with neat arrangements of fancywork, quilts, afghans, and rugs. These examples of craftsmanship were impressive in their intricacy, and what was particularly pleasing was knowing that many of the wonderful old skills continued so that younger generations were inspired to take them up and continue the tradition. The hooked rugs we saw at Dover seemed more unique in imaginative design than any other area.

Most of the usual fair programs prevailed at Dover-Foxcroft, but because it was smaller in size than most, an auto thrill show was usually not offered. However, we were there the first time this type of show was attempted. The standard horse-racing track is a half-mile, and about half of this is required for the presentation of an auto thrill show. At Dover-Foxcroft there was no racetrack, only a horse pulling area, which was woefully inadequate to stage a proper thrill show as it provided less than a quarter of the space essential for the cars to perform properly.

The auto daredevils must have been greatly concerned when they saw the tiny area available to them. But, in true the "show-must-go-on" spirit, they spent the day preparing for their evening show. Painstakingly they stacked and changed placements of ramps as they measured and remeasured. They frequently huddled, wore harried expressions, and cast looks in the direction of what they had to accept as absolutely the only stopping place available—a place immediately in front of a cattle shed full of cows.

To perform rollovers, and sliding broadside stops, a certain minimum speed is necessary. But at the required speed, the cars also needed a minimum amount of space to come safely to a halt. Adequate stopping space was clearly a problem. There wasn't any other shelter for the cows so they had to remain in place and take their chances. The cow owners agreed to this only if enough backstop material could be provided for safety. Unfortunately, the only material available for a backstop was some shavings and copious amounts of cow manure—at least the cow manure was heavy stuff and a vehicle plunging into it would be buried in it before leaping over it.

The drivers hauled and piled manure all afternoon. This promised to be an auto thrill show fraught with complications, and we made it a point to be on hand.

The auto daredevil act requires a good deal of swashbuckling. The background announcer is keenly attuned to that fact and attempts to swing the audience to his level of high-pitched excitement as he wrings his hands and expresses grave concern as to whether the drivers can possibly survive their next stunt, and, if they do, it will be absolute proof of their immortality.

The thrill drivers were dressed in snow-white shirts and jodhpurs with shiny black boots molded from knee to high heel. At the end of each breath-taking maneuver they slid sideways in a mighty spray of sand and dust, flung open the car door before it came to a complete stop, and stepped out, turned to face the crowd, and gave a grand flourish, their arms reaching skyward and their teeth flashing. Given the "arena" size, there was barely a chance to get rolling before it was time to hit the brakes and so this final splendid gesture was nearly always accomplished in the depths of the backstop. It is difficult to exude gallantry and bravado, or do much swashbuckling as usual while wallowing about in a great pile of cow manure. It was a great show and although the daredevils' spotless white and shiny black became a muted shade of brown from the manure, their good sportsmanship exceeded even their skill.

On the last night of Piscataquis Valley Fair was a supper of the season's final sugar and gold sweet corn, fresh and succulent and grown on a nearby farm. A good friend and sheep exhibitor from New Hampshire used to say, "Have the water boiling before you pick the corn, and if you trip and drop it on the way to the kitchen, throw it away and run back to pick some more." Freshness was the whole key, which is actually true, for corn quickly loses its sugar content after being removed from its stalk.

After supper, the four of us went for a last-night stroll around the midway. On the way back we caught up with Frank at a coffee and doughnut stand, preparing to bring his evening snack back to the barn. As we walked along with him we passed the "girlie show" tent. The current show had just ended and spectators were leaving from the exit side of the tent. Among them was Denny Bascom, trying to slip through the crowd and shifting his eyes furtively in the hope that nobody would see him. Frank spied him, and called out, "Been in there preachin' to them about their sinful ways, have ya Denny?"

That first year, as we would in the future, we continued our fair travels for the rest of summer and into the fall. Even when Connie and Debby Jo were school-aged children, the school systems understood the valuable lessons of 4-H and the benefits of attending fairs and let them miss school, although teachers gave them assignments they needed to complete.

Each year we returned to the Union Fair, the site of our very first sheep competition, and again to the Blue Hill Fair, where eventually we would look forward to our annual meetings with the author E.B. White. When I would read *Charlotte's Web* aloud to Connie, I always pictured the fair set at Blue Hill. It was delightful to learn from this gentle and wonderful man, who lived in that area, that the Blue Hill Fair was indeed the one he had in mind when writing the book. We even sold him some sheep for his farm.

After the Blue Hill Fair, always Labor Day weekend, fairs included the Oxford County Fair, the Farmington Fair, and the Fryeburg Fair. The first frosts of the season generally occurred while we were at Farmington, located in Franklin County. The draft horses would be pulling their stone drags across the crystal-laced fields, puffs of steam coming from their noble noses. The days were luminous with sapphirine skies and surrounding hills of sun-washed gold. On the pine-forested edge of the grounds I always gathered a small bouquet of purple, lavender, and rose-colored wild asters and a few brassy goldenrod for contrast. The powdery-blue grapes growing wild on the perimeter fence decorated a fruit basket nicely, and their rich, wild taste was superb. Chill evenings were comfortably spent in the warmth of the camper reading, before being lulled to sleep by the pastoral murmurings of the cows who were almost our bedfellows.

One of the highlights of Farmington Fair was its informal pet show. It was limited to children as owners, but the pets could be any member of the animal kingdom and generally featured cows, sheep, horses, goats, dogs, cats, mice, bunnies, and birds. There were always a large and varied number of contestants. Pets and owners formed a big circle, and the judge, usually a local dignitary, stood in the center of the ring to watch the animals parade. He would ask each owner about his or her pet and make a short acquaintance with the pet itself.

One year the judge was a very tall, distinguished-looking man with an air of pleasant dignity. After lengthy consideration, of the contestants he awarded the one and only prize to a petite toy fox terrier whose weight could only have been calculated in ounces.

At the judge's invitation the young winner brought his happy smile and tiny dog to stand by the judge in center ring. Looking out at his audience, the judge went on at some length describing his reasons for choosing the winner. As he gestured and smiled and got into the spirit of his hearty speech, the little terrier made several close circles around the judge's ankles, carefully savoring the odor and texture of his well-shined shoes. Satisfied with his investigation, the dog lifted his small leg and dampened the judge's knife-creased trousers. It was not until the dog had lifted his leg for a third time that the judge looked down in response to the stifled laughter of the crowd. His made his retreat with aplomb and a tight little smile.

───

The Fryeburg Fair, founded in 1851 and proclaiming itself the largest livestock fair east of the Mississippi River, was the last fair of the season and was always eagerly anticipated. Fryeburg sits on the Saco River and is nestled along the New Hampshire border and in the shadows of the White Mountains. The fair is held in the foliage season of early October in one of Maine's most scenic areas, and it is the settling ground of all the summer's livestock competitions in the East. The melancholy aspect is that it is the last fair of the season in Maine.

All types of weather have their beauty, but the pristine clarity of an early fall day is hoped for on the way to Fryeburg for it is a time when nature is at the height of her flamboyance.

It took us about three hours to traverse the hundred miles to Fryeburg. Every bend of the road brought an offering of indigo lakes, red-and-ochre farmhouses, fields of emerald spotted with copper cattle, twisted apple trees, and faltering stone walls. Nearer Fryeburg are moody coves of the sand-bottomed Saco River and navy-blue lakes with blurred reflections of autumn orange about the shores. Then the powerful rising outline of the White Mountains flashes through the dark pines, interspersed with flaming maple torches and the birch leaves that glow like Egyptian gold. We usually arrived near sunset when thready webs of steam roved the lavender mountain slopes, their shadows sometimes pierced by the last blazing shafts of the sun.

Days were mostly warm and bright at Fryeburg, but the nights could be downright wintry. Several times we have had to light small bunches of hay under the outdoor water faucets to thaw an ice blockage so we could water the sheep. Some years it was so warm during this first week of October that it was a pleasure after sheep trimming to go swimming on the secluded beaches of the Saco's sandy coves.

Fryeburg Fair lasted a full ten days, and is the most well attended fair in Maine. Perhaps because it is the last fair of the season, but also because the foliage is at its peak during this week, and the surrounding White Mountains are at their best. There is a keen and joyful competition among the exhibitors to decorate their sheep and cattle pens, and we found that this had to be done before the fair officially opened as the crowds became so thick we could hardly get near our animals throughout the day.

The largest pulling horse competitions in the East were held at Fryeburg Fair, and the horse barns stood close by the camping sites. At night there is a constant but somehow soothing, thumping as the great animals kick the barn walls with monotonous regularity, perhaps to ease their boredom. From dawn onward they are hitched to exercise, and with harnesses cheerfully jingling, and stone boats hissing over the sand, they pass by all day. Splendid in their power and size, their grace and docility is such that they are often led by young children, or support a rider on their broad, bare backs.

The International Ox Pull was sometimes held here. This is basically Maine and New England oxen against teams from Nova Scotia and New Brunswick. The Canadian oxen are colorful with their head yokes painted bright reds and blues and banded with brass-studded leather harnessing, as opposed to the well-known neck yokes of our

New England oxen, which are plain and naturally polished with the body oils of the beasts who wear them.

The Canadian teamsters with their clipped accents, subtly redolent of Old England, are friendly and low key. Their oxen are especially fat and sleek. But I had to think they were more "exhibition" animals than our rangier Maine oxen, many of whom truly did work their way in this world in the winter wood lots and around the farm. Most of the teams went by our trailer exercising as the horses did. Their wonderful bells didn't resound with musical echo, but clanked with an old and flat melody that called to mind peaceful and fertile fields inhabited by enduring bovines.

Many times ox drivers kept their animals hitched to the sides of their trucks when not working. As we watched them from our camper at mealtimes, a couple of them stand out in my memory.

One pair of exactly the same color must have been together for many years for their every move seemed to be in unison. Tied to the truck, they ate their hay contentedly, reaching for a fresh mouthful at the same moment, and chewing to the same measured beat. They swung their tails together in satisfaction and now and then flipped them with a light twist at the very tip. To my complete fascination, even this odd little move was performed as if at the direction of a choreographer bent on perfect timing. No doubt they had been raised and trained together from calf-hood (look-alike calves are often selected to be a future team).

Also I remember a grand, molasses-colored ox. He was lying down, forelegs tucked under like a cat. He had the ageless eminence of the Sphinx. His ivory, black-tipped horns curved long and outward. His long, gold-lashed eyes were slitted tranquilly against the westering sun, which splashed him in bronze rays as it lapsed behind the pillars of Fryeburg's pines.

There were snatches of conversations among the drivers about their "off ox" or "near ox." Their real verbal performance comes in the ox-pulling ring, and I could listen to them all day, for each one has his own way of cajoling his animals to victory. It is theater and opera at its country best.

Some drivers just swung a small quirt in circles above the team's heads and said little; others shouted, "H-i-i-i-ke!" with a voice that could be heard in the next town. There are those who leaned on the hindquarters of their "near" beast pushing with all their might and sobbing in apparent agony the names of their team with every inch of the draw, "Sam, Dick, Sam, Dick . . ." with hardly a pause for breath.

One of my favorite drivers, who was at most fairs, got in front of his team and spread his feet as far apart as they would go. Without bending his knees, he jumped up and down rapidly, and as high as he possibly could, while in a high falsetto he hurled naughty words and names at them so fast they were nearly (and perhaps fortunately) unintelligible. I have often thought about what fun it would be to see and listen to these teamsters and their cattle training at home. On a given day they must have struck on a powerful word or gesture that brought results and so stayed with it. Although typically not people with an inclination for public display, the competitive spirit gives them a remarkable ability to discard "stage fright," and enter the ring with an "it's just you and me boys" attitude.

At the Fryeburg Fair, I stood in front of the carousel on those final days of the season to saturate my heart with its music. I would store the moment in my mind to make it last through the long winter. And Jim and I always walked the fairgrounds together on the last night, sharing the same melancholy with other exhibitors. This was the end of the season, a season we all loved so well.

CHAPTER 17
Back to the Chickens

IN THE EARLY 1960s, our fair traveling was still in its early stages and while seen as a critical way for us to earn money, we certainly could not make enough to pay all of our ongoing bills or our debt. The chicken broiler business remained the most critical and largest source of our income. This income also remained the same flock after flock, meaning we received half-pay and every once in a great while a bonus. But even when we did receive a bonus, the bonus didn't come close to matching the income we would have received had the one-cent-per-bird-per week payment been made. So at the time, our ten weeks of fair income each year plus the sheep sales that resulted from it, combined with the town roadwork that Jim did with the farm equipment supplemented the chicken business to keep us from falling off the edge. The problem was the hits never stopped coming. We could never settle into the chicken business because we were constantly asked to make changes—to spend more money in order to keep the chickens.

In 1962, Penobscot Poultry sent a representative to give us an ultimatum—the company could not afford to send grain, heating oil, and sawdust, and pick up mature chickens so far away from its processing plant in Belfast unless we had enough chickens to make it worthwhile.

Jim and a helper working on the new chicken barn in 1962. The addition of this barn increased the farm's chickens capacity to thirty-five thousand.

They had done "a careful study" and were asking their best producers (we were known as "growers") to add on or build additional buildings to house a minimum of thirty-five thousand birds. If we were unwilling, or unable to find the extra space needed, then we would not receive any more chickens and effectively be shut down. Along with the ultimatum came a promise that renewed efficiency in their operation would reduce their costs to the point that we might receive the full penny per bird as originally planned. Once again there was no contract, and the "promise" was without bond or even a handshake. We were in no position to demand assurances beyond spoken words.

Together we spent long hours pulling the proposal apart from every angle. Could we believe their promises yet again? What influenced us to drive further into the Dismal Swamp of Debt was the clear knowledge that we would drown anyway if we lost income from the twenty thousand chickens. There was no other way we could replace that income. After all the sweat, love, and tears of frustration we had put into building North Country Farm we were not about to give it up.

Our existing chicken barn was on a corner of our property and there was no room to add on to it. However, we had plenty of land along the road and there was a good, level place beyond the sheep barn to build another barn that would house fifteen thousand more chickens.

Once again, Jim gathered his drafting tools and spent hours designing and making lumber and equipment lists. We had visited the Farmers Home Administration about money for the project, and they were willing. They were loaning to others in the business who had received the same news from other chicken companies, so they already had a nifty little twenty-year repayment package. We were basing our hope for future success on the government's apparent faith in the broiler companies. We had less than six months to get a new three-story barn built and ready for the chickens. For the third time in the last ten years or so we were surrounded by lumber. We hired neighbors to help Jim build the balloon-framed building he had designed, and it was up and running before the six-month deadline.

However, even after the first flock arrived finish work remained so we hired a man to help feed the now thirty-five thousand birds. He

North Country Farm as it looked from Route 32 in 1964. The main house is far left followed by the sheep barn and the newest chicken barn. The old cattle barn was located to the left of the house from this angle.

was a retired fisherman who had helped his father go seining for herring and sardines all his life, but farming was not his forte; we could fill several hanging feeders while he was still working on the same one. He would look at each row of feeders and try to remember which ones needed how much, rather than just carry a bucketful with him. The grain chute that ran vertically through the center of the building was supplied by the bulk grain bins built under the roof. By the time he went for the grain and went back to the feeders he had forgotten which ones needed to be filled.

After we received the first couple of thirty-five thousand chicken flocks, the company did indeed pay us the one-cent-per-bird-per-week as originally promised—and our spirits and courage soared. At last it appeared promises were being kept, and it seemed we might have a chance to earn a decent living in this business after all.

Our euphoria was short-lived.

Suddenly, all the chicken processing companies did the same thing to their growers—they dropped pay back to one-half cent. We were told that the expanding southern poultry business was giving Maine heavy competition. They said that southern producers could sell their chickens for less because grain was more cheaply available, and they incurred no heating oil costs in winter. This issue was always there, but it seems the Maine processing companies didn't realize it until we growers were more deeply in debt. We had the figurative bear by the tail and there was no letting go. We were now in the same mess again, only on a bigger scale. We knew that driving forward and doing the best we could, sprinkled with lots of hope, was our best option.

CHAPTER 18
Scot, the Border Collie

WE KEPT EXPANDING our sheep flock, and sales were excellent. Experience taught us that the sheep were a separate "basket of eggs" that we could control when it came to management and marketing. Unlike the broilers, we were not at the mercy of the chicken processors decisions.

We now had the sheep-raising routine under control—lambing, vaccinating, shearing, dipping, haying, and fencing. Weather occasionally delayed some things, but it all got done. Fencing was constant, either to increase pasture size or repairing. If there was any weakness along the fence line a sheep would always find it, quickly followed by more, maybe even the entire the flock. We spent hours and would run miles ahead trying to get ahead of a group to turn them back, the only way it worked. We were still in good shape, but running until you are about to drop is not only tiring it is also time consuming, and we were always short on time. So on Labor Day 1962, when we were managing the sheep dog trials at Blue Hill Fair, we decided it was time to splurge on the luxurious necessity of a border collie.

A good breeder and handler from Ohio was also a commercial shearer. He sheared sheep the entire year, on the farms spring and

Scot, our first border collie.

summer and in the stockyards during the winter. He ran a dog in the trials named Scot, who was very impressive. We asked Scot's handler if he had any dogs for sale that we could afford. He replied that Scot was for sale. He was "burned out" by the heavy year-round demands, but he still had plenty of vigor left for easier work on a family farm. His price was more than reasonable, and he soon was ours.

Scot was six years old and had been brought up the old-fashioned way as earlier border collies were. His owner told us to keep him in a doghouse, never let him off his chain unless he was working, and don't try to make a pet of him; he was a working dog only. (None of the dog handlers subscribe to this theory anymore and haven't for years.)

We were aware of the commands, all continued from the old Scottish terms: "To Me," for coming to you; "Way Back," or "Get Away Back," for going out into the field or wherever, to get ahead of the sheep; "Away To Me" for turning right; "Come By" for turning left; "Lie Doon," for making a sudden stop and lying low; and "That'll Do," for leaving the job when finished.

So many of the dogs were imported originally from Scotland with an understanding of these commands that the handlers had to use them and then became so accustomed to them they continued when breeding their own dogs. We asked Scot's owner if Scot would become confused if he we gave him the wrong command. The owner smiled and said, "Don't worry, that Scot dog won't let you make a mistake, if you do, he knows sheep, how they think, and what to do." He also told us that Scot had never enjoyed a family life, was a "one man" dog, and wouldn't be interested in me, a woman.

Scot quickly bonded with Jim, and while he showed no animosity to Connie, Debby Jo, or me, he did ignore us for a while. We had a nice little house formerly home to a couple of pigs that was titled "Pork Chop Palace," so we chained Scot there the first night.

It was also the last.

We could not bear to own a dog and not treat him like a member of the family, so we brought him in the house the next day. It was the first time he had been in a house. He lifted his leg twice, and when Jim reprimanded him with a sharp word, he never did it again. He slept quietly on the carpet in our bedroom, and eventually moved to the comfort of a chair. He was never again secured by a chain.

One night a couple of weeks after he came to live with us, we were sitting on the living room couch watching a TV show when Scot walked into the room and shoved his nose under my folded hands on my lap and asked for attention. Then he did the same with Connie and Debby Jo. We happily responded and we were all a team from then on. He just needed time to trust and accept his changes.

Scot's first six years had obviously been tough. When he finally accepted and enjoyed our petting, we discovered that all of his ribs had knobby protrusions where they had been repeatedly cracked. In the stockyards he had worked the crowded flocks by walking on their backs and leaning over to direct them by pushing his nose on theirs. He often fell between them and got trampled, thus the injured ribs. His tail was in a zigzag from beginning to end. These dogs rode on the pick-up truck floors, never asking to look out the window, and often the owner slammed the truck door not realizing the dog didn't have a tail all the way in. He clearly fell victim to this several times.

When we first took Scot down to the pasture to move our sheep to a new field, we were excited, but our old attitude was still there. When we did it ourselves, if everything didn't go exactly right we spent the entire afternoon chasing sheep. That was all about to change. We stood in the lane, next to the fence, and Jim said to Scot, "Get Away Back." He sailed over the fence as if it didn't exist and became a black-and-white streak heading for the sheep at the far end of the field. We then went to the gate where we wanted the sheep.

The flock threw their heads into the air, packed themselves together, and eyed this dog creature coming at them. *What was this?* It seemed like they thought, *surely we aren't expected to be subservient to a dog!* Jim commanded him "Lie Doon," and he dropped as if shot. He followed every command swiftly and instantly. With quiet ease he moved the sheep to us and straight through the gate. They filed past us trotting along like a bunch of ladies. They were not terrorized—the respect sheep have for a dog is instinctive and it happened quickly. We stood there in awe. The sheep had been moved in minutes, we weren't hoarse from screaming across the fields, we weren't struggling for breath, and we had not run a single sprint. Only heaven could beat this.

Just the week before we had chased a ewe—a "fence jumper," which comes along occasionally. We used every ploy we could but ended up following her down the lane and through the woods to a very steep bluff above a wild shoreline. We had chased her at least a mile and a half by then, and as we had pounded through the woods we lost sight of her but were able to hear her crashing along. We stood breathless at the top of the bluff and looked down the very long and steep banking to the shore below.

It happened that a lobster fishing friend was pulling a trap right next to the shore, and Jim yelled down and asked him if he had seen a sheep. He laughed and said that there was one standing on the rocks right near him and she seemed out of breath. We caromed down the precipitous slope, and then spied her standing on a ledge under an overhanging hemlock bough. She was breathing heavily, and her next step would have put her into Muscongus Bay.

She allowed Jim to slip the halter on her, but she wasn't about to follow us in a civilized manner. He pulled from the front, and I pushed from the rear. We would heave and grunt for a few feet, stop for a short rest, and then drag and shove a few more feet then stop and pant. We made our way grabbing bushes, protruding ledges, and tree trunks for handholds. It took us more than half an hour to bully this beast up over that high bluff. She let us have her full weight of about one hundred seventy-five pounds and would not help us by taking a single voluntary footstep.

We started to see whirling lights in front of our eyes when we finally got to the top and stopped to catch our breaths in sobbing gasps. The ewe stood there quietly. Suddenly she flung her head in the air, snatching the halter out of our unsuspecting hands and raced back down that incline again until she once again stood on the same rock at the ocean's edge.

I nearly cried in rage and weariness. Jim said, "We ought to just leave her, but she's a good ewe, we'll have to try again." So we worked through the same procedure again, but this time kept a death grip on the halter until we got her home. Those kind of experiences helped us truly appreciate our Scot dog. That ewe would never have gotten beyond the lane if he had been with us then.

Pastures must be alternated regularly to keep them from being overgrazed, and the second time Scot moved the flock for us, our big three hundred pound ram, Rambeau, decided his ewe flock should be protected from this possible predator, and he took a stand in front of the sheep, stamping his front hooves as Scot approached. Scot kept on coming, slowly but surely, and then the ram made his move. He lowered his head and came thundering toward Scot, folded his legs under him, and gave Scot a mighty blow with his full weight that threw the poor dog into the air and rolled him end over end several times.

It happened so fast we were powerless to stop it. We were certain Scot was mortally injured and might never rise again. But before we could reach him, he rose to his feet and took off after the ram, who by this point was headed back to his ewes feeling victorious. Scot's feet were hardly touching the ground and when he reached the ram he leaped onto his back. As he had done back at the stockyards, he moved up to the ram's neck and reached over to grab his nose. He didn't draw blood, but he pinched Rambeau's nose hard as he pulled his head around to the direction he wanted the ram to go. When the ram changed direction, and the ewes started to follow, Scot jumped off and moved to the rear of the flock to keep them moving.

Miraculously, Scot was unhurt, and his authority was never questioned again.

Scot was our family dog and a valued partner. One of his favorite treats was going down to Long Cove so he could swim and chase incoming waves. The first time he went into the ocean, he took a drink, no doubt thinking it was in freshwater like in Ohio, but he quickly gave up because of the salty taste. We took Scot to fairs with us, and he proved a great help loading and unloading sheep. He also went to the Blue Hill Fair and visited with his previous owner. We never put him into the trials, because we not only managed them, Jim sometimes judged them as well. Instead, Scot went up the mountain with us to pick blueberries and had a joyous time roaming the hillside. We laughed to watch him gathering his own blueberries, using his teeth to grasp thick bunches and then pull them from the bushes.

At the age of fourteen, Scot died peacefully from a sudden stroke, and as with every dog we have loved, a piece of our hearts died with him. His eight years with us were wonderful. He had shown us the joy of moving and handling sheep and brought forth from us the love and respect that every good working border collie deserves.

CHAPTER 19
Island Sheep

ONE OF OUR major sales of North Country Cheviots was to the owner of Bartlett's Island, a twenty-five hundred acre island in Blue Hill Bay. Richard C. Paine Jr., the gentleman who owned it as well as nearby Hardwood Island, did not live on the island but still wanted to have a rugged flock of sheep capable of fending for themselves. His goal was keeping the island's open pasture from becoming overgrown. There was a barn for shelter, and he would bring a supply of hay to the island to help through the winter. We knew this breed could live on the island and survive on their own just like deer, because that is how they lived in Scotland. In the Highlands, they had no shelter, broke through the snow for forage, and lambed on their own.

Our primary concern was how we could get a starter flock out to the island, but Paine assured us it was no problem. He owned an old Navy landing barge and knew a man who could run it. We could drive our truck right onto the barge, and when we reached the island shore, he would drop the barge gate and the truck gate and the sheep could step right onto the shore and in their new world.

Our big dump truck, loaded with sheep, was a tight fit on the barge. But still all was going well until one of the barge engines failed.

Both engines were necessary to maintain steerage, and with only one we traveled in circles with little control.

At the time, we were about halfway between the island and the mainland and were fast approaching a group of moored boats. Among them was a large, unoccupied sailboat with a long and noble bowsprit that was on a direct collision course with the radiator of our truck. The man running the barge was not a mechanic, but he was doing his best. Jim hastily joined him to help with the troubleshooting. Jim had experience with diesel engines, and he soon discovered that one engine had lost its fuel prime, so they worked quickly to restore it. By the time the bowsprit and the radiator were barely feet apart, I began wondering what the accident report would look like. Perhaps something like, "The front of our truck is impaled on the bowsprit of a large sailboat, and the incident happened while both were in the middle of a harbor." Just then the second engine came to life. The remainder of the trip and the landing went smoothly.

After landing, the sheep quickly spread out into the sweet, wild grasses of the island grazing with obvious delight on these fresh and virginal pastures. There was no fencing, but they had a big barn for shelter, and about two thousand acres of spruce forest for shade in summer. There were no predators to harm them. We had raised them all from lambs, and admittedly I felt a pang of concern about leaving them. Deep down, we knew that it was a fine, free life for them and exactly what their breed were built for. We would not see them again until spring, when we returned to shear them and dock their lambs' tails.

In June the following year, we packed our camper trailer for the several days' sojourn. Jim sharpened the electric shear cutters and combs, we rented a gasoline-powered generator, and the four of us, along with a young lad who liked adventure, set off to shear the North

The North Country Farm truck driving onto an old barge en route to Barlett's Island to tend sheep there.

Country Cheviots on their new island home. The island owner had a spot on the shore for us to park the truck and camper trailer and a boat ready for us to use to get to the island. The plan was to round up the sheep, get them into the big barn, shut the doors, and shear until they were done, then sort out the lambs. The ewe lambs would have their tails docked as they would stay and grow with the flock. The ram lambs' tails would remain, as they would be going to market in the fall.

With the equipment landed, and with Scot at our side, we set out to find the sheep. They were bedded down in the big, main pasture

The barn on Barlett's Island in Blue Hill Bay.

under a small grove of spruce trees, "shading up," as we say in the world of sheep. With the exception of someone bringing hay to the barn on occasion, the flock had not seen people in nearly a year. As Jim was just preparing to send Scot on a long outrun to quietly get ahead of the sheep and turn them toward the barn, the sheep spied us. In a flash they jumped to their feet and started running for the woods. Worst of all, just before they reached the woods, they split into two groups and dove into the forest.

This was no ordinary woods, but evergreen growth such as can only be found on a Maine island, branches so thick and low to the ground that you couldn't walk through them standing up. We made progress only by dropping to our hands and knees and crawling along. We all looked at each other in despair knowing the flock had as much as two thousands of acres of woods to hide in. There seemed no possible way to gather this flock without dozens of people and dogs. Scot was begging to go after them, so Jim gave him the order to "Get Away Back."

When Scot disappeared into the greenery, we thought it might be days before we saw Scot or the sheep again. He was not in sight or in hearing range to receive a command, and since we didn't even know the location of the sheep we couldn't have given him one anyway. We stood there for about twenty minutes trying to formulate some sort of plan. Suddenly there was a loud crashing in the woods, and out came the entire flock of sheep, all back in one group with Scot hot on their heels. We have always wondered how that dog ever got those two groups together in such dense woods and brought them out completely under his control. But, oh the relief!

With the sheep back, we all took our planned places. Jim guided Scot and the flock poured into the barn at a dead run. The ram, however, was not yet ready to give up his freedom. He headed for the back of the barn at top speed and sailed through a window, taking out the glass and sash in the process.

Scot tore outside and went after him. We saw them disappearing toward the shore, and when we knew the flock was secure in the barn, we followed them. After awhile we found them. The ram stood at the far end of a ledge that extended into the sea; he could go no further. Scot stood on the shore blocking his return from the ledge, just watching and giving him the border collie "eye," which says, "You will do as I wish you to!" The ram was so exhausted that he plodded back to the barn with Scot keeping a gentle but firm distance behind him.

For the first couple of hours the sheep were difficult to handle. They had developed the attitude of deer since they had been living like them. Later we found places in the spruce where they had "yarded up." This is a grouping of animals in one small area where there is feed, and in a deep snow they keep the "yard" trampled down for easier movement. Snow mostly blows away on the islands, and, of course, there was none now. We knew about the sheep yards because the spruce in these areas were without foliage up to an even height of how far a sheep could reach to eat it. We admired their instinct to not depend on the barn for shelter since they might have gotten snowed in and been unable to forage for food.

As the day progressed, they calmed down and regained some memory of this procedure. We were impressed by their condition. They were not fat but were firm and wonderfully muscled. Along with the good island grasses, they had grazed on herbal plants such as bayberry and sweetfern, which kept them from having internal parasites. Since all animals love salt, they also indulged in seaweed. This diet produced the most beautiful fleeces we had ever seen—bright, lofty, and featuring an amazing tensile strength and abundance.

The most desirable, and feasible, living lamb crop is projected at 150 percent, meaning that a given number of ewes will have twins. This flock, with no help from human hands, had produced a surviving lamb crop of 98 percent. The lambs were vigorous and solidly well fleshed, and their mothers had produced plenty of rich milk.

The shearing and tail docking took three days. The work was intense, but we enjoyed the wild and magnificent beauty of the island, with its ivory ledges, dark spruce, rippling field grass, and an early morning sea the color of smoked silk. All of its sounds and scents became absorbed into our being. We thought of the families who had once lived here amongst this glorious beauty. There were a couple of empty houses and several cellar holes. The community was founded in 1765 by Christopher Bartlett and his wife Freelove who built a log cabin. The island reached a peak population of more than one hundred in the late 1800s, but times and the economy changed for the islanders until it was no longer possible for them to farm and fish and still make a proper living.

At the end of the third day, we gathered the wool bags and our equipment and made several trips to the mainland. As we left the barn and pasture area with the last load, the sheep who fled into the woods at first sight of us now lined up in single file as sheep do instinctively so that only one track is made and their forage is not trampled. They followed us to the shore and gathered around us as we loaded the boat. When we left, they stood on the shore watching us for a long while, then turned and followed their narrow path back to the pasture.

Spindrift.

CHAPTER 20
Goodnight, Sweet *Spindrift*

IN THE MID-1960S, the chicken broiler business continued at basically half-pay. Our long-term loans with Farmers Home Administration were such that the interest we paid annually was in the thousands of dollars, while the principal taken from our payments was only in the hundreds. The light at the end of that tunnel was decades away. Payment received from the chicken company went toward, but did not completely pay, the mortgage debt. We had to make additional payments to the company to pay for the feeding and watering equipment, meaning we received no compensation for our labor in taking care of thirty-five thousand chickens. It was deeply discouraging.

Also, we knew we owned an asset that was no longer vital to us financially. What we needed do with it was in both our minds, but neither of us could voice it for a long time.

We must sell *Spindrift*.

After Jim stopped lobster fishing, he had put a tuna pulpit on her bow, and when we could find the right day and a few free hours, we went out to hunt tuna fish.

213

On hot days we found them "finning" or lying near the ocean's surface with just their fins showing as they basked in the sun. After spotting them, Jim would leave the wheel to me and we slowly slipped up to the tuna. He moved to the pulpit and stood poised with harpoon in hand, trailed by a coil of rope and an attached barrel so we could locate the fish when it finished its post-harpoon run. Tuna are clever, and it was tricky, but we did get a few. Tuna brought decent money, but nothing compared to what they did in later years.

In the spring of 1963, we scraped and painted *Spindrift* for the last time. We placed an advertisement to sell her in a fishing industry publication. Through the years her hull and her engine had never suffered from lack of attention, so her condition was superb. *Spindrift* was quickly sold to a gentleman who planned to use her for sport fishing. Before the new owner came to take her away we visited her together one final time, touching the surfaces we loved so well. We thought of all the good times with her; the beautiful and prospering days, the hurricanes, the gales, and the bitter cold and heavy seas. Always she performed as she had silently promised us she would when we first saw her lovely hull in Leslie's workshop surrounded by shavings.

After we sold *Spindrift*, it took more than two years before I could speak her name without it catching in my throat. Like all good boats, she had a soul, and it was part of us. And in memory, it still is.

CHAPTER 21
Jocko

TEN MILES OR SO from the farm, in the town of Bremen, a couple preparing to move away called and asked if we would like to have their burro. The burro had been given to them as a joke, but they were very fond of him. He couldn't move away with them and they wanted him to have a good home. We felt that Connie and Debby Jo would enjoy riding him, and he would fit in nicely with the sheep. His name was Jocko.

He was not the usual small, gray donkey with a dark cross on the back, but a larger donkey with a rich chocolate color. He had big white circles around his eyes, a white nose halfway up his face, shaggy ears, a sweet but mischievous disposition, and a loud, comical bray. We had to put a jacket over his head to get him on the truck, but once at home he soon adjusted to the sheep and seemed happy with their company.

Although Jocko had never been ridden, he accepted a saddle and Connie and Debby Jo upon it. When he had enough of being ridden, he didn't try to throw the girls off, he simply insisted on slowly going under a spruce tree so they would be swept off by its branches, or quietly folding his legs to lay down.

Jocko, the family donkey.

We had put fencing right to the sides of the house enclosing the backyard and joining it to the sheep pasture, as it had been a dry year and we needed all the grazing land possible. Jocko loved this because he could come to the back door for cookies or bread. He accepted each piece by wrapping the long, loose end of his nose around it. His nose was almost prehensile and he loved to explore our faces with it, huffing and snuffling as he did so. This was pleasant because his soft nose felt like sheared velvet and smelled deliciously of freshly brewed tea. You may have heard of someone grinning and looking like a "mule eating thistles." Well, thistles are stimulated by sheep manure, and our pasture had its share of both. Jocko loved the thistles, and it was incredible to see him lift his lips and nose so only his square teeth showed as he gingerly munched on these fearfully thorny plants.

Jocko watched us at mealtimes and at night while we washed up before going to bed by laying one big, white-ringed eye to the window. When the bathroom light went out, and the bedroom lamp came on, the eye appeared in that window as well. And when the bedroom light went out, he gave several nasal brays as a goodnight.

Our outdoor cellar entrance was a bulkhead with very old wooden doors built on a slant from the house, and it covered huge stone steps. Jocko loved to thunder across these wooden doors early in the morning to get us all up and going. One bright moonlight night he must have thought it was dawn, because shortly after midnight he started pounding on the bulkhead so hard we heard a crashing, splintering, and cracking, followed by mighty thumps of a body hitting stone stairs. Then from the cellar, immediately under our bed, came braying so loud it might have awakened the neighborhood.

We hurried to the cellar expecting to find him in a broken heap, but instead he was just standing there roaring in panic. His tail was high in the air and he was emitting an unbelievable stream of manure. Although his droppings were very similar to a horse, we had noticed that when he became startled or frightened, typically during a thunderstorm, all became liquid. And there was lots of it.

We went to the barn, got his halter, and moved the broken doors away and Jim urged him to come out of the cellar and back up the steps. Jocko responded by doing what donkeys do best, digging in with all four feet and not moving. He was not going to do stairs.

Nothing could convince him, gentle persuasion or even a pan of grain held tantalizingly in front of him. Even covering his eyes didn't work. We tried it all for nearly two hours, until Jim said, "Probably the best thing to do is to leave him alone with the cellar light on. He can see the stairs and the way out, if not, at the rate he's pouring out his deposits, he'll elevate himself out."

By noon the next day, Jocko was in the cellar still braying and still defecating. Jim figured he might have to bulldoze the cellar steps away so Jocko would have a level exit.

Then, just as he was figuring how best to approach this project, the burro made two mighty leaps and lunged up the stairs and out into the pasture. We then spent several hours cleaning up all the donkey manure in the cellar and soon invested in steel bulkhead doors.

Over time, Jocko's name became shortened to Jock. He provided an almost daily laugh with his antics. If Jim were fencing, he might snatch the pliers out of his back pocket and run with them in his knock-kneed fashion, his brown eyes rolling merrily and his tail twisting in the air. We do not smoke so we didn't know that Jock also loved tobacco. One day a prospective sheep buyer came into the sheep barn with a large, fat cigar in his mouth. He had not yet lighted it and did not do so given he was in the barn full of hay. Instead, he leaned on the fence looking at the sheep and sucking on his cigar.

Jock loved visitors and made sure to come front and center seeking attention and admiration. As he did with everybody, he put his nose to the visitor's face whuffling over it. Before anyone could divine his intention, he used his broad teeth to neatly snap the man's cigar in half, then stood there blissfully munching it down. A good sport, the gentleman joined in the laughter after removing the remainder of his cigar from his mouth. He also bought several sheep.

One day Jim was out on the hayfields baling, while I was preparing to round up a crew to bring in the hay, when I looked out the window and saw Jock meandering along the tar road. He found a gate mistakenly left open and decided to go exploring. I quickly started after him, but when he saw me coming, he decided it was time for a game of chase and picked up his pace. As I was passing a house with new neighbors I hadn't yet met, I was yelling at the top of my voice pleading, "Jock, Jock, come back to me, please don't leave me like this, I'm alone and this is hard to deal with!" No luck. By now he was out of sight and I slowed down. I lowered my voice slightly and changed my tone saying, "You are a miserable, wretched, jack-ass, Jock!"

As I said this, I became aware that the new neighbor lady, who obviously had not seen Jock race by the house, was watching me with a strange and disapproving look. I didn't have time to introduce myself, because I needed to catch up with Jock. I ran back to the farm, jumped into the pick-up, and, after turning around when I passed him, literally herded him home with the truck.

Within the week, I learned that the neighbor's nickname for her husband was "Jock."

CHAPTER 22

My God are We Broke!

THERE WAS LITTLE change to our seasonal routines through the mid-1960s; Jim plowed a section of road for the town in winter, we worked haying and attending fair circuit in summer, and we ran the two large barn operations for chickens and sheep. It was all physically demanding, as was the bookkeeping. But the most mentally exhausting part of it all was that our income was constantly negative.

A typical diary entry of the era read: "My God, are we broke!"

This, of course, was largely because we still provided the major part of our labor to the chicken producers gratis, a situation we were helpless to change unless we gave up the farm.

In the mid-1960s, we worked with Lipman Poultry of Augusta, our third chicken processing company. By this time, the chicken processor business had consolidated to five major companies, including Lipman in Augusta and our former chicken processor, Penobscot Poultry.

And the business had been changing, mirroring our situation. In 1966, broilers were the second-most valuable farm product, trailing only potatoes, with a value of $66 million. The number of broilers produced in Maine was now 72.5 million, up from 16.9 million in 1950 and 54.1 million in 1960. In 1966, Maine was the ninth-largest broiler producer in the United States. Despite the growth in chickens produced, the number of farmers had decreased from 911 in 1964 to 750 in 1967 and most were within fifty miles of the chicken processor, thus Waldo and Kennebec Counties accounted for forty-two percent of all farms. To handle the increased production, the farmers had to built more barns, and the amount of space alloted per chicken had decreased from 1 square foot per bird to 0.85 square feet.

The chicken processors, who held all the power, continued to fine-tune their operations. And so it was in 1967 that a state poultry specialist told us that he believed the broiler processing companies would soon drop all chicken growers located more than thirty miles away from their plants. The nearest one to us, and the one we were currently raising for, was forty-two miles away from the farm. It was a deeply disturbing statement and also profoundly prophetic.

By the fall of 1967, the latest flock of broilers had gone to market, and we had cleaned the barns and were ready for the next flock. Jim was in the field, cutting some second crop hay. The telephone rang. It was Lipman Poultry. I expected them to give me a date when the baby chicks would arrive. Instead, I was told we would not receive anymore birds; they were indeed dropping all growers beyond their newly established thirty-mile limit. In all, area farms beyond this limit with a capacity equally 500,000 birds were also out of business. Just. Like. That.

We always knew it could happen, but the suddenness was smashing. I stood there reeling, and I asked if there was a problem with our bird quality. We had always been praised for the efficient figures of our flocks. I was assured that was not the problem. It was simply that a new policy had been put into effect. Eliminating the growers more than thirty miles away would reduce operating costs and allow processors to survive against Southern competition. We had heard about the stiff Southern competition each time we were told we must enlarge our capacity, which forced us to borrow more money to handle more chickens. This time there was no request to expand. And no amount of pleading or begging would change their minds. This was a "show no mercy" proclamation delivered by a telephone call—the cowards. Not to mention the news was delivered by a member of the company we had never met.

Although Jim and I always tried to wait for the right moment to exchange bad news, I could not bear to know this edict alone while waiting a few hours for him to come home. I drove several miles to the field where he was working and sobbed out my anguished report. He always received even the biggest problems with equanimity, and this time was no exception. His position was that we had recently been told this could happen, now it had. We would move forward as we always had, and somehow the good Lord would inspire us with a way to save our farm. We both knew that what we faced now was going to take iron in the will and granite in the soul.

We took no comfort in the fact that several of our neighbors and other chicken farmers just like ourselves around the state were also being financially executed.

A story in the *Maine Times*, a weekly newspaper based in Brunswick, described the situation that developed in Maine like this: "The broiler grower finds himself being squeezed by one of the strangest feudalistic economic systems ever contrived, a system that has reduced his lot to something akin to that of the sharecropper in the South. His income from the broiler business has diminished to poverty or near-poverty levels."

Although we knew it was futile, we contacted the other few chicken producing companies in Maine to see if they would supply us with chickens. The first question they asked was about our location. Indeed, it seemed they all had imposed a thirty-mile limit, and we, of course, were beyond it.

It must be said that the way had been well paved for the poultry companies to institute this policy. *The Maine Times* wrote a story in 1969, that read: "In this instance, the FHA's role could be described as that of an unwitting accomplice caught in the middle of a situation created by the companies that dominate the industry, the broiler processors."

By dropping growers like us, the processors weren't giving up the capacity they needed because they constantly loaned money to new growers who operated within the new limit. In effect, the companies had at their call brand-new buildings, built to their ever-changing specifications for heating, ventilation, and insulation. The taxpayer was the ultimate supplier of this money to build this capacity because those farmers who lost their contracts and could no longer pay their FHA loans were simply told to leave their farms and, if they did, their debt to the government would be wiped out. The harsh reality is that eventually even newly-built, FHA-financed facilities suffered the same fate when the chicken producing companies ultimately went bankrupt, leaving hundreds of poultry barns in the State of Maine standing empty.

At the time we received our final blow, an excellent demonstration of FHA's outrageous irresponsibility was playing out just a few miles away from our farm. On a piece of land within sight of a suddenly empty chicken barn, a brand-new thirty-thousand-bird capacity barn was being built by a prospective broiler grower financed by FHA.

Since FHA district directors were transferred so often there was little continuity with any particular one, but one person we dealt with numerous times toward the end of our farming days was supervising the building of this new facility. We went to see him and asked him what company was going to put birds into this new barn, which stood in the midst of so many now empty ones. And since this building was also beyond the thirty-mile limit, how about that company taking us on, too.

The director, per usual, gave us double-talk and non-answers until he tired of our persistence and promised he would bring the representatives of this processing company to see us. Sure enough, on a rainy day, two of them eventually arrived in the director's car wearing business suits and trench coats. We gave them a brief but sound description of our experience and a tour of our clean buildings and equipment. Their inspection was perfunctory and they were clearly bored. They declined our offer of coffee or even a short conference, instead returning to the car with the FHA director.

We accompanied them and, through the car window, Jim asked the chicken company men, "Can you tell us if you would have us raise broilers for you?"

One of them replied, "We can't give you an answer on that right now."

Persisting, Jim asked, "Are you going to put chickens in the barn currently being built by FHA money for Mr. Stanford?"

The two company men fumbled for answers, until at last one admitted, "Well, we don't really know."

The FHA director slumped down into his seat, slipping his chin into the collar of his trench coat. It was clear he didn't want to hear the answers to these questions.

Whatever It Takes

Going for broke, Jim said, "Come on now, you certainly know whether or not you are going to put birds into the new Stanford barn, why not just state your plan one way or the other!"

They looked at us a moment, then the company representative turned to the FHA director and said, "You may as well know. No, we are not going to contract that building for birds, it is too far away from our plant."

With that, the company man turned to us with a cold look and practically sneered, "Does that answer your question?"

Smiling grimly, Jim and I nodded.

The FHA director, pale and tight-lipped, closed the window abruptly and drove away. The Stanford building, which cost tens of thousands of dollars, never housed a broiler. The owner suffered a heart attack and then died shortly after that from a stroke.

CHAPTER 23
A New Plan

SINCE THE FARMERS Home Administration was no longer receiving their weekly "assignment" check from the poultry company for our chickens, they soon notified us that without fail we needed to pay the balance of our loan by the end of the year.

There was no way we could do it.

Even if we both took jobs, we could not make enough to handle that kind of debt. We tried not to let black despair and hopelessness consume us. But these were very dark moments for us.

We figured that if we paid FHA with our sheep income, we would not be able to operate the farm unless we raised a great many more sheep. And even if we did that, we would still only be able to pay a small part of the debt demanded. Acquiring more sheep could be an answer. Our sheep operation had always been in the black, it was work we understood and loved, but we would need to have hundreds of them, and we couldn't produce those numbers out of our own flock for years to come. Also, the bulk of such a flock would be for commercial production—the meat market, in other words. Purebred sales brought more money but would not provide the required volume.

Of course, the key problem with this idea was, "Where do we get the money to buy three or four hundred sheep?"

Borrowing was the obvious answer, but given our situation we were a terrible risk. Since the local bank wanted nothing to do with us before, they would surely snort in derision now. That left, once again, only the FHA. We formulated a plan. We felt since the FHA had put us into the chicken business, and because of their indiscriminate loaning of money to please the poultry companies, they had essentially put us out of business. This is how we saw it, anyway.

We sat down with our detailed sheep farm records and put together what we considered a realistic plan to generate enough income to handle our debts and allow us to live. Our living would be frugal, but we were accustomed to that. Our biggest criteria was always where we lived, not how well we lived. Each night we worked on estimates—costs of feed, additional sheep, production per ewe, and marketing.

We knew where and how to market purebred sheep, and we also knew how to market meat lambs. At the fairs we met a buyer from Boston who would buy all the meat lambs we could produce. His reason for coming to the fairs was to line up farms that would sell their lambs. Our lambs that did not meet strict breed standards and did not fill our own freezer were sold to this man's company. His business integrity had been excellent. We also knew there were others like him who would buy market lambs, so we would not be limited to only one buyer.

In addition to money, there was also the issue of finding adequate space and grazing land, a problem Jim soon solved. Jim, developing an idea sparked by an article in a sheep magazine, decided to replace the wooden second floor of a poultry barn with open grid metal flooring. As a result, since sheep manure would pass down through the heavy wire grid, the sheep would not need bedding, and would remain clean.

The droppings would land on the cement floor below and could be easily cleaned out. This system would require far less footage than a conventional barn. We would have separate barns for the purebred sheep and the commercial sheep.

We put together pages and pages outlining our plans and financial estimates and took it to representatives of animal husbandry at the University of Maine, University of New Hampshire, and University of Connecticut for criticism before presenting it to FHA. They all deemed it feasible and were interested in the concept. FHA had a different opinion. They had not financed any similar sheep operations in Maine and were not about to use us to gain experience.

Their only solution to our miserable state of affairs was quite simply and firmly this—abandon your farm.

They essentially told us, "Bring us the keys to your farm, move away, and find jobs. We will sell your farm and apply the proceeds to your debt. Any unpaid balance will be wiped out as a government loss. This is the solution that other people are taking, and you both just need to face it."

We didn't grovel, but we implored the committee to study our proposal and examine its merits. Compared to the revenue an expanded sheep operation could provide for repayment, the sum we were asking to borrow was not huge. Not only could we not bear to lose our farm, it was against our rock-hard principles to leave any debt unpaid. They assured us this would not be a blot on our record since it was happening to so many others. They even made a couple of thinly veiled suggestions that our barns might catch fire, a fate suddenly being suffered by some other barns around the state. We did not believe in that either.

We returned home deeply discouraged. The FHA could not force us to leave the farm for another year, but still, we needed to find a way to stay legally and soon. We believed in our sheep farming idea, and we weren't ready to let it drop without a fight. It occurred to us that some fight was just what we needed to show. The FHA had made some unsound moves, and we felt this agency bore a goodly amount of responsibility for its irresponsible actions and their devastating results.

Our opinion was solidified when we learned a chicken farm was sold to a fisherman for five thousand dollars. The only condition required to acquire the farm for such a ridiculous price was that he not raise chickens on it. That was easy; there was no chance. We knew the outstanding debt on that particular farm was fifty thousand dollars, meaning forty-five thousand dollars of taxpayers' money was thrown to the winds so the FHA could get an outstanding loan off its books.

We were outraged, and this situation gave us ammunition. With a fire in our bellies, we contacted our state congressman and gave him a complete history of our relationship with FHA and the broiler business and outlined our plan to repay our debt. He was impressed and willing to help in whatever way he could. He promised nothing, just said it would take time for him to look into the situation. He suggested that we had a right to meet with the New England Regional FHA Director. We soon learned that this director planned to visit the University of Maine shortly.

We successfully made an appointment and were in his office at the required time armed with our neatly typed figures and plans. A man of lesser rank screened us and our paperwork in a cold and clipped manner. When the director came into the office, he ignored us at first and asked the other man, "Have they got figures?"

May and Jim tending their sheep in 1967.

The man rolled his eyes and, with a sarcastic smirk, replied, "Have they got figures!"

The director's attitude was also cold, his eyes were shark flat, but he did listen and he did review the plan, although perfunctorily. He leaned back in his chair and told us what we had already heard: "Turn over your farm keys, and forget the whole thing."

We stated our beliefs and informed him about the broiler farm that had been quickly sold to get it "off the books" for five thousand dollars. He replied that this must be nonsense, that would have been just the down payment, and we had it all wrong. We told him it was a documented fact and gave him names and dates. We asked him if he thought that was the proper way to handle taxpayer money. We have always wished we could have found a way to record his next statement. After the other man had left the room, and there was just the three of us, he smiled and said, "It's only government money, and who cares about government money?"

His final words echoed the local FHA committee. "No."

If we were going to fight, we realized that we needed to use every weapon possible.

We knew not to display anger or insolence, instead the best way was to continue presenting the facts to all who would listen. To this point, only those of us who had been in the broiler business and who were indebted to the FHA knew what was happening; quick and quiet sale of the farms was the FHA's way of keeping the whole expensive mess out of the public eye.

We placed a call to the *Maine Times*. They were interested and came to interview us and then others as well. They printed an excellent article that clearly outlined the plight of all of us who had been caught in this grave situation. The article was headlined: "HAS FHA LAID AN EGG?"

Not long after the story ran, we received a notice from our local FHA office asking us to attend a meeting with them. The local director introduced us to the state director who wasted no time in stating his position. Tall, stern, and silver-haired, he stood over us shaking his finger in our faces as if we were two naughty children. He fairly shouted as he told us we were irresponsible for asking FHA for financial aid to expand a sheep operation. He demanded to know what made us think we were any better than all the other people walking away from their farms.

Finally, when he started to run out of steam, Jim calmly and firmly told him that the FHA would have to drag us from our farm feet first, and, before that, we would spend every last cent we could lay our hands on to visit Washington, D.C. and make our case. We would meet with all fifteen Agricultural Committee members in Washington, and we would describe in detail the entire unsavory history of the FHA and its outright betrayal of Maine's chicken farmers.

It was delightful to watch this man change from belligerent to concilliatory. His tirade was clearly an opening gambit to intimidate us into leaving with our "tail tucked between our legs," but when he saw that he had failed, he took a different tact. He said, "Well, we'll have another look at your sheep proposal. There isn't much point in you folks getting your congressman all shook up."

Indeed, our congressman had come through and had apparently already spoken of a "shake up." That combined with the newspaper article, and our visit with the Regional New England Director, probably helped convince FHA officials that this story would be told as far and wide as we could manage.

By the time we left, an appointment had been arranged for us to return with our sheep figures. The State Director rose, shook our hands and, in kindly tones, thanked us for coming to talk with him. This was our first experience with politics!

The local FHA officials and their committee reviewed our request, and their final decision was that they would loan us enough money to buy the wire flooring for the barn and one hundred sheep, not the four hundred sheep we felt was required to generate enough income to pay our debt. The setup we had in mind was labor intensive, but much less so than thirty-five thousand chickens. By cutting the financing for the number of animals we could buy, it was like loaning money for a hotel, but only letting the borrower fill the rooms to one-quarter capacity. We explained all of this, but the committee was firmly in a wait-and-see mode. A quarter of a loaf was better than none, and at least we bought more time.

CHAPTER 24

Royal Winter Fair

We were officially out of the chicken broiler business and started to build the sheep business even bigger. We now had about 125 head and even sold some to as far away as Iowa.

We had decided that our commercial sheep should have as much Polled Dorset blood as possible, since this breed can produce lambs twice a year if properly managed. They were not the same rugged grazers as our North Country Cheviots, but that wouldn't be necessary in this case.

First, we tore up the wooden second floor in the oldest barn, fastened the wire grid to the floor timbers and welded them together. Jim did this all in record time. He also built large bulk feeders that would hold several days' feed, so sheep could freely eat again. Animals cannot produce if they aren't fed properly. We found good and affordable Dorset ewes, many of them purebred with papers, and a purebred Dorset ram. Finding purebred sheep was necessary to keep the double-lambing propensity in their genes.

There was a window in time before we started the new sheep operation that allowed us to attend the Royal Winter Fair in Toronto, which claimed to be the largest indoor livestock show in the world

May posing with trophies won at the 1967 Royal Agriculture Winter Fair in Toronto Canada.

with twenty-seven acres under one roof and more than 17,000 entries. We had always wanted to do this, but couldn't when we had chickens. "The Royal" is held in mid-November. In those years, the Canadian Government selected the best animals, sheep, cattle, and goats from each province and paid rail transportation for both livestock and owners to attend the fair. Separate dormitories were provided for men and women and the fair lasted ten days. Americans had to provide their own transportation, understandably, but were welcome to enter the competition.

The most attractive part of this fair to us was that a livestock auction called The Sale of Stars followed the competitions and buyers from around the world came to participate. Prices at the fair were excellent and North Country Cheviots were in high demand. Prize money at the show was also excellent. We sent in our entries and went through the federal blood testing required of all the animals we were showing and selling. We washed, trimmed, and cleaned our show flock and sale animals, and packed for ten days. Early on a crisp November morning, the truck and stock trailer were loaded and the four of us were off to Canada.

The facilities at the Royal Winter Fair were unlike anything we had ever seen. The other side of the sheep penning area was barely visible the distance was so vast. Beef cattle were being judged in carload lots, rather than individually, because their numbers were so great. The show rings held six, six-horse hitches and wagons at one time. Everything was on a grand scale, and more than once we asked ourselves what we were doing there. We were just small farmers from the coast of Maine. On opening day, uniformed officials came and swept all the sheep exhibitors against the wall, telling us not to move away from it until we were told. Soon, Prince Philip, who was officially opening the fair, came through. He was very gracious and stopped to shake hands with several of us. Connie was one of the fortunate ones.

The dormitories were interesting, Jim stayed in the men's dorm, while Connie, thirteen, Debby Jo, nine, and I stayed in the ladies dorm as required. There were cow ladies, goat ladies, sheep ladies, and horse ladies in the dorm, and we heard accents of all sorts. All of us worked on and showed our particular types of animals throughout the day. By the end of the fair, the mixture of all our work clothes perfumed the dorm with such a profound mix of bovine, equine, ovine, and goat odor that it was nearly overpowering. We all good-naturedly thought our animal scent was the most endurable.

The classes were huge and the sheep spectacular. We held our placings in the top ten until it came to the ewe lamb class. The judge

kept shifting the line-up until he was satisfied, and I saw Jim standing at the end of the line of ninety ewe lambs. Judging a class of that
size can take the better part of two hours. Ours was a classic of her
North Country Cheviot breed, and I couldn't really believe she was at
the back of the line. Some judges select either the top or bottom animals first, not always following the same pattern from class to class.
They will go down through the line re-examining and shifting places
sometimes quite radically. Sheep become tired of being held in position to say nothing of the crouching exhibitor.

Tension built with every switch of the judge. We knew a fine rep-
utation could be made in this contest. When the ribbons were handed
out it became clear that our ewe lamb was at the top of the line and
had won her class. We were overwhelmed, and further so when she
was named Reserve Champion Ewe, the equivalent of being named
the best ewe lamb in North America. The honor was splendid, and
the money that went with the win even more so. We also won first
place ewe lamb, third place yearling lamb, and second place ram lamb.

At the end of the show we talked with a competitor from Manitoba. He had some fine sheep, and we told him that we felt guilty
coming to his country and having our sheep place ahead of him. He
appeared to live a simple life, as did we, and we knew that this was all
about prize money and sales. He smiled and said, "Oh, don't worry,
I have eight oil wells!"

And he did! He served in the Royal Air Force during World War
II and one of his veteran's benefits was the opportunity to buy a great
deal of land cheaply in Manitoba if he wished. After his war experiences he wanted solitude and to live peacefully with his wife while
shepherding his own flock of North Country Cheviots. The deed to
his land did not stipulate that mineral rights belonged to the Queen.

Jim with Reserve Champion Ewe from the Royal Agricultural Fair in Canada.
The equivalent of being named best ewe in North America.

So when he decided to drill for oil on his land, and hit it, it was all his. The eight wells supported him in grand style. We were happy to think that this man who had fought for his country was rewarded by it.

The sheep we brought for The Sale of Stars were all sold at excellent prices—some of them even went to Cuba—and we were able to bring home much-needed money to pay operating bills.

———

Meanwhile, back in Maine, the wire floor operation worked as we had hoped, and the production of market lambs reached our expectations. We couldn't come near making the original FHA payments with only one hundred or so commercial sheep, but we hoped our initial success made would prove to the FHA that our the plan, if fully funded, could work.

Because there were some purebred Dorset sheep in our new commercial flock, we were able to add them to our show string, which helped to improve our income. Dorset sheep date back to the seventeenth century and are highly prolific breeders. We were now washing, trimming, and showing about thirty-five sheep every week during fair season. There were times it was hot and tiring, but we were hanging on to the farm, even if by a slender thread. It was worth whatever had to be done.

In spite of all we did do, income was still seasonal, and operating expenses for the farm were pared to mere portions of what was really needed. The FHA, which remained adamant about not further financing our sheep farm, apparently saw the handwriting on their wall as the Maine broiler business continued to struggle and loans continued to sour. The bad loans on the books just weren't a good image, and how the books got cleaned up didn't seem to matter as long as they were no longer visible.

As a result, they began talking more and more often about their desire for us to abandon our farm and simply walk away. We remained steadfast: No way!

CHAPTER 25

Arctic Prawn

GIVEN THE SEASONALITY of the sheep business, we were always looking for ways to earn money in the off season. By the late 1960s Arctic prawn, or what we know as Maine shrimp, began appearing off our shores in great numbers. They came down from Arctic waters from winter until early spring to spawn in the comparatively warmer waters off the Maine coast.

These relatively small, but firm, pink shellfish have a delicate taste akin to lobster. They are not flat tasting or iodine flavored as are some Southern varieties. The cold, fresh Northern waters are probably responsible for their fine quality.

It seemed these spawning shrimp appeared in great numbers for a few years every few decades and when they did, they were very helpful to people on the coast. Lobsters were scarce in winter, and most lobstermen put their boats and traps up on the shore until spring. However, the arrival of these shrimp inspired them to rig up their boats and drag for this new harvest. Steel A-frames and galluses were welded for support of the drag doors and the nets. Jim was able to pick up a few welding jobs to earn extra money. If we had still owned *Spindrift*, he certainly would have rigged her and joined the fleet.

But there was still money to be made. Jim put the farm dump truck to good use when a local lobster and fish buyer hired him to make the five-hour run hauling shrimp up to a fish processing plant in Eastport.

The boats dragged all day and didn't return to the New Harbor dock until after dark. After our truck was loaded with thirty thousand pounds of shrimp, Jim made an all-night run to Eastport, returning in the afternoon of the following day. Jim would catch a few hours sleep, and then drive back to the dock for the next load.

Eastport is the easternmost town in the United States, and it is where the sun first hits the East Coast in the morning. The road to it is long, narrow, and winding, and late at night not even a small coffee shop remained open. Jim took thermoses of coffee and sandwiches for the trip.

At the time, Machias had a long, narrow old steel bridge that spanned the Machias River. Two cars could barely pass on it. One night, a night when the temperature plunged to twenty below zero, the truck lights went out shortly after Jim drove onto the bridge. There was no cars in front of him to follow and no oncoming traffic to help light the way. In total darkness, he had to creep across the bridge foot by foot until he heard the rumble of tires on steel grids give way to tires on pavement. Remarkably, after Jim reached the paved road, the lights just came back on again.

Most of his trips were made in cold, even sub-zero weather, and the shrimp would freeze solidly to the truck bed. Fire hoses were sometimes used at the processing plant to break the shrimp loose to unload. Deliveries had to be made regardless of the weather, and Jim drove through blizzards and icy rain. One night as he was leaving the dock in a howling Northeast snowstorm, a fisherman friend said to him, "Mossified Christ! You ain't leavin' on an ass-hole of creation night like this, are you?"

But he did. I didn't go with him, because there were sheep to feed, and Dorset ewes that could have lambs. I always breathed a sigh of relief when I heard Jim's truck come growling into the farm-yard the next day.

Jim earned money trucking shrimp for just one winter, and then the fish buyer installed sucker tubes to unload the boats instead of bushel baskets. These tubes also loaded the shrimp into the trailer trucks he now used to handle the increased volume of shrimp.

But we still found a way to earn money from shrimp. Several local people with pick-up trucks would load shrimp into coolers and then head for other states such as Vermont, New Hampshire, and Mas-sachusetts to sell them in parking lots or along the side of the road. They usually went on weekends when shoppers were out looking for something different to spice up their dinner menus.

Through friends we learned of an abandoned gas station in East Hartford, Connecticut that was located next to a shopping center. It seemed like a good location to sell shrimp. So, we made a trip to Connecticut to get permission to park at the station and to obtain a seafood vendor's license.

And just like that, we were ready to peddle fish on a street corner. My mother and father who lived near our farm, came over to watch Connie and Debby Jo, and we provided the sheep with enough feed to last for a few days.

We bought the fresh shrimp, so fresh they were still wiggling, in New Harbor late on Thursday afternoons. We packed the shrimp in ice coolers, and then around midnight we left for East Hartford, arriving early on Friday morning. We could then be set up and ready to sell to early shoppers and people just passing by.

We made high sideboards for the truck that proclaimed: "FRESH MAINE SHRIMP." We made smaller, separate signs reading "2 LBS. FOR $1.00." The truck tailgate sporting a clean covering was our counter. We used a cigar box for our cash register with a big iron bolt to keep the money from blowing away. Sales were brisk for this was a new product in the area. One obstacle was that many people wanted to know how they really tasted. Jim solved this by setting up a tiny propane burner and small pot to cook them and provide samples. The secret to cooking an excellent Maine shrimp is to drop it in boiling water for just one minute and then quickly removing it, thus providing a shrimp with firm, sweet, almost lobster flavor. Once our potential customers tasted the shrimp, they were believers and we nearly always sold out by Sunday.

Days spent peddling shrimp were long and tiring, although it was always fun talking to the customers. The cheap seemingly cardboard-walled motel we stayed at was a haven come 10 p.m.

We had experienced plenty of cold weather in our lives, so we stood outdoors at the truck's tailgate all day regardless of conditions. I have often thought how the good Lord was with us on those weekends, because it seldom rained or snowed to dampen the sales we needed so badly. However, we did experience bitter cold, and it seemed more penetrating just standing there in Connecticut than it was in Maine. We tried to dress for it—Jim with his buffalo plaid wool Maine Guide shirts, North Wool green pants, heavy gray wool, red-banded socks above his L.L.Bean boots, and red-and-black mackinaw and wool cap.

I wore my L.L.Bean boots and wool socks as well. One of the things we laughed about was that people would sneak a look at the

L.L.Bean boots and then lean down surreptitiously to peek under the tailgate to see if the truck was really licensed in Maine. I had tried the wool jackets, but I didn't seem to have the same resistance to cold that Jim did, and each trip I found a new way to keep warm with some very old clothing.

My mother had a long fur coat of great age and indeterminate origin that had hung in her attic for decades. The fur was worn away in patches here and there, but it was whole and the most wind resistant covering I ever wore. It hung down to my ankles. The boots took care of my feet as L.L.Bean boots with sheepskin inner footpads are unbeatable. I wore old fur mittens to keep my hands warm, but nothing I tried could keep my head warm. Finally, I mooched around in mother's attic and found a Persian lamb fur cape. It was well worn with bare spots, like the coat, but by making and trying on patterns of old cloth, I fashioned a bonnet that strapped under my chin, around my neck, over my ears, leaving just my eyes, nose, and mouth exposed to the elements. I trimmed it with a small strip of bunny fur from Connie's baby coat. It was quite bizarre, but oh, so cozy!

Looking at myself in the mirror as I tried it on, I thought of a businessman we knew whose eccentric brother insisted on wearing, winter and summer, an old leather aviator's helmet-like cap that strapped under his chin. It was his trademark, and his well-dressed brother would say despairingly, "I'd pay anybody anything to keep that sunuvabitch on an island so he wouldn't come into the store and call me "brother.' " Our customers probably understood the reason for my backwoods outfit; regardless, it didn't hurt sales.

On one trip we brought a big cod fish that had been caught with the shrimp. We put a reasonable price on the fish, but because of his size and because it was a whole fish with head and all, people didn't know how to judge the value. We weighed him many times, and knew his weight to the decimal, but each potential customer needed to see him on the scales.

Each time, Jim would say enthusiastically, "Well, let's see what he weighs!" as he slapped him on the scales. I would giggle thinking, "That fish could find his own way to the scales by now." Eventually a gentleman not afraid of cleaning a fish bought him.

On one January shrimp-selling weekend, we had left home in the snow, hoping it would soon clear. Instead, rather than clearing, we drove into an ice storm in East Hartford. We had the shrimp, so we just had to sell them if at all possible. We slid into the old gas station and prepared our place of business—the tailgate. Freezing rain seemingly fell in sheets, and everything both horizontal and vertical was icy.

The gas station and truck were located on a hilltop along a busy street, but most of our customers came from the shopping mall at the bottom of this steep hill. We sat together in the truck cab thoroughly disheartened. There was not a soul in sight—no cars, only an occasional service vehicle passed by. We could just as well have been on an uninhabited planet. We feared this would be the time we would finally go home with a full load of shrimp.

For almost two hours we sat in this miserable weather fearing the worst. And then miraculously we saw a person coming out of the mall's grocery store. Yes! It was a man carrying a small sack and making tiny, exploratory steps over the slippery ice. What direction was he taking? No, he would never try to get up over this hill and pass by the truck. Moment by moment we watched his erratic progress until finally, yes, it did seem he was preparing to tackle the hill.

As we watched, he had slowly made it more than halfway up the hill. Unbelievably, this lone soul did appear headed toward our truck.

Hope glimmered, and Jim said, "Well, I'll get out and stand beside the truck so he'll know we're here."

He opened the door, and swung his long legs around from the seat to step out. As I watched, his entire body just slowly rippled and undulated over the running boards with his hat being the last thing to disappear under the truck. His feet never got a purchase on the ice, and he slid in slow motion until he lay spread-eagled on the glazed pavement.

As the approaching man purposefully headed for the truck, Jim was valiantly trying to gather himself together so he could gain his feet. I was already silly from the long, sleepless, icy drive. I knew Jim wasn't hurt, but seeing him lying there with his arms stretched out, I thought it must appear to this potential customer that Jim had thrown himself to the ground in an imploring gesture of desperation to please buy our shrimp.

The good man did buy several pounds, and while Jim was waiting on him, I was laughing in near hysteria. I could not suppress my howls even though I was sure the man must think I was crazy. That thought made me laugh even harder. The more I know the occasion is such that I should not laugh, the more the uncontrollable the urge is fueled. By mid-afternoon the sun came out, the ice melted, and customers appeared as if from a swarming anthill. Again, we went home with an empty truck and a full cigar box.

We sold shrimp on the street corner for three winters before the volume of spawning shrimp went into a declining cycle. Prices rose and sales fell and our winter income from shrimp sales was over.

CHAPTER 26
Rabbit, Rabbit

THE QUESTION THAT squirreled around in our minds every day in the late 1960s and early 1970s was, "How can we use all the empty poultry barn space on this farm to make money?" Two floors of the older barn were now being used for the commercial sheep business, but there were still two other floors, and an entire three-story building that sat empty.

During our travels showing sheep, we learned of a Massachusetts man who used his former poultry barns to raise rabbits. We visited him and he was kind and helpful in sharing his rabbit raising experience. It seemed rabbits definitely had a value beyond charm.

We knew marketing rabbits to sell for meat would not be a problem because our Boston lamb buyer was always asking us if we knew where he could buy some because demand far exceeded his supply. He bought the rabbits live and processed them at his plant.

Given what we learned, within a couple of months we were in the bunny business. The major investment required was a building, which we already had in place. We bought rolls of wire and, using wire cutting shears and J clips, Jim soon had the third floor of the original barn filled with hanging wire cages. He built wooden nest boxes

Rabbits at North Country Farm.

for each cage, and we bought small crocks for water and feed in each cage. The wire cages allowed the rabbit droppings to pass through, and this system helped keep the rabbits clean and healthy.

Our shrimp peddling efforts provided enough money to buy the equipment and several dozen rabbits, but given our limited money and lack of experience we decided to start on a small scale. We figured if everything we heard about how fast rabbits multiply was true we could increase numbers in a reasonable time. Like sheep, every breed of rabbit has a particular advantage. We were told that Californian rabbits were to the meat rabbit world what Angus and Herefords are to the beef world. Compact, muscular, and solid, they were also beautiful, sporting white with dark eyes, ears and noses. They almost had the markings of a Siamese cat. We found a breeder of excellent Californians and they became our primary breed.

As time went on, and as we met with other rabbit breeders, we added other breeds like the big giant chinchilla, not to be confused with fur-bearing chinchillas. These were a lovely salt-and-pepper gray, and very large and with sweet dispositions. One breeding doe, which Connie named Gretchen, would stand on her flat, furry hind feet, put her front paws on each side of our faces, and lick our chins and noses when we opened her cage to dispense feed and water. The breeding does and bucks never went to market, of course, and we were successful in establishing a small but thriving market for purebred rabbits that we would sell to other breeders. We shipped our rabbits in wooden vegetable crates to breeders as far away as California.

We subscribed to a couple of rabbit magazines that were helpful in many ways, although they tended to be "cutesy-pie." At the risk of appearing that way also, I might as well admit that something within the center of my being has always melted at the twitching nose of a rabbit, its velvet chops, receding chin, powder puff tail, and long ears. They groom themselves meticulously, and I loved watching them grab their big ears and pull them forward to be licked clean.

We found that breeding rabbits could be a comical experience. The buck has to be taken to the doe's cage, and you must stay and keep watch, because if the doe is not in the mood she can, and often will, attack and kill the buck. If she begins to act ugly he must be quickly snatched away.

Mating can take place very quickly, but often we had to stand watch with each doe for up to half an hour while she played hard to get. Recognizing the buck's success was easy, and always amusing. When his service is completed, his ears fall forward, his eyes go completely out of focus, and he rolls over on his back with all four feet in the air in a short faint. The doe is then returned to her cage and her record chart attached to it is carefully marked with the date and the number of the buck. We tattooed all the rabbits in their ears.

Rabbits bear their young in thirty days after mating. This is called "kindling," and there are generally ten to twelve rabbits in a litter. Near the time, we put fresh hay in their nest boxes, and the doe would begin pulling fur from the big roll of skin that hung under her chin and over her chest. This apparently exists as an extra source of fur for the purpose of making a soft, warm nest for the young.

Most people picture rabbits as gentle creatures. And basically they are, but they can bite and scratch severely, so you must quickly learn the proper method of handling them. Feeding a mother rabbit can provoke a biting attack. Occasionally a mother rabbit will even eat her own young.

We certainly received our share of deep arm and hand scratches from the powerful kicks and long nails of the rabbits before we mastered how to pick them up by the loose skin of their backs and tucking them quickly into a crooked elbow. Long sleeves and leather gloves were a must.

No, it was not easy taking these lovely creatures to market. But to survive on a farm, the fate of some animals must be accepted; the food chain is a fact of life on this planet. Like the sheep, we enjoyed the comforting side of the breeding program, which was the purebreds that went on to live out their lives.

Initially to feed the rabbits, we carried hundred pound sacks of grain up to the third floor of the barn where the rabbits were housed, and eventually the crated rabbits weighing hundreds of pounds had to be taken down to the main floor. Carrying all this up and down the stairs didn't last long, and we wouldn't have either, so Jim designed a platform elevator operated by a chain-fall.

Handling rabbit manure was another matter. The elevator was not feasible for this, so Jim cut a door at the back of the barn so the tractor bucket could be raised to receive the manure and, when full, transfer it to the dump truck or manure spreader. Rabbit manure is highly valued by farmers. At the end of a year we had around two hundred and fifty breeding rabbits, and they had produced copious amounts of manure, which had to be removed as often as possible due to its weight on the floor under the cages.

Some of my diary entries regarding rabbits read as follows:

"Began cleaning rabbitry today, wheelbarrow and manure forks, heavy, brutal job."

"Another deposit check in the mail today for purebred giant chinchillas, bless their furry little souls!"

"Up at 4 a.m. Took 98 rabbits and 12 lambs to Boston. Shipped giant chinchillas to a breeding farm in Maryland yesterday."

"Shipped twenty-five Californians for breeding to Saskatchewan."

"95 rabbits and 44 lambs to Boston by 10 a.m. "

The sheep and rabbits were producing well, and we were making more money with them than we could possibly have made if we both had eight-hour jobs. But contrary to popular opinion, rabbits breed quite seasonally especially in winter of northern climates. This is probably nature's way of keeping the young safe from extreme cold and lack of food. In a controlled temperature environment, if we could have provided heat, production would have improved greatly. But the economy of this was out of the question.

Even with the rabbit and sheep business doing well, we were only scratching the surface of our debt and making just token payments to the FHA. They continued to rumble that it would be best for us to "turn over the keys," and we continued to point out that our sheep figures proved we could have made our debt payments if they would have loaned us the necessary money. We were clearly at a stalemate but one that we knew we could not maintain forever.

It was now the early 1970s; we were both in our early forties, and hanging on the best we could. We knew that while the FHA was reluctantly giving some time, their patience was running low and we needed to make some real money soon or we would be forced to give up our dream farm—our home.

It was time to look once again toward the sea.

CHAPTER 27

Why Not a Trap Mill?

THE WINTER OF 1971 was severe even by Maine standards, but snow didn't help us financially anymore. The town no longer divided its roads into sections and hired local people to plow; rather it awarded a contract to the single company submitting the lowest bid. We didn't have the necessary equipment to make a bid, nor could we afford to buy it.

I wrote in my diary that January: "Sweating the money situation out horribly, day-to-day. For inspiration, we two waded through the snow in our big, lovely sheep pasture."

Lo and behold, a few days later inspiration arrived.

Jim met a lobsterman friend who complained that he couldn't get enough oak trap stock to build his lobster traps for the coming season. Each lobster season, wear and storms destroy or damage a portion of a lobsterman's traps so they must be replaced or repaired. Typically, during the winter, lobstermen rebuild their trap supply either in barns or in fish houses down at the shore. There were already a few working mills making wooden trap stock, but demand exceeded what supply the existing mills could produce in timely fashion.

As he recounted this conversation, Jim noted that we had a huge, empty building (our "new" chicken barn) just screaming for something to be done with it. Here, he said, was an industry in which existing suppliers could not keep up with the demand, meaning the market already existed. Not only did we have the facility, but Jim had experience working with wood and sawmills. Unfortunately, we didn't have equipment or the money to buy mill equipment. However, we had found ways to overcome such obstacles before, so why stop now? Jim scoured the newspapers and auction notices looking for used mill equipment. We reasoned that if we held back some FHA payments, we could use the money to get the mill running. However, it would be a gamble and we needed to move swiftly (and successfully) or undoubtedly the FHA would finally drop the sword hanging over our heads.

Starting a sawmill to make lobster trap stock required several pieces of equipment, but four items were essential to begin. First, we needed an adequate power supply. Specifically, we needed three-phase electricity, which was not available in our area, and it would cost us more than twenty thousand dollars to have the electric company bring it to us. It may as well have been twenty million dollars. Jim looked for another way. He knew a friend who owned an old Buick Straight 6 engine that he no longer wanted. We did want it, so we trucked it home. The six-cylinder Buick would provide us with power.

Second, we needed a bolter saw, also known now as a slasher saw, that could cut the bolts up to six feet in length, which is all the length needed for trap stock. Third, we needed a rip saw to slice the wood delivered from the bolter into one-inch thick planking. Fourth, we needed a resaw saw to cut the planks into the widths and thicknesses needed. We found the rip saw and the resaw at a used machinery company in New Hampshire. They were old, but seemed to have some life left. Regardless, the price was right. We found an old bolter saw in Mariaville, a beautiful area of blueberry barrens in Hancock County, at a small wood working company that made yo-yos. All these pieces found their way onto our dump truck and eventually into the old poultry barn using the big farm tractor, chain falls, pulleys, and rollers. Jim worked night and day to position the pieces correctly and wire them to the old Buick engine, which had neither clutch nor transmission. Its power was initiated and transferred when the engine started. Jim installed a "panic switch" that could stop the engine and the saws all at once.

Once the saws were working, Jim built a "brow," a kind of land dock outside where the bolts, or logs, could be unloaded from the wood trucks. From this dock, the logs could be rolled through a cutout in the building and straight onto the bolter saw. Oak is brutally heavy wood and we could not lift these by hand.

At the agricultural fairs, we met and made friends with numerous draft horse people who competed at the fairs. Often, they also owned and operated woodcutting operations, so Jim contacted them to deliver the oak bolts. We would use both red and white oak. The first load of three cords was soon delivered, and Jim wasted no time shoving the oak through the mighty, singing forty-two inch saw, an awe-inspiring piece of steel that commanded mortal respect. As the planks arrived at a safe distance from the saw, I took them away and piled them up. Then we worked together to feed the planks through the resaw, which, with six blades working at once, was capable of producing sixty laths per minute. The laths had to be graded, counted, stacked, and tied. I typically handled that work.

As soon as we opened, word spread swiftly amongst local lobstermen that trap stock would soon be available nearby. We received orders nearly every day for the rest of the winter.

Laths, which are used to both build new traps and repair old ones, were not the only pieces of stock needed by fishermen. Those building new traps also needed the heavy framework, or sills, for each side of the trap, as well as runners and crosspieces to complete the frame.

We also needed to make the complicated half-round bows used as the top framework in the popular "hog-yoke" trap, so Jim worked on an invention to steam and bend the bows. Jim designed a steamer and controlled its intake of water by using an old toilet tank valve. Anything that would work was fair game to Jim. The steamer heated and softened the pieces of oak until they were pliable enough to bend over a rounded tank. They were then left to dry into the bow shape. Initially, too many pieces of wood resisted the strain on their fibers and split in the center, rendering them useless, so Jim then devised a system of individual steel straps that went over the bows and held them in place until they were dry and firm. This system reduced breakage to a minimum. Every second of Jim's time was directed toward improving and expanding the mill project, all necessary if this were going to work.

As soon as the power supply fired up and the saws were working, sawdust became a problem. Shoveling sawdust, which I did for hours and hours, was much more pleasant than shoveling chicken manure, but still monotonous until Jim created a blower system that automatically blew the sawdust out the back of the building.

Every day we produced trap stock, counted it, and tied it with hay string from the sheep barn. Our machinery was old and tired so Jim spent seven days a week from dawn until nearly midnight coaxing it along. Eventually, we became so busy we needed to hire a worker.

Steaming the oak to make half-round bows was tricky, so Jim created a way to hold the wet wood in place using steel straps until it dried in the needed shape, greatly reducing breakage.

I loved helping in the mill, but there were still sheep and rabbits to care for every day. Connie and Debby Jo, who were now teenagers, were wonderful help after school and on weekends, but there were still not enough hands to handle all the work.

A local lobstermen said he would like to work for us, and this was a great thing, for he understood the product. The mill only ran during the winter months because there was no demand for stock during the summer, by which time traps were built and in the water and the lobstermen spent all their time hauling traps. It would be late fall before demand started again. This worked out well, because we earned our summer income at the fairs and by selling breeding stock, lambs, and rabbits.

The initial figures from our makeshift mill enterprise were promising. And we had so many of the required elements—a building with water, a heating system, and room to expand. We could get good wood supplies from our fair-going draft horse friends and we could easily find skilled labor looking for winter jobs. We combined all that with Jim's ability to put anything together and make it work, not to mention our combined determination and optimism that, someway, somehow, we were going to save our farm.

Despite the promise and hard work, we just didn't have reliable machinery, a decent power plant, or, of course, money. In April 1971, the mill was humming along with plenty of customers, but the rip saws just kept going kaput and the Buick power plant simply wanted to die. In other words, to put it plainly, we were working with equipment close to junkyard condition. Jim managed to keep running, and added other important pieces as time and money allowed, but we really needed a proper power source to generate our own electricity—we had to have a real generator, and soon.

———

By the end of May, the mill closed for the season and would not reopen again until fall. Haying season and the fair season were ahead of us, and we had good purebred sheep sales lined up that we had to process. As this money came in, we put every dollar into the sawmill.

We put out feelers in every direction and read every newspaper ad looking for an affordable generator. Finally, when we got to the Blue Hill Fair on Labor Day Weekend our outreach paid off. A fair official told us about a shuttered zinc and copper mine in Brooksville, on the Cape Rosier peninsula. He thought they had an old standby generator that they might be willing to sell. We jumped into the truck and went to check it out. The old Callahan Mine operated for a while in the late 1800s and then reopened in 1968 as an open pit mine. Nearly 800,000 tons of ore and five million tons of waste rock were removed from the pit. It closed in 1972 and was eventually flooded when the Goose Pond dam was removed.

Anyway, it was closed and unflooded when we visited. At the end of a winding, narrow trail that snaked down into the deep open-pit mine sat a colossal diesel generator covered in heavy tarpaulin and tied with old rope. You couldn't tell much by looking at it, but we did realize that it probably weighed about ten tons. We found the person responsible for the generator and he let us uncover it for inspection. It was a Dorman Diesel and the man told us it produced six hundred volt, three-phase power.

It was a foreign generator, which meant obtaining parts would not be easy, and it rarely had been used. In fact, the Dorman, kept only for emergencies, had not been fired up for at least five years. It could be ours, as it sat, for five hundred dollars—no warranty.

The price was attractive, but the condition and lack of maintenance made it a gamble. Since there was nothing better on the horizon that we could afford, and we needed to reopen the mill in just a few weeks, we made the decision—buy it.

We told the company representative that we would return soon to get it and he said someone would be available to help load the generator onto our truck with a crane still at the mine. Mike Weston, one of our wood suppliers volunteered an old pulp truck to haul the load home. The truck, which had been retired, was long and tough with a wood platform body that was well-worn and gouged by thousands of cords of wood. It couldn't handle daily work anymore, but it had the strength and capacity to haul our ten-ton generator.

Jim asked Mike if there was anything special he should know about it. Mike replied, "There ain't no knob on the gearshift, the horn don't work, the fuel gauge broke a long time ago, and you got to use this hammer to release the emergency brake. Don't forget to hold this handle to the south'ard or the door won't shut. Just drive her like you hate her."

Jim secured the chain and rope and wooden chocks to the truck bed and we began the three-hour trip to Brooksville. The old truck roared and clanked along, and as we descended the narrow, circular trail along ledges cut into the sides of the mine, we wondered if given her length she could negotiate the turns. She did. When we drew alongside the great mass of the generator, the crane, also well-used and decrepit by now, lifted it onto the truck.

When the generator was hoisted and lowered to within about four feet of the truck body, something slipped on the crane's mechanism and the generator crashed onto the truck body sounding like an exploding bomb. Dust and splinters from the wood body flew everywhere, and we were sure the generator would crash right through to the ground. In our minds, it seemed the generator landed on the truck's body center and both the front and rear of the truck rose from the ground before settling back down again. Luckily, there didn't appear to be any scattered or broken parts around the generator, and soon we were working our way back up the treacherous walls of the mine. The truck groaned all the way home to Round Pond.

The generator was fastened to wooden skids, and when we backed our bulldozer up to the log brow, Jim was able to slide the generator off the truck. The next day we uncovered it, nervously searching for anything that might have broken when it dropped, but all seemed to be in place. Since this was a water-cooled engine and was not yet hooked to a water supply, we could not run it. But it could be "turned over" for a few seconds to verify that it would run. We were most anxious to know if we had bought something useful with our five hundred dollars.

Jim brought a can of starting ether, hooked up a battery, and prepared to engage the starter. We looked at each other with an unspoken prayer. The Dorman gave a few grunts, a couple of mighty belches accompanied by big black clouds of exhaust, and then she settled to a great, smooth purr. Jim shut her down immediately, but our grins were broad and bright. We owned a real generator.

"She's a big babe!" Jim said.

We agreed that would be her name: Big Babe.

When the fair season ended, Jim began wiring the sawmill for three-phase power and built a small attached shed to the rear of the barn to house Big Babe, insulating it for sound and cold protection and a platform to keep her away from the spring runoff. Meanwhile, I scraped Big Babe's peeling paint, scrubbed off all of the grease and grime, and painted her a soft gray. By the time I was done, I knew every crevice, curve, and protrusion of the massive machine.

When the sawmill reopened in early November, we already had good orders in place. The lobsterman, Kenneth "Stubby" Leeman, who we called Ebby because he hated "Stubby," returned to work with us again. He was soon joined by another lobsterman, Howard Smith, who worked at the big saw with Jim.

That first real year of operation, we were sawing three to four cords of wood per day, cutting 3,500 lathes and making 450 to 500 hundred bows. Depending on quality, we would pay up to fifty dollars per cord for bolts of oak.

Everything proceeded along reasonably well until early January.

My diary entry for January 7, 1972, reads: "A really TOUGH day. No electricity from Big Babe. Jim spent the whole discouraging,

The 42-inch main saw at North Country Wood Products demanded respect.

depressing, heart-rending, body-breaking, BLACK day trying to get the DC exciter off the motor."

Two days laters, I wrote: "Jim put DC exciter back—checked everything—NO electricity. Oh God. Called generator expert in Portland, Dale Simms, who charges seventy-five dollars per trip plus time. Dale said, 'Don't worry, we'll get the old son-of-a-bitch going!'"

Dale was somewhat elderly but spry and brilliant and seemingly born with an electrician's manual programmed into his brain. While working on Big Babe, Dale told us how he had once responded to a call from a wealthy owner of an island whose generator had failed. Things at the island house were uncomfortable, and the owner was not about to wait for service. Dale packed his tools and rushed to the job. When he approached the generator and began assembling his equipment, the island homeowner said, "Now before you begin this work, I insist on knowing what your qualifications are." Dale replied that he was a licensed master electrician with a lifetime of experience.

The gentleman went on, "No, I mean I want to know what your educational background is, your college degrees, assurance that you really know what you are doing."

His attitude was so haughty that Dale replied by telling him the truth: "I got through the third grade, and that was all I wanted of school. From there on everything I know is experience."

Dale began to repack his tools. The island owner looked aghast and asked what he was doing. Dale said, "Well, I guess I'm leaving, you don't seem comfortable with my background, and you see, you're the one in trouble here, not me."

The man, apparently accustomed to treating local help shabbily, backed down quickly and assured Dale he would stay out of the way until the job was done. Dale had his generator going in no time.

He also had Big Babe running again in no time. Thank God!

We took care of animal chores at dawn and worked in the mill all day and then again after supper each night. By the end of January, we had four lobstermen working with us at the various machines, with Astor Prior and Clyde Campbell joining the team. I took laths away from the saws, graded and tied them for as many hours as I could each day. But the bookkeeping was becoming more and more time-consuming because we now had a payroll and all the additional work that goes with it for government records and taxes. I also had to keep up with sheep and rabbit pedigrees not to mention handle the winter lambing Dorset sheep to check at night. We took turns at this.

We were busy with the sheep in the sheep barn, the rabbits in the old barn, and the sawmill in the "new" chicken barn that we had built in 1962.

As the sawmill business got going, we had three hundred rabbits in the barn that we were breeding, with about seventy percent of them purebred Californians and thirty percent giant chinchillas. We sold both breeds as purebreds and to the commercial meat market. Even though the rabbits seldom produced in mid-winter because of the cold, we were still able to take ninety to one hundred live meat rabbits to our Boston buyer several times between early spring and July, when production slacked off again because of the summer heat. But this worked out well, because the fairs began again at the end of July. We shipped the purebred rabbits for breeding via Railway Express as far away as California. It was a small market, but good. The rabbit business was always profitable for us.

However, as the mill work increasingly demanded more of our time, it grew more difficult to justify keeping our rabbit business. The mill generated more money and had much greater potential. We decided to sell the business. We searched for a buyer and by late spring had sold our entire rabbit operation. My feelings were mixed. Rabbits were so pleasant to work with and unfailingly delivered a small profit, but we just didn't have the time.

We still had the sheep, and they accounted at times for maybe half of our income. Sales of purebred sheep were single sales of rams or ewes or small beginning flocks of both Dorsets and North Country Cheviots. We had about 150 sheep of both breeds in the mid-1970s and were selling them in Maine and shipping to Indiana, Illinois, and New York, as well as Canada.

One frigid night when it was my turn to check the Dorset sheep, I threw a coat over my nightgown and followed the icy track to the barn to find a first-time lambing Dorset ewe in hard, complicated labor. She was definitely going to need help. This usually involves two people, but I was reluctant to wake Jim. His day had been long and exhausting unloading truckloads of wood onto the brow in below-zero cold.

Connie, still a teenager but highly experienced in all aspects of sheep delivery, woke with her usual happy smile, and we piled on a bunch of clothes and attended to the ewe. The ewe was having twins that were breeched, so it meant a lot of reaching in and turning lambs around. While she lay stretched out, one of us would hold her head and stroke it while speaking to her softly. The other would kneel and with face laid to the sheep's rump would reach inside the lamb to assess what parts belonged to which baby lamb and sort them out before we began a gentle pulling process timed to the ewe's contractions.

These contractions continued throughout the sorting out, and they can be so powerful they will numb your arm and hand and are actually capable of breaking fragile bones. It's a tiring job. Connie and I frequently exchanged places until we successfully delivered a fine pair of lambs, got them to get their first important drink of milk from the ewe, made sure the placentas had cleared, and ensured the ewe's comfort in a private pen with feed and water.

CHAPTER 28

Delivering Firewood

SOME OF THE wood trucks that came to the mill had a loading and unloading boom attached to the truck, but most did not. And after scaling (measuring the cordage of the wood), it was a long and back-breaking job to get the bolts of heavy green oak off the truck with hand-held pulp hooks. It was also far too time-consuming. It quickly became evident that we needed to buy our own loader, that also unloaded. We felt it would work out well because we were also developing a firewood business on the side. The mill produced so much scrap wood, the unusable slabs from the bolts and edgings of the planks, that we decided to sell them too. We installed a swing saw to cut the wood into stove lengths, and a conveyor to carry it outside where it could be dropped into the dump truck. If people wanted to cut the lengths themselves, we used the pulp loader to drop it into their vehicles. We found a loader on a truck that was ready for antique status, but the loader mechanism was fairly good as long as we could keep its parts replaced.

Firewood sales were a minor part of the operation, but they did bring in a few dollars. The loads were huge and the price minimal. Oak burns hot and long and we always had orders. We would deliver within a fifty-mile radius and we made a few trips each week, weather permitting. We delivered the firewood at just about sunset, after regular mill work ended. I joined Jim whenever I could. Not only were the winter scenes, snow-crusted pines, and glowing rose sundowns beautiful, but we had a chance to talk over the day's events. The people we met and our experiences were sometimes interesting and even poignant. Two experiences particularly stand out.

One day, I received a nearly indecipherable note, along with a wrinkled, grimy check in the mail. The note was written on the back of a small grocery list, which consisted mostly of cat food. The note, from a man named Ed, requested we deliver a truckload of wood to the man's trailer located down a single-track dirt road several miles away. The note was signed, "*Yr friend.*"

We delivered the wood on a bright Sunday morning after a heavy snowfall. Ed's fifteen-foot trailer was ancient and battered and stood on the edge of a lonely but lovely back road. The trailer was overhung by spruce trees with alders nearby. At one end of the trailer under a little porthole window was a bumper sticker that advised, "Vote for Ed Muskie."

Ed came out the only door, presenting a slight figure, with extremely hunched shoulders, probably caused by rheumatism. His head was bent with gray hair that curled out from his red and unbelievably greasy cap. He sported at least a week's beard, and his eyes were very red-rimmed and watery. He seemed frail and gentle.

As he stepped out through his door, a grayish, furry mass came out around him making his legs invisible from the knees down. Upright tails rippled and waved about, and whiskery faces rubbed against his legs. The mass surged forward with him until Jim raised

A loader made it much easier to load and unload the oak bolts for the saw mill. Previously, it was done by hand with hooks and chains.

the dump body of the truck. The noise sent the cats hastily seeking safety inside the tiny trailer.

When the load was dumped, Ed came around to the truck cab to thank Jim and wish us well. Jim returned the wish then asked, "How many cats have you got, Ed?"

"Saven," Ed replied, pronouncing the first "e" in seven as the "a" in the word *at*, as many Mainers do. "But," he continued, "they're a lot of company."

Sensing an almost apologetic note in his tone, I leaned around and said, "Sure they are, Ed. We love cats, too!"

He replied, "I do. I love 'em. Christ!" The last word was with a nod of his head for emphasis and delivered in an almost reverent tone.

The cats had returned to surround him. Waving to us Ed turned and picked up an armload of the freshly dumped oak wood. With his attachment of gray and tiger-striped companions he disappeared back into his trailer.

As we drove back up the long, narrow road, we commented that even though he lived in the most frugal of circumstances, he lived in clean air, pristine beauty of the woods and enjoyed the company of sweet creatures he loved.

A second firewood delivery also stands out in my memory. There was a phone call one evening from a well-spoken young woman who stated that she and her friend were taking care of a house and the wood supply left for them had run out. They were now going into the woods and cutting dead branches, which were not burning very well, and beyond that the stove was operating extremely poorly.

They had enough branches to last overnight but begged us to bring them a big load of wood the next day or she believed they would surely freeze.

The lady sounded desperate. She said she couldn't describe just where they lived; she would have to meet us at the junction of two main roads and guide us in from there. We arranged a meeting time and place for the following afternoon.

The day had been bitterly cold, and even the pine trees looked dark and frozen by 4:30 that afternoon. The sunset was crimson and gold, its colors sharpened by the freezing air. We looked for a car at the appointed meeting place, but there was only a girl, between eighteen and twenty-five years old, sitting on a frozen snow bank and leaning against a road sign. She wore a long coat, and her head was wrapped in a woolen shawl. She jumped up and hailed us, saying how happy she was that we were on time. She had no car and had walked four miles to meet us. She was cold from the walk and was glad to get into the dump truck, which had a fine heater.

She had been right; not only could she not have described how to find the house, it is doubtful we would have believed her directions. We traveled short back roads branching off from one another, unpaved and narrow. The last turn was into a heavily wooded track that was little more than a trail. The truck was wide, high and heavy, and we just didn't need to get stuck. Jim stopped and asked the girl if this road was passable, and if it had been plowed all the way through. She assured us on both counts.

It must have been plowed with the smallest of Jeeps, because it was just a narrow ribbon of sheer ice with great trees crowded to the edge. As we progressed slowly, the track continued to narrow until the wheels were straddling the plowed area and digging through the frozen snow on both sides. The trees became ever thicker and closer, their branches now sweeping the sides and top of the truck. Jim and I exchanged looks, but we were committed. There was no hope of turning around anyway because of the thick woods and frozen swamps on either side, which, if spring-fed, wouldn't support us. It was another case of the only way out was onward. After more than a mile of creeping along in this fashion we came to a tiny clearing, where with skill and luck, Jim might possibly turn around.

There was still no dwelling in sight, although a path seemed to continue beyond the clearing, stretching up a nearly perpendicular hill. Jim asked the girl where the house was, and she replied that it was up over the hill and beyond, and did we think we could please get the wood to the house? Jim said he would continue hoping to find a better place to turn around. He shifted into a low range and lunged at the hill. We only made it partway because of the deep snow, so he backed down, shifted to a lower gear and roared up the hill again. Once at the top, there was still no house in sight and still no place to turn around. Clearly the next move would be down the other side of the hill, but it was too steep. If we got stuck, there wasn't a piece of equipment, short of a tank, that could get us out of this place until spring. Finally, Jim said he needed to see the remaining terrain before he went any further. We walked down the steep hill and at the bottom was a little, old house. There were broken panes of glass, bricks were falling off the chimney tops, and the house hadn't seen paint for decades. It was obvious that if we slid the truck down the hill to the house, we would not make it back up through the ice and snow.

Jim said he needed to back the truck all the way back to the small clearing and hope there was room to dump the load there. The girl apparently hadn't realized that a dump truck couldn't travel on a footpath. By now darkness had settled, and the night was lit only by a pale moon, which provided barely enough light for Jim to back down the hill and through the trees. He succeeded, dumped the wood, and pointed the truck back down the trail toward civilization.

The girl said she and a friend had come from New York City a few weeks earlier to care for this, well, shack is really the only word for it, in the wilderness. There were two goats and a horse as well. The owner was a minister, and at the moment he, his wife, and six children were touring backcountry churches in the hills of West Virginia. The girl's speech seemed to indicate she had a cultured background, and she and her friend had believed they were setting out for a fun adventure in the Maine Woods. It was an adventure, all right.

She said payment was at the house, and would we please come and see why the stove wasn't heating properly. We asked how they planned to get the wood to the house and the girl said they had a child's wagon and would transport it up over the hill and down the other side. Each of us picked up an armful of wood and started over the hill. While it was a sad-looking affair on the outside, it was even more depressing inside. The weathered door opened into the kitchen. The floor was wood and hadn't seen soap and water for years. There were no curtains at the windows and little plaster left on the walls. Some of the interior walls had been torn out so that the place was really an empty shell.

A small black iron kitchen wood range sat in the center of the floor and was emitting streams of smoke from around each stove lid, crevice, and crack it possessed but little heat. Sitting dejectedly next to it was another girl with long, tangled hair, and red-rimmed eyes. A big yellow dog was leaning against the stove shivering, and two little kittens were nestled directly beneath the firebox.

Writings about LOVE and PEACE adorned what walls existed. Old clothes, boots, and tree branches (for the stove) lay about with a couple of sacks of grain here and there, presumably for the horse and goats. Jim took a quick look at the stove, flipped some dampers and drafts, and smoke disappeared instantly giving way to a crackling fire. It was a good little stove, but they were trying to operate it with all the drafts set to banking a night fire, which choked off the heat.

The girls told us of their woes. The hand water pump had frozen at the black iron sink even though it was only two feet from the stove. The sink was filled with rusty looking, food-encrusted pots that had been soaking in water but were now encased in ice. There was no sign of an evening meal; I thought perhaps because there were no clean dishes left. One girl remarked that everything had gone wrong today. Looking around it didn't seem that "today" was any real exception. Since the pump had frozen they attempted to get their water from a dug well but lost a twenty-foot birch log down the well trying to break the ice below.

They were young, strong, and obviously educated so their philosophical choice of this current lifestyle was apparently their own. We did feel sorry for them and did not accept any money for the wood. We stayed long enough make sure they understood how to use the stove without burning down the house. With drafts properly set, the house was warming up nicely. The girls' moods brightened, the dog stopped shivering, and the kittens wandered out from under the now-hot stove to stretch. We left feeling they were now a little better off. Warmth makes anything easier to cope with.

As we trudged back to the truck we saw a small, doorless outhouse huddled under the trees, but saw no signs of a horse or goats. It all made us think of our log cabin days, but we were brought up knowing how to rough it, so that made a difference. When we walked back into our farmhouse with its shiny, varnished wood floor and braided scatter rugs and smelled the supper cooking in the oven it gave us more reasons to count our blessings.

At the sawmill, our crew worked hard and steady and were dedicated. They worked well together although there was always a lot of teasing, which helped cement the relationships, at the morning coffee breaks (mug-ups) and afternoon cookie breaks. The work was heavy and steady and such breaks were important.

In March, we traded our 1968 Chevy truck for a one-ton Ford truck that could also haul sheep. I couldn't help but shed a few tears for the Chevy, which had given us 125,000 miles and ran without incident during all those shrimp peddling trips to Connecticut. The Chevy did perform one last service for us before we traded her—Connie drove her to get her driver's license.

When I mentioned our truck change at the mill during a coffee break, it prompted a lively discussion of Ford versus Chevrolet and which brand started better in winter cold.

Clyde said of a Ford, "You can probably get 'er to start if you go out every twenty minutes during the night like the mail delivery man did. He was so afraid his car wouldn't start in the morning that he went out all through the night every little while and started 'er up. Kuh-rist, come time to leave in the morning he found he'd run 'er out of gas. He struck off to get some and by the time he got back she was froze up!"

Ebby reached for a doughnut. Knowing he was diabetic, Astor Prior said, "Thought you wuzn't supposed to eat nothing sweet?"

Ebby looked contrite and said, "Can't help cheating. I know I'm shittin' in my own nest, but ya can't just die altogether!"

Clyde Campbell remarked, "Far's it goes, Astor, you're just like a seagull, eat, squawk, and shit. But then I know when I come in from lobstering, I could eat the hide off'n a skunk. Can't eat a heavy meal at night, though. I'd die the death of Old Mother Dumplin's duck. Got to cut out eating as much as I do," he said and placed his hands on his round tummy, "Why, I'm like a barrel of shit with the middle hoop broke."

Just then a gentleman who had moved to Maine from "away" came in to ask about firewood. He was making an earnest attempt to appear like an old salt with his denim jeans, suspenders, and rubber boots. But his haughty bearing, "from away" speech and "pork pie" hat just didn't come across. When he left, Clyde said, "Don't I wish I had two hats just like that one! One to shit in and one to cover it up with!"

Talk then turned to a local attractive lady who had had a few husbands and was now having her twelfth child with her latest one.

Clyde said, "Guess she's been around."

Howard remarked in his slow, quiet way, "Why I'd say she's been around more than the button on an outhouse door."

Occasionally when I would come into the mill in the morning, I would see big, fluffy tufts of black hair lying in the snow. I puzzled about its origin until one evening as everyone was leaving after work, I stepped outside and Astor, who sported a wealth of black curly hair, was bent over double brushing his hair in a forward direction. He then took out his jackknife and, grabbing great handfuls of hair, hacked it off. He was a fine worker, and had a poet's heart under his rough exterior. He could sing songs that he had composed describing the Maine coast that would bring tears. He also had a severe sinus problem in the winter that he couldn't seem to control with a handkerchief. Out of Astor's hearing one day Ebby said, "Jeezus, he sounds just like a toilet being flushed."

Lobster trap orders began to slow down by mid-March as most of the fisherman had bought their stock through the winter and were nearly finished with building and repairing their traps. Still, we wanted to keep the mill running as long as we could so we scoured the trade publications for lobster dealers along the New England coast who handled trap stock for the convenience of the lobstermen. We also invested in a small advertisement. It seemed that we were on the right track with this approach because a big truck came from Downeast and took away thirty tons of laths. We also began hearing from lobster dealers further south who were interested in fall delivery of trap stock.

This was all good news to pass on to FHA. We had been paying them as much as we could while still leaving enough money to operate the mill. When big loads of oak came down the road, we had to purchase it whether we could afford it or not. Wood lot operators depended completely on the weather to get logs twitched out of the woods—too much snow and it is impossible, while during mud season they didn't even try. To be without our raw material was unthinkable, so we had to stockpile it.

Stockpiling wood requires capital and cash flow. When I would hear a big logging truck grinding its way to us over the hilly Foster Road, my heart would sink as I mentally calculated the limited funds in the check book. Having to buy the wood so far in advance was the crunch and this was true because we were trying to pay for a huge, defunct business and still leave enough to operate the new one. The FHA grudgingly acknowledged that we were making every effort, but they still rumbled darkly about the future. They really just wanted all the messy broiler business cleaned off their books.

Jim and May celebrate their 25th anniversary in October 1973. Earlier that year on her birthday, Jim wrote: "Our love has deepened and strengthened beyond anyone's imagination, for a lifetime of devotion is all I can give you. You are my life, my being, my strength, everything that I have and hope to be is you. We have had our struggles, but it has made us more aware of what we have. Our beautiful children, our wonderful farm and our way of life, as we want it, free in spirit and soul."

CHAPTER 29
Julie and Star Glow

SPRING. THAT EXQUISITE season that I yearned for each winter. As the days lengthened, I anxiously searched for every sign that meant the coming end of winter's long siege of ice, snow, and bitter cold—not to mention the March mud and slush. As we climbed over March Hill once more, the sky brightened its blue, the seagulls were sweeping along the fresh air currents and making their spring cry—no longer a mournful mewing, but one that was quick, loud, and happy. The Balm of Gilead trees on the front lawn filled the air with the deliciously spicy smell that emanates from their sticky buds.

Meanwhile, our goat Julie had just defied statistics by having her third set of quadruplets. Julie was a Nubian goat given to us a few years earlier. Jim had delivered a small flock of North Country Cheviots to a hobby farm in Massachusetts. The family was large and charming and each child had their own types of animals for 4-H projects. Julie was a by-product of this and was one more goat than they needed. She was fashioned in large splotches of brown, black, and white, with the typical long Nubian ears that could wrap around her nose and halfway back up her jaws again. The farm lady said that Jim should take this tiny and engaging creature home to Connie and

Debby Jo. Jim chuckled, and said, "Not a chance; we have too many animals now."

On a future visit, the lady described what happened when Jim was ready to step up into the truck and leave. She just came to him with Julie in her arms, and passed her into Jim's arms. He just said, "Thank you," and placed her on the seat beside him.

Connie, Debby Jo, and I were ecstatic when he brought her home. She was affectionate, intelligent, and full of sprightly fun. When she bleated she made a hysterical sound that reduced us to helpless laughter. When she drank water she could hold her great ears out like airplane wings. The rest of the time she swished them around in delight, as would a girl with long hair who knew she was beautiful.

By the time Julie was four years old she had been in heat several times and obviously longed to literally have "kids" of her own. She would wander over to the rams' pens and climb up the partition as far as she could with her front legs hanging over and her ears hanging down. She would gaze longingly at the rams, swinging her lovely ears and bleating seductively. They thought she was nice, but just not their type.

Eventually we took mercy and boarded a Nubian buck goat for the winter. His name was Star Glow, and he was also a character. He and Julie were very fond of each other, but Star Glow was always looking for new adventure, and he was an accomplished escape artist. We came to believe that a four-sided pen built of twenty-foot brick walls could not have contained him. His favorite place to visit was the barn with the wire floor and commercial ewes. There was no romance here for goats: sheep do not mix that way but he was curious. One day our neighbor called to say that Star Glow was up on the barn roof. It was four stories high and this didn't seem possible, but he had climbed the stairs, found a series of ledges outside an open window, and was indeed standing on the barn roof with his front feet in the rain gutter. He returned by this same route.

Connie was fond of Star Glow but he gave her some bad moments. He followed her to the school bus in the morning and waited for her on her afternoon return. The bus driver always managed to close the doors just before Star Glow jumped inside. When he was in his rutting season, this buck goat had a musky scent so overpowering it could almost be touched, and it permeated everything he came in contact with. Like a dog, he urinated on the borders of his territory, but also on anybody he happened to really like. This act left his pungent aroma wherever it landed.

One morning Connie was in the commercial barn sitting on the stairs and feeding a special bottle lamb before she went to school. She hadn't realized that Star Glow had absconded to this barn through the night and was now approaching her down the stairs that rose behind her. He was so happy to see her that he urinated on her head. The school bus was due before long and Connie smelled like a "he-goat." After a long shower with lots of shampoo, I drove her to school.

We found good homes for all of Julie's kids, and when she had produced her third sets of quadruplets we believed it was time she retired from motherhood.

For a few weeks that spring we pursued another way to generate some income and we went "sundowning." This is an Australian term meaning traveling sheep shearing. The four of us did it on long weekends, and it paid well as there were not many sheep shearers. We drove to farms around New England and to other islands similar to Bartletts Island in Blue Hill Bay. Jim had taught Connie to shear, and

Debby Jo in the sheep pens in 1972.

though she was as slender as a willow wand she could shear sheep of any size in double quick time. It was all Debby Jo and I could do to keep up with the two of them, skirting, folding, and tying fleeces. We met some fine people, including a wonderful lady who went lobstering by herself for a living and kept her sheep on an island.

We also sheared the sheep we had sold to Andrew and Betsy Wyeth on their farm in Cushing. It was a delightful experience, and we were privileged to see the Wyeth studio, including an in-progress portrait of Richard Nixon that was never finished.

Through their work on the farm and their years in 4-H sheep projects, Connie and Debby Jo became professional in their ability to handle, trim, shear, and show sheep. They had won bundles of trophies and champion ribbons to prove it. They were raised in the hard, demanding work of farm life, and they never approached it in any way but with willing hearts and love of what they were doing. We worked and played together with our daughters and they were always a source of glory and happiness to us.

Connie drove the farm tractor before she rode a bicycle, and by the time she was fifteen could back the manure spreader into the barn, use a front end loader to fill it, and take it out to the fields to spread. She inherited her father's expertise with machinery.

Debby Jo loved all animals, but sheep were her passion from the time she could toddle out to the barn. Her fine sense of humor was fulfilled by the antics of the sheep, and her love of beauty in all things was rewarded by their response to her care and attention.

As with all children, their growing-up years went too fast, but it is the way of all our lives and must be accepted. In the summer of 1972, Connie, who had just graduated from Lincoln Academy that June, met Tim, a young man two years older who was shepherding a New England show flock of sheep for the summer. Their romance progressed through the season as we all traveled to the same fairs. Their interest in sheep and farming were a bond, and instead of going to dances they worked together preparing sheep for show or reading farm magazines. Tim was attending an agricultural college so it would remain a dating situation for at least a few more years.

In the last years of Connie's 4-H project, a new class was introduced to promote an important image of sheep and wool products—the "Ladies Lead Class." It required a clean and finely groomed sheep that would lead in a mannerly fashion on a halter. The "lady" was to be dressed in a practical one hundred percent wool outfit that could be worn on a special occasion. Many of the awards Connie won in these contests included lovely pieces of wool cloth to make dresses and suits. She was a high school honor student and excelled in Home Economics, so she could cut from a pattern and whip up an outfit on the sewing machine in an evening's time.

In 1974, Canada's Royal Winter Fair was sponsoring its first Ladies Lead Class. It was not 4-H, but it was open to anyone. It was a challenge that Connie accepted, and one we considered exciting. She chose a pattern for a floor-length, princess-like dress of white wool with a high neckline trimmed in white fleece, as was the flared bottom of the dress. Her chestnut hair swept into a chignon, her lovely face, large brown eyes, and flashing smile completed her outfit. Her big North Country Cheviot ewe, Leah, was as snow white as Connie's dress and was led on a white leather halter. Connie and Leah loved each other. Connie would call her by name, and the ewe would follow Connie through the sheep pasture lane and down to the shore and hop over the rocks beside her as they explored tide pools together.

We thought they presented an elegant pair, of course, and to our everlasting, bursting joy so did the judges. Out of twenty or so contestants from the Canadian Provinces, Connie won the class—the first American to do so. The Canadian folks were most gracious and provided a wonderful buffet and dance after the ceremonies. One heartwarming result was that although my mother was dying of stomach cancer and could not attend The Royal, she had been just on pins and

Connie, white gown in the middle, in 1974, with her sheep Leah, was the first American to receive a silver bowl at the Royal Winter Fairs and Sheep Lead Line Class. The class was formed to promote wool and to show it could be used in formal as well as casual wear. The contestants had to make their own garments and own their sheep.

needles waiting to learn the results of Connie's efforts. When I telephoned her that night we shared tears of delight and pride, for Connie, who called her Mamma Jo, was her beloved also.

My mother died a few months later on July 19, 1974. She was just 69. She and my dad had been married for forty-eight years. She was a fountain of love and giving, beloved by us all. Mom loved to sing and, incredibly, she burst into song as she was drawing her last breaths; she looked so happy. As a result, we were left with beautiful thoughts of what she was seeing that prompted her joyous outburst. My Dad was a strong man in all ways, but Mom's death hit him particularly hard. It was clear, we all needed each other at this time. At the time Mom died, the fair season was just starting and we persuaded him to come along with us for the first time. By 1974, we had traded the tent for a nice trailer that provided a comfortable space for him to stay. Dad enjoyed the cattle and he had great talks with the fair exhibitors his age. That fall, all of us being together as a family, Connie, Debby Jo, Jim, and Dad helped us begin our healing process. About two years after Mom died, Dad sold Ocean Reefs Inn and moved into a house that we had built for him on our land. He lived there by us until he died in October 1989 at the age of 94.

After Scot Dog was gone, we sorely missed his mastery at handling sheep and knew we needed another border collie. At the Blue Hill Fair's Sheep Dog Trial in the early 1970s, a breeder of especially fine dogs had a sweet-natured female named Tess with a litter of pups only days old. She ran in the trials and was swift and sharp. Tess was bred in Scotland and shortly after being imported had whelped in Ohio. Her pedigree and performance were impressive. Her owner offered us the pick of the litter. One classically marked female, white neckpiece, tail tip, chest, and paws seemed to send out a vibration. Her eyes weren't open yet and she fit neatly into the palm of Jim's big hand. After the four of us held her, we named her Nell, handed her back to Tess and began the six-week wait until she could be flown to us.

By the time Nell arrived at the Portland Jetport, she had spent two days in the air and at various terminals being rerouted by mistake. When Jim opened the sky kennel, Nell stepped out, gently climbed on his chest, and nestled in his neck. We all took turns for a cuddle and the bonding was instant. When we got home and this little puppy came into the house, she made a doodle on the floor. We expected we would need to house train her and we planned on a long and patient siege. We said nothing, but before I could get a paper towel, Nell ate what she had done in apparent horror at her sin. We felt terrible because we had not uttered a word or made a gesture. That single incident was Nell's total housebreaking; she never made another mistake, she was a lady to the core.

Jim worked with her in the sheep barn and the pastures when he could find time. At six months, Nell would sail over the fence and put the sheep anywhere we wished them to be. A border collie with good breeding and background has such a profound instinct for their work and "I live to please you" attitude that training is a pleasure. She barked perhaps twice a year and then only when she had a really good reason. She slept in our bed and kept gentle but firm law and order among all the barn animals. If two drakes got into a fight over a female she would step between them and use her nose to push them apart.

CHAPTER 30

So Long Big Babe; Hello, Mrs. Murphy

TIME ROLLED ALONG without incident, and by the winter of 1975 the mill was doing nicely and the wood supply was plentiful. We could hardly keep up with demand. Not only was our faithful crew back with us, but we had to hire an extra man to take Jim's place at the bolter saw. There was just too much for Jim to do to stay confined to one machine. Loads of wood came in to be scaled and unloaded, customers arrived to load their trucks, machinery needed repair. After work, Jim would be on the phone with lobstermen discussing trap designs and taking orders until well after 10 p.m. Not unusual was a gentlemen from Downeast who called us at 4 a.m. explaining: "Just couldn't sleep, so thought I'd call and talk to you about my trap stock order." He and Jim had a pleasant conversation for the best part of an hour.

By now, there were seemingly saws of every type and size in the mill, and because of frozen wood, and the grit and dirt in the bark, the blades constantly needed to be sharpened. Sending the blades away was expensive, and the work was not always satisfactory. Jim read about an accelerated three-day saw sharpening course offered by the Foley company in Minneapolis, Minnesota, so we piled into the pick-up truck and headed west. We, of course, hit a snowstorm in Minneapolis that was so nasty several massive snowplows had veered off the road or turned over. In Minneapolis, Jim crammed through his schooling and learned how to properly sharpen the saws. This new skill lowered our expenses and improved our saw quality by a large degree.

We also learned a little more about politics, something that never held any interest for us beyond town meetings and national elections. The FHA was beginning to realize that just maybe the Davidsons had been worth extending the time on their debt. They still weren't rid of all their embarrassingly empty chicken barns, and here we were a possible example of how a good potato may still be pulled out of the burning pit. Visitors came from other counties to see our commercial sheep farm (even though the FHA wouldn't loan us enough to make it fully viable) and every so often FHA committees and visiting dignitaries came for a guided tour through our now humming lobster trap sawmill.

The mill was working, but we were always searching for more business and growth. Our informal market research clearly indicated that out-of-state business could be attained if we had a proper delivery system. Neither our dump truck nor pick-up could handle it. We needed a low-bed trailer (one close to the road to allow for a high load) and a serious truck to pull a heavy load. We found a used but rugged "tug"—a single axle truck that pulled mobile homes—and a flatbed trailer. The trailer was long and low but not as heavily constructed as we could have wished, but the combination was affordable and gave us a start. Once we bought the new truck and trailer, we immediately expanded our market into Massachusetts.

North Country Wood Products was going regional.

The sawmill was a growing regional business, certainly, but it remained a family-like atmosphere. One year just a few days before Christmas a fine snow was falling, and the forecast called for it to increase its intensity throughout the day. I knew the crew would be hungry, so I walked the short distance up the road to the mill with the usual morning coffee and doughnuts. Ebby greeted me at the door with his warm smile and declared, "Jest look at that hog swizzle coming down! This'll be an ol' baster before it's done!"

Clyde was getting over a cold and I asked him how he was feeling today. "Oh, finest kind," he replied, "but I'm still headed down the dark road to death and ruin!" He turned to Jim and said, "After coffee guess we'd better swamp out a road in this snow for that load of oak Mike's bringing in today."

Just then we heard Mike's big truck lumbering down the road followed by her brakes groaning to stop the heavy load outside our mill. When Mike came in, stamping the snow off his feet, Jim told him to join us for coffee before the wood was scaled and unloaded. It was Mike who had loaned us his old truck to bring Big Babe home from Cape Rosier and had become one of our wood suppliers.

Mike owned several teams of splendid draft horses that he used in his wood operation. His horses could get into difficult places not accessible by skidder machines to twitch logs out of the woods. For this process, chains were fastened around the logs and the horses pulled them out to the roadside where they could be loaded onto a truck. During the summer "offseason," Mike entered his horses in the pulling contests at the agricultural fairs, which earned him a nice return since they were hard teams to beat.

As talk turned to horses, Mike told us about a recent experience he had with one of his teams. When training a new horse he paired it with one of his experienced animals. He was working with such a team, and the "green" horse was doing well with the older, calmer, or "clever" one. Or so he thought. At the end of the day he brought the team out to load onto his truck to be taken home but realized he had forgotten to bring his chainsaw out of the woods. It was only a short distance back, so he looped the reins lightly around a tree and dashed back for the saw.

A car raced past the horses blowing its horn for some reason, startling the green horse. The horse began prancing and rearing and soon pulled the reins away from the tree. Sensing freedom, he bolted, forcing his teammate, who shared the harness, to run with him. When they had reached full speed they came to an obstacle in their path—a convertible owned by Mike's young "chopper" who was still in the woods.

The car's canvas top was in place and all the windows were closed. The angle of their approach was such that the wild horse ran past the car while the clever one was forced to climb up over the car's trunk. The stress caused the harness to split allowing the green horse to continue his flight, while the quiet one's momentum carried him right up onto the canvas roof where he promptly fell through. His front feet were in the front seat, and his hind feet in the back seat. His head hung over the windshield, but he was unhurt and not a window was broken.

Hearing the commotion, Mike rushed to the scene. The horse stood calmly as Mike considered his next move. Mike said, "There I am figgerin' what the hell to do next, and Barney, he drives up in his pulp truck and looks this all over, laughing fit to bust himself and says, 'Condrumated Christ, Mike! If I'd known you was so desperate to give that hoss a ride home, I'd a' loaned ya my truck!'"

"Well," Mike chuckled, "I felt some foolish, kinda like I didn't know if my ass was bored or blasted. But you know I opened the door of that car and that hoss swung himself around so that he could get his front feet onto the ground and follow his back feet into the front seat and bring himself clear. The other hoss saw him and he come back on his own."

With that, Clyde turned to Mike and asked, "Couple weeks ago you wuz sayin' you had to take a load of lumber out to Vinalhaven. Did you make it out there?"

"Ayuh," Mike replied, "what a Christer of a day that wuz, though. Wind wan't too bad when they loaded my truck onto the ferry. She was freighted with green lumber. Being first in line when the boat come in they put me up on the bow, first to unload. When we got out beyond the Rockland breakwater the wind come up and before long the swells commenced to spray over the windshield and green water wuz sloshing round the wheels. They told me to get out of the truck, she'd be first thing overboard if the chocks broke loose. We wallowed hard rest of the way. Wasn't I some Jesus glad to get that load off when we hit shore. "That trip wuz jest like marriage. It was so goddam calm at the dock!"

⸺∘∘∘∘∘⸺

Later that winter, I was sitting at my desk writing payroll checks and glancing at the ever-increasing snowfall, when I heard a strange whining noise that increased in intensity with each passing second until it reached a near-deafening roar. It seemed to come from the sky in the general direction of the sawmill, and all I could imagine was a jet plane losing altitude and crashing into the farm. Just then Connie burst through the door, pale and shaking, and taking my arm said, "Mumzee, something terrible has happened at the mill!"

My entire being felt as if it had been sliced through by frozen steel. I can remember almost pushing Connie away in denial of what she was about to tell me, for all I could picture was a mortal injury to someone, and I whispered, "Not Daddy?" She hastily assured me that nobody was hurt, but that Big Babe was blowing up and she had called the fire company.

As it turns out, we were filling a large order and all the machines were in use. Jim was working on the forty-two inch main saw, and everything was going smoothly until all of a sudden the big saw began to speed up. The saw was only hammered to turn about twelve hundred RPMs, but it began to go into such a speed-up that it was making a sound like a siren.

Every machine powered by the generator started doing the same thing, simply running amok with increasing speed. The generator was increasing its power from six hundred volts to seven, eight, and even nine hundred volts, and it was those volts that controlled the speed of the motors. Clearly a spring had broken. Without the governor to control it, the engine increased in speed, and as it gained in speed the generator couldn't stand the increased voltage. As soon as the saws began to race, both Clyde and Jim ran for the main switches slamming them into shutdown position, then raced for the generator room. When they got out there, the generator was roaring toward a crescendo. They didn't dare enter the room, because by that time a thousand volts or more were coming out of the generator, and it wasn't made to withstand that kind of speed. The windings on the generator were starting to break apart, and the heat caused by the increase in the electricity was melting all the windings and fittings in the generator itself.

When they opened the generator room door, it looked like the Fourth of July. Rockets of sparks and flame were shooting everywhere from the machine and it wasn't possible to get near it. We had several fire extinguishers near the door and we played those on the generator, but we couldn't stop the generator's action because the Dorman was running away. This is actually a technical term and is not an uncommon occurrence with diesel engines. Its speed was causing the electrical windings of the generator to catch fire, which produced an intense amount of black smoke, and the diesel engine with its air intake inside a closed room was sucking in the heavy black smoke and fueling itself with it. The more smoke it took in, the more it made and the faster it went.

A diesel engine, once it is fired up and running, will burn any kind of fuel from kerosene to low-grade fuel oil. The Dorman continued to accelerate to ever higher speed until iron and steel could no longer withstand the stress and, with a thunderous crashing and banging, Big Babe wound down to a grinding clatter. Rods, bearings, and pistons were shattered and gone. The Dorman was a heap of broken rubble inside.

Our five-hundred-dollar gamble had given us several years of unfailing service in return for the TLC Jim had given her. We couldn't have asked for more.

Our wonderful Bristol Fire Company responded to Connie's call, but the flames had succumbed to the fire extinguishers, and all that was left was the blackened, charred body of the generator and Big Babe herself.

Merry Christmas to us!

We replaced Big Babe with a colossal, bright-yellow diesel generator made by Murphy, which the crew christened "Mrs. Murphy." She was not new, but she was well taken care of. The price was horrendous, but so was the need; the sawmill could not function without a generator. Of course, we didn't have the money, but by now there was another bank in town. Three years earlier, a group of Damariscotta businessmen recognizing that fishermen, farmers, and commercial people needed a forward-thinking financial institution, formed The Damariscotta Bank and Trust. Because of that bank, the life for many people changed for the better, including us. This bank reviewed our figures, our past, our situation, and the fact that we were now employing area labor and loaned us the money to buy Mrs. Murphy.

Losing Big Babe was big, but, the major event of 1975 was the marriage of Connie and Tim in April. It was a small but beautiful wedding performed at the Methodist Church in New Harbor with a reception at The Willing Workers hall. In addition to family, the sawmill crew, who all loved Connie, were in attendance. For Jim and I, it was a bittersweet day. Connie and Tim left that afternoon for Cozad, Nebraska to start a new life on a sheep ranch where Tim had obtained a job. As is true of parents in such cases, big pieces of our hearts went with her. We worked so closely in our daily farm life and shared similar philosophies. She was our beloved oldest child, but also a friend and partner. Luckily, we had a sharp memory—Jim and I could remember the sheer joy of starting our life together and how much we enjoyed looking ahead to adventure and independence. In this way, I guess, our pain was healthy.

It was just part of the changes rolling our way. Debby Jo was now seventeen and would graduate from Lincoln Academy the following spring. An independent soul, she left home soon thereafter and lived for a while near Augusta, where she maintained some animals. She always loved sheep.

In just a matter of two or so years, my mother had died, my dad sold the inn and moved onto our property, Connie married and moved west, and Debby Jo graduated from high school and struck out on her own. It was a sad, proud, and emotional time, recognizing the constant, relentless march of life.

By 1976, we were making regular deliveries of trap stock to other New England states. We headed out with loads almost weekly from December through April to Massachusetts, Rhode Island, New Jersey, New York, and Delaware. We often drove all night and made no stops other than to unload, but sometimes we did get a hotel room to take a break. The mill business had expanded to the point that we now employed twenty-five people during the busy season.

The tug, a Loadstar, had a bench seat, which according to Clyde, "must be beatin' you to death." And he was right. Every ridge in the cement road sections seemed to bounce us in the air and slam us back down onto a slab of granite—especially when we were driving the truck home empty. However, making deliveries of stock had opened yet another way to expand our business. Lobstermen in other states loved the splendid Maine oak, and many said they wished we built traps as well, because, if we did, they could go ground fishing in winter off the Massachusetts and Connecticut coasts instead of spending time building their own lobster traps.

Jim and May preparing to deliver a load of traps to Massachusetts.

It didn't take us long to figure out that selling finished traps could be a steady sales outlet for our stock and would help further expand the mill business. Our crew members were already skilled at building traps and certainly could teach others. We placed a small advertisement in *The National Fisherman* and the orders rolled in from as far away as New Jersey. We added more workers so that we had twenty-five employees during the busy season, and Jim reorganized the second floor of the mill into a trap building operation complete with a chain hoist elevator, similar to what we had used for the rabbits, to get the heavy stock upstairs. We soon billed ourselves as "New England's Largest Producer of Quality Built Lobster Traps and Stock." We sold forty-inch offshore traps complete for $22.00, which included three heads and four bricks, and we sold a forty-eight-inch version with four heads and four bricks for $25.50. We would also quote a custom-built trap based on a customer's design if they sent a picture and a description. We required a one-third deposit to start the job and then payment in full upon delivery. We charged for delivery on a per-mile basis.

We both went on deliveries because these were long trips, with quick turn-arounds, and it took two of us to unload them and share the driving duties. Jim would drive the heavy load to its destination, and then I would drive the empty truck home so he could catch a few hours of sleep. During the days between our deliveries, I attended to the ever increasing bookkeeping and payroll, and we somehow managed the sheep chores.

However, as we did with the rabbits, we eventually realized we couldn't continue the commercial sheep business, also because there just wasn't enough time. So we sold all the grades (unregistered sheep) and kept just enough of the purebred Dorsets to fit in comfortably with the North Country Cheviots so that we were tending just one barn of animals. We basically cut the number of those sheep in half to seventy-five head each. Our days were filled beyond capacity, and there was no time for recreation of any sort. Although, since the sawmill business still did not operate during summer, we always had the fairs to look forward to. It was a different kind of intense work, but one that offered more chance to relax.

Still, there were, as there always had been, moments of joy. I wrote in my diary that spring, "We kicked over the traces and took a walk out into the pines behind the house. It took us nearly two hours, but after twenty-five years of living here we finally got to the stone wall that marks the back line of our property." It had been a long and beautiful walk in our kingdom and a fresh inspiration to work as hard as was needed to be sure we never had to leave it.

For a small family celebration of spring, we had a sunset cookout at the farm pond's grassy shore. Jocko, the donkey, joined us. Crimson cloud draperies streamed above the dark spruce, and the Evening Star drew a silver line across the pond. Fragrances of hot dogs, rolls, and corn rose from the charcoal cooker. Jim took an ear of corn and held it for Jocko to peel off with his big square teeth. The burro's brown eyes rolled in pleasure.

That May we put the truck loaded with traps on the Islesboro Ferry. We stood on the upper deck so we could look down upon the ferry and out toward the flaming blue sea and sky. There was not a cloud in sight. A handsome gentleman standing next to us expressed curiosity about the load of traps below, and we explained that we had built them and were delivering them to the island.

The man was Robert Goulet, the famed and wonderful singer originally from Lewiston. After a firm handshake, we remarked that this was the kind of day for his song: "On a Clear Day You Can See Forever." Goulet thrilled us by singing a few bars of his song:

On a clear day, rise and look around you
And you'll see who you are
On a clear day how it will astound you
That the glow of your being outshines every star
You'll feel part of every mountain, sea, and shore
You can hear from far and near a world you've never heard before

His golden voice rang out over the length of the ferry and across the expanse of Penobscot Bay.

CHAPTER 31

Tears of Humiliation

By November 1978, we already had enough orders for finished traps to last us the winter. The greater part of the finished traps were now going to the New Jersey and New York coasts. Given the increased business and distance of deliveries, the old Loadstar tug and low-bed trailer were no longer big enough. We needed a bigger horse and wagon, as Jim would say. Jim looked through used truck magazines and decided to seek more information about a 1973 Kenworth with a 671 Detroit diesel. It had been used for the light duty of hauling mail, so it didn't appear overworked. We arranged with Damariscotta Bank and Trust for a loan and rode a bus to Cherry Hill, New Jersey to look at the truck.

It was love at first sight.

The truck was a rich maroon, tall, stately, and rugged with a big, shining radiator. It had a single rear axle, huge tires, and no sleeper, but air seats that would float us over the road, and a ten-speed shift. Sinking into the comfortable seat, I turned to Jim and said, "Please, oh, please!"

We took her for a road trial, and her power steering, which the tug didn't have, was intriguing. The rolling purr of the Detroit diesel was steady and powerful. She passed every test Jim could think of. We called the bank, the money was wired, and a few hours later we were on the road home. I had brought a cassette tape we had just bought—since this truck had a cassette player—and on the tape was the song "Send in the Clowns." We played the tape on the ride home and I forever associated this gentle, haunting melody with that wonderful truck.

> *Isn't it bliss?*
> *Don't you approve?*
> *One who keeps tearing around,*
> *One who can't move,*
> *Where are the clowns?*
> *There ought to be clowns.*

We also stopped in Connecticut to look at a forty-two foot drop-deck Fontaine trailer. It was new, heavy, and rugged, and we knew it could hold four hundred traps and that the Kenworth could pull it. We told the dealer we would come back to get it and asked if he wanted a deposit. He talked with us awhile, and said, "No, I would rather make a deal on a handshake with a man from Maine than take a cash deposit from somebody from anywhere else."

We were honored. The next week we brought the Kenworth back down to get it, and we were ready to begin our first real trucking experience.

Our first big load with the new rig was destined for Belmar, New Jersey. It was early on a crystal-frosted morning, and a white vapor trail streamed from the truck's tall stack. As we approached Brunswick on Route 1, the truck started losing power and the engine died completely. We looked at each other with an "oh-my-god-what-now" expression and suffered the stricken feeling that maybe there was something about this truck we hadn't been told.

Jim had pulled over, got out, and climbed under the big hood. He came back smiling and said a shackle pin had fallen out of the throttle mechanism and he could fix it in a jiffy. He went back to the load and removed a cotter pin from one of the cargo straps. We were soon on our way, and the truck never faltered again.

The family to whom we delivered the traps had been lobster fishing for one hundred fifty years. They sold live lobsters to restaurants and lobster meat to seafood establishments along the New Jersey coast. They helped us unload and asked us to stay for a meal. When our visit with Peg and her husband, Bill, ended and we returned to the truck we found a group of their lobster fishing neighbors admiring the new traps. In a short while, we took orders for hundreds more traps on the spot. They had all tried the new wire traps and were not happy with them because the traps rolled on the sandy bottom of their coast. Not only that, the plastic covering wore off the wire, so it quickly rusted through and disintegrated.

They were impressed with the quality of the oak and the way the traps were built. We went home in a state of euphoria; it seemed we might have struck the mother lode in this territory. Even without a load, the truck rode softly with the air seats, a welcome change. At mug-up the next day, the crew was happy to hear about the job security of the new orders and all about our trip. Clyde said, "Well, better you than me going down there, after all the traveling I did in World War II, I'd as soon count rat turds on Southern Point as leave the State of Maine again."

Our next lobster trap delivery was to Tom's River, New Jersey. We stacked four hundred traps on the trailer, four rows high and each row cinched and ratcheted down with nylon cargo straps as this open load could not be allowed any shifting room. It was Thanksgiving and we had sent turkeys home with each of the crew, but didn't have time for one of our own; that could wait until we got home. Thanksgiving night we headed out, Jim liked night driving in the congested areas of Connecticut and New York when there was less traffic in the predawn hours.

As we unloaded the traps the next morning, a group of lobstermen gathered around us as they had at Belmar, and we were again delighted to take home more orders. It had been a long night and we were weary as we headed for home. When we started back along the New Jersey Turnpike (I'll never forget the oil refineries and the insanity of the traffic), I had an uneasy sense that things were not right in my inner regions. By the time we reached the turnpike's last rest area, I had to admit to myself that this stop must be made.

For twenty minutes or so I couldn't leave the restroom, dashing back each time I tried to reach the truck. Eventually I decided I couldn't spend the night there, so I informed Jim of my problem—which was growing worse—and suggested we find a motel soon. He gently explained that there was nothing in the immediate area, which I knew, but that soon we would cross the George Washington Bridge, and be in Connecticut where there was a Holiday Inn. He assured me that the George Washington Bridge was barely twenty minutes away. I decided that with considerable will power and phenomenal luck I just might make it. Maybe.

We had driven only three miles when the highway became a vast parking lot as far as the eye could see. To me it appeared that half the cars in the nation were returning home after Thanksgiving and they were all on the New Jersey Turnpike. Even the breakdown lane was bumper-to-bumper, so Jim couldn't even pull over if I was forced to abandon ship. Jim's "twenty-minute trip" to the bridge took two and one-half hours. Jim tried to soothe me with light conversation and encouragement, but my replies were made through clenched teeth as the turmoil within my body began considering all exits.

For a while, I achieved some sort of self-hypnosis; I knew there was no way to park this vehicle or for me to leave it, so my mind became a sort of vacuum. When at last we started moving, we rolled through a series of tollbooths, but the road from booth to booth was pitted with potholes, and air seats or not, they jarred me so I felt my inner world was coming to an end. And finally it did. Just outside a tollbooth, I pointed mutely to the side of the road. Jim stopped quickly and I climbed down to the ground and took a quick look around. There wasn't a bush, a tree, or a rock on the horizon, just hundreds of cars creeping slowly toward the toll booths, and everyone was staring straight at me.

I could not wait another second. I crawled behind the big wheels of the tractor and sat under the overhang of the trailer where it was hitched. But for all the overhang that hid me from view of fellow travelers, I might as well have jumped onto the empty trailer and danced as if on a stage. Under these circumstances, crouched under the trailer hitch, I proceeded with my two-way performance in full view as they crawled past the truck.

I felt terrible in all ways possible, but partway through I began to laugh at the gross indignity of my situation. Then my laughter turned to tears of mortification and embarrassment, followed by recognition of the gross humor of the whole thing so I laughed in near hysterics.

Finally, I was sobbing tears of humiliation as I climbed back up into the truck. I sobbed out to Jim that I knew my clothing was no longer fit for me to be sitting in the truck. He hugged me and said, "Just sit on it, and don't worry, I'll have us at the Holiday Inn in no time now!"

While Jim was parked to register, I scouted the nearest shrubbery. When he zipped by toward the parking lot he tossed me the key. My hand was trembling when I found the lock that matched the key. It was a rough night, but I had clean clothes, and by 3 a.m. I began to feel that I may actually survive. By 6:30 a.m., I volunteered that we should start home to beat an impending snowstorm.

The waitress at breakfast that morning took a long look at my ravaged countenance when I refused to order and volunteered to bring me some tomato juice with ice cubes.

"It always helps!" she assured me.

My final humiliation was realizing the waitress thought I was suffering from a volcanic hangover.

CHAPTER 32

Captain Jack

BRINGING HOME OUT-of-state orders was great, but our expanding business was not without its headaches. Our core group of lobstermen who were turning out trap stock on the first floor were able to teach new help how to build traps, but building them efficiently required us to buy more equipment such as power nailers. We also needed to hire people to knit lobster trap heads. Luckily, our crew knew some women who did this kind of knitting for their husbands and others who did it commercially. They all worked out of their own homes, and we would supply the nylon twine and pay them by the piece.

Further, complications were caused by local fishermen who wanted their stock and wanted it "Now!" even though much of the stock was needed upstairs to build finished traps for other customers. This tension created divided loyalties between the building crew and the stock crew. The stock crew wanted to see their lobster fishing friends happy, while the building crew leader wanted to see traps quickly built for their customers. Meanwhile, we wanted to see both crew and customers happy, but we stepped into the middle of a turf war nearly every time we came home from a delivery. Members of each crew would approach us essentially saying, "If you don't fire so-and-so because he isn't cooperating, then I'm leaving." We needed them all, and we spent considerable time soothing, smoothing, and placating staff.

The new help upstairs were mostly young people, some of whom tended to forget to bring lunches. I frequently found myself hastily putting something together for them to eat, until I realized it was easier to just keep a big pot of soup simmering on the woodstove. Sometimes eight or ten people walked over to the house for lunch, and at times it seemed as if we were running a soup kitchen, but we did most anything to keep the crew happy and productive.

The other problem was, of course, the same one that had existed for years—money. Business was great and we handled decent amounts of money, but there was never enough cash available. There were two major reasons for this: One, we couldn't buy our wood inventory as needed, instead we were forced to buy it whenever it was available and in whatever amounts that may be. This tied up a lot of operating money. Two, much of our existing cash flow was still used to pay FHA for a chicken farm business that no longer existed. It was a real Catch-22 situation. As with everything else we had ever attempted, we took the same motto: "The only way out is onward."

During that winter for the most part, we managed to satisfy all the local customers and keep the out-of-state deliveries going, although even those customers were starting to fight with each other. Each delivery we made brought a new group around the truck wanting to place orders. On one delivery, a fisherman shoved another out of the way to place his order first. The one shoved shouted, "I was first in line, and unless you want me to chop you a new asshole, get back where you were!"

In theory it was fine to be fought over, I guess, as long as we weren't fought with!

Most of the time the fisherman receiving a delivery helped us unload, but sometimes he was out fishing and his wife would just tell us where to pile the traps and we had to unload them alone. After driving all night to make a delivery, unloading hundreds of traps was a tiring job. The traps, depending on their size and style, weighed between fifty and eighty-five pounds each. I, and all my five-foot, two-inch, 110-pound body, would stand on top of the load sliding each trap down to Jim, who carried it to the designated spot.

One delivery we unloaded together was at the edge of Boston Harbor. It was a cold and teeth-chattering job. There had been an extended period of cold weather and the harbor was mostly frozen. On this particular day the windchill seemed like forty below zero. Knowing the cold we would face, I resorted to my old shrimp peddling outfit featuring the ankle-length fur coat and fur bonnet. Both our faces were chilled to marble white when we were finished.

If time allowed we stayed in a cheap motel, and we ate most of our meals at Arthur Treacher's, which we called Treacher's Creatures. Many times we rolled home weary but happy, sometimes singing, "Wabash Cannonball" together during the final miles.

> *Listen to the jingle, the rumble and the roar*
> *As she glides along the woodland o'er the hills and by the shore*
> *Hear the mighty rush of the engine hear those lonesome hoboes call*
> *Traveling through the jungle on the Wabash Cannonball.*

In early June, we had a high and heavy load of traps bound for Atlantic City, New Jersey. They were going to a Captain Jack and his beautiful big boat, *November Gale*. Captain Jack lobstered two hundred miles offshore in what was known as The Canyons, which are off the Continental Shelf and run several miles deep. The lobsters that lived there were huge and, according to Captain Jack, "thick as lice." The size of the lobsters and the fishing bottom required larger four-foot traps that had earned the nickname "bear traps" because they were indeed a bear to handle.

Atlantic City was a strange combination of glittering opulence on its shorefront and poverty just a few blocks off the shore. To reach Captain Jack's, we drove through a particularly poor area on a roasting hot afternoon. We had driven all night and were anxious to unload and return home. This was our last delivery of the season, and our hayfields were waiting to be cut.

Captain Jack's dock area was enclosed by cyclone fence topped with barbed wire strands—much like a prison. When the traps were unloaded, Captain Jack insisted on giving us a tour of the nearby Resorts International Hotel, which housed a casino. He supplied lobsters to the hotel restaurant so he was privy to all areas of the place. We were dressed in our lobster trap unloading costumes of jeans, sneakers, and denim shirts, but Captain Jack insisted on treating us to a gourmet dinner and a tour of the various gambling locations. He provided us with a few chips to play in a game or two, which yielded no winnings. We were content to watch the tuxedoed men and beautifully-gowned women who ran Baccarat and other table games where thousands of dollars were being wagered. Cameras and security were everywhere. The plushness of it all—carpets, wall hangings, furniture, and atmosphere—was overwhelming.

When we left with Captain Jack for this adventure we expressed concern about leaving the truck untended. He assured us that it would be safe behind the securely locked gates of his shore compound. We wanted to be on our way, but he was so eager to show us part of his world that we joined in the adventure, always ready for a new experience. As we left the casino we went through a jewelry store where ladies in elegant gowns were draped on mauve velvet stools examining exquisitely gleaming jewelry. Gentlemen hovered over them eager to spend their winnings. It was a far cry from Lower Round Pond—all fun to see, but it made us all the more eager to climb into our Kenworth and head north.

As we approached the compound to get to our truck we were greeted by hundreds of people dancing in the street to a rock 'n' roll band. They were having a grand old time and the noise was horrendous. But the noise wasn't a problem; the fact that the band set up right in front of the locked gates where we needed to exit was a problem. There was no other way out. Captain Jack said he had forgotten about the street concert, but said it would be over by midnight. He let us into the compound through a locked door in the fence and then we had no choice but to just sit in the truck and wait for the concert to end.

It was well 1 a.m. by the time the band left and Captain Jack opened the gates and let us out. We were bone-weary but anxious to leave. We followed the same route out as we had entered. We had hoped maybe everybody had gone to bed, but not so. The streets and sidewalks were filled with people drinking and partying. There was so little other traffic at this hour that our rig stood out as an object of interest.

We drove slowly for two reasons: The streets were filled with people not overly anxious to move, and we hit a red light every couple of blocks. It was not a comfortable situation. As we were stopped at one red light, a group of teenagers and even younger kids jumped onto the empty forty-two foot trailer. Jim opened the window and yelled at them, but they replied with the famous finger and more of them got on. We drove carefully to the next light, considering how we were going to handle this.

There was not a police car in sight. Jim said we could stop and get on the CB radio asking law enforcement for help or we could just keep going and hope our uninvited passengers would realize they were simply getting further from home and abandon ship. The problem with the first choice was that it might be a long time before law enforcement came to our rescue. The second choice was not good either, because there was constant danger of somebody falling off. They were all dancing around and shouting on the trailer. We feared what might happen to the person who fell and to us if someone did.

At the next light some folks jumped off, but even more took their place. A car pulled alongside us with a middle-aged couple inside who were screaming obscenities at us for giving all these kids a ride. Jim told them the actual circumstances and suggested they try to encourage the kids to leave. It seemed the couple knew some of them and told them to get off the trailer. There was a fair response, but about two dozen remained. We were stopping at every red light even though there was no traffic because keeping our Class One licenses clean was vital for insurance reasons as well as our own self-respect.

Jim said, "There is only one way to handle this that I can see, and that is at every red light you look your way, I'll check mine and we'll keep rolling at ever-increasing speed until they get the idea there will be no stopping."

He rolled down the window and yelled back to the ugly group, "Get off this truck now or you are going to Maine, non-stop!"

They just hollered.

The truck doors were locked and the windows were up. We quickly scanned the side streets at the lights and Jim gently, but positively increased our speed. After going through a few red lights the troops apparently began to believe Maine was indeed the next stop and started leaping off, until finally the last two jumped off and rolled end over end on the ground. We watched until we saw them come to a stop and get on their feet so we knew they were okay.

By this time, we had not slept for more that twenty-four hours, but we were so pumped with adrenaline that we planned to stop only for fuel until we crossed the glorious borders of Maine.

CHAPTER 33

And Finally, the End Does Come

WHEN WE RETURNED from Atlantic City, once again the sawmill was not a place of peace and tranquility. Another insurrection had taken place and resulted in an all-out battle between the stock-producing and trap-building floors. It was exhausting. It had all been so simple when it was just us and our four lobstermen, but they were now gone, as always in spring, to tend their lobster traps for the summer.

We had employed every act of diplomacy and tact we could to keep peace. Which would not have been so bad in itself, but along with this whole operation came a tremendous amount of bookkeeping. We did our own tax returns and had never hired an accountant until recently. He was not really affordable, but the tax laws, now that we had twenty-five employees, were beyond my scope of understanding or time to learn about.

It was now 1979. It had been a quarter-century since we had gotten into the chicken business and it had been a period of both intense physical labor and a constant mental battle to pay a debt. I would turn fifty in May and Jim would turn fifty-two in August. We no longer had the energy of twenty-year-olds, and we were both exhausted by the constant pressures on mind and body and the idea that it was not going to change, no matter how hard we worked. The trap mill was a fine business, but it operated at the maximum edge of our financial and physical capabilities. Nor had we figured out how to manage a large crew, especially when we were frequently gone. We realized it could not offer us a long-term solution to our situation without a massive infusion of capital from somewhere. And we didn't see how that could happen.

As weary of it all as we were, it never crossed our minds to sell the farm and forget the whole thing. After all, keeping the farm was the reason we were working so hard in the first place. Selling it smelled like failure. We were determined, as we had told FHA years ago, to only leave it feet first. Finally, sitting across the kitchen table from each other one morning after yet another sleepless night, we stared at one another and one of us voiced both our thoughts. "There must be a better way."

We discussed our options and threw out ideas. Recently, we had been approached by people who wished to buy the sawmill, but we had rejected them for several reasons—not the least of which, the mill was part of the farm. Also, if we did sell, how would we earn a living to supplement our sheep business? And what would be a fair price for the mill that would also improve our situation? And most of all, could we be assured that those workers who has been loyal to us could return to their jobs if there was an ownership change?

Amazingly, the first question was fairly easy. Making trap deliveries in our Kenworth had been adventurous, and the road took us far away from our problems both physically and mentally. It was short respite, but it offered a glimpse into another world. Maine was, is, and, always would be our world, but there was a tremendous amount of the country to see. We were physically able to handle the trucking business, if we could just unload the burden of financial stress. At the time, America was still in the midst of a fascination with trucking as well, coming off hit movies like *Smokey and the Bandit* and *Convoy*, which was also a hit song. We thought: Maybe we should give long-haul trucking a try? We had talked with and listened to truckers on our CB radio, and their experiences held a certain appeal. We could be paid to see places we had never seen and still have summers free to attend the fairs with our sheep, because we could hire a driver when we needed to be home. It seemed like a fine plan, but it had to be implemented.

First, we paid a visit to our accountant who reviewed all our figures and came up with a price both fair to a buyer and ourselves. We had built a viable business with plenty of potential. The selling price would allow us to pay the FHA and still have enough money to purchase a truck.

Next, we met with a realtor who specialized in selling Maine businesses. He was impressed with the figures and paperwork on the sawmill and thought the price reasonable enough that the business would sell within a year. In our discussions, we had been thinking in a timeframe of three or four years. We insisted that any buyer keep our older original employees for at least a year.

We hoped we were doing the right thing by selling the mill, but we weren't immediatley concerned because we were sure a sale was a fair piece down the road.

That spring, the haying was done, and everything was in order for fair season. A couple at the mill would tend our remaining sheep flock of about seventy-five between our return trips. Before we left, we received the sad news that our dear Ebby Leeman had suffered a stroke and was in the hospital. When we visited him he was in tears, and so were we for he was now partially paralyzed—his lobstering days were over. He could still speak well enough to be understood and we did a lot of reminiscing about the mill.

That summer, Howard Smith passed away, or "got through,"as we were told. In the spring, Ebby said he had stopped to pick him up at his driveway as he often brought him to work. Howard was lurching around the edge of the road already drunk. With a big smile he said to Ebby, "I'm hooter than a drunk owl, and today is my birthday, and it's my last one so I ain't coming to work 'til tomorrow." He saluted Ebby and stumbled back up his driveway.

It was, indeed, his last birthday. He was a good man and a great worker.

That same summer, Astor Prior met a lady and moved up the coast, and Clyde Campbell fell seriously ill. It was sad and painfully obvious that our original crew would not be returning to the sawmill regardless of who owned it.

The fair season, so beloved by us, went well and we had a show flock that really earned its keep in the prize money. Frequent visits to the mill showed that the building of fall trap orders was progressing nicely despite a few problems. We also received a telephone call from our realtor who said he had a potential buyer for our mill and asked us to come in for further discussion. The buyer seemed seriously interested and visited the mill to see how it operated. We provided a thorough tour and additional information.

Then, on November 10, 1979, the realtor left a shocking message on our answering machine: "Break out the champagne! The buyer's loan to purchase the mill has been approved."

We were stunned. We had thought this would take years, and maybe deep down we had hoped it would. Jim had built the mill not "from the ground up," but from "below the ground" up using discarded equipment with barely any life left.

We had worked hard to develop a strong and growing market, and now we felt sudden apprehension about change, not to mention parting with an entity that had been "our baby." Yet we knew the sale would offer much relief and mean an easier life that our tiring souls yearned for. We also relished the adventure ahead.

We had no way of knowing at that moment, of course, that the wooden trap era would soon end and give way to wire traps, which would come to completely dominate the lobster fishing industry starting in the 1980s. It was just good timing on our part, but sad to see the end of the iconic wooden lobster traps as part of the Maine identity.

The sale closed on November 26, 1979. We sold the sawmill and three acres of our land for $175,000. We still owed the FHA $62,500, in large part because we often paid late and were mostly paying interest on top of interest, thus never really attacking the principal. We also owed $25,000 to the bank for the truck that we used to deliver traps and a short-term $15,000 loan we used to buy wood stock. We paid it all off.

There were some pangs. I had loved the snarling song of the saws and the smell of the oak sawdust falling from them in moist, pink crumbles, their unique fragrance both sweet and bitter.

But as I have said, this debt, which we carried for more than two decades, often felt like near death—it always felt like our farm, our hard work and dedication, our future, were on the verge of turning to dust. It is tough to describe the constant anxiety of it all. I am sure part of my feelings were based on the "debt is sin" mindset that my parents so forcefully instilled in me while growing up back in the 1930s and 1940s.

Even though I had dreamed about it for years, when we made that final payment to the FHA, I was almost overwhelmed by the feeling of relief. We had felt like prisoners for years, then suddenly, now magically we were set free—no more would these dark words echo in our minds, "Turn over your keys and walk away from the farm."

Incredibly, we had waded through the Forbidden Swamp of Debt and walked out the other side into sunshine. We were humbled by our great good fortune knowing how many people, including friends of ours, had been forced to hand over the keys to their beloved homes and walked away with only a few belongings and no real prospects. We were sad for them but overjoyed we had saved our farm and we were free of a debt that for so long seemed impossible to pay.

As Jim always said when changes occurred, good or bad, "This will be another step upward on our staircase to the future."

Well, the future was now.

In our innocence, perhaps ignorance, we had thought the FHA supervisor who was also a neighbor might write us a note in recognition of our achieving this feat as we had promised we would—a simple "atta boy" knowing that thousands and thousands of dollars were never paid back to FHA, partly, in our minds, due to their poor lending practices and an all-too-cozy relationships with the chicken processing companies.

But never a word was spoken nor note written, just the return of loan papers gloriously marked "PAID."

And truthfully, that was good enough. As good in our minds as finding the Holy Grail.

CHAPTER 34

White Line Fever

THE NINE YEARS we ran the sawmill had been exciting and challenging, but running it successfully required nearly every waking moment of our thought, effort, and devotion. I loved the singing of the saws and the smell of sawdust. We enjoyed many laughs and happy memories at the sawmill, but life is a constantly changing adventure and there always comes a time to move on. We planned to move mentally and physically—literally traveling our country from sea to shining sea.

Nearly as soon as the sawmill sale closed, we left for Boston to look at a 1980 Kenworth Aerodyne truck. We decided to take $50,000 from the sawmill sale to make a down payment on the truck and a refrigeration unit. We would use another $22,500 to pay for the permits, registrations, and insurance needed to operate an independent long-haul trucking business.

Our 1973 Kenworth had been good to us while delivering lobster traps along the northeastern coast, so we decided to stick with a Kenworth. At the time, there were only thirty-five Kenworth Aerodyne trucks in the country. Although it had nothing to do with our choice, this same truck model was featured in the popular television show *B.J. and The Bear.* Our new Kenworth was silvery, crystal-blue, and we lettered our names and address on the side, along with larger letters that read PINE TREE EXPRESS. It was not a long-nose truck but a cab-over-engine design. The cab was tall and featured two windows near the front of the roof that allowed the entry of pleasant light. Two big sleeper berths were located one above the other with large, soft rolls of padding similar to that found on a water bed to prevent occupants from falling out. The entire cab interior was padded and covered with dark, soft leather; it had a wonderful new car smell.

A small twelve-volt refrigerator slid out from under the lower berth, and the seats (which were adjustable and air-controlled) were as comfortable as armchairs. The seats sat six and one-half feet above the ground, providing a view of the road that was spectacular. The engine was covered by a doghouse located between the seat, and I protected its leather covering with a rubber backed, loop-pile rug that matched the interior because Nell would ride in this comfortable spot when she wasn't sleeping in my lower berth.

The truck, or more properly, the tractor, was colossal. Our old Kenworth was a single axle with dual wheels, but this truck had a double axle with two sets of dual wheels, and double chrome exhaust stacks. I stood in front of the radiator and my head was nowhere near its top. A four-hundred horsepower Cummins diesel with a thirteen-speed transmission powered this mighty beast. When sitting in the driver's seat, it looked as if the passenger's seat was fifteen feet away when in reality the cab fit comfortably within the road's width. It was such a different visual to look directly down upon the road from the front seats, rather than at a hood stretched out ahead of us. I loved the truck but believed it would be a long time before I would summon the courage to drive it.

Pine Tree Express in 1980.

As we brought the truck home, I was still awestruck by our height from the road; we could look right down into cars as we passed them. On the way home, we also stopped to pick up a forty-three foot Great Dane trailer with a Thermo King refrigeration unit that we would attach to the Kenworth, allowing us to haul perishable goods. The combined rig could extend to more than sixty feet with hitch adjustments. It was massive, and my fears about driving it only increased.

We did considerable research before making this investment. Our objective was to see the country while earning a living, and what surfaced as the most lucrative load combination was hauling perishable

The cockpit of the Pine Tree Express.

products to the West Coast, and then returning with fresh produce. Of course, we also could haul nonperishable goods, if necessary, giving us great flexibility. We knew a key to success was never pulling an empty trailer. We sought out and signed an agreement with a frozen fish company in Gloucester, Massachusetts. Our agreement did not limit us to hauling just their loads, as we had decided that never again would we invest in a business in which our livelihoods were controlled by a single company, as it was when we raised chickens.

We were what was known as independent operators. This meant we were not committed to any company but could take any load anywhere we wished. Signing a contract (not a lease) with a company meant that they took care of the necessary state permits and you drive for them, when, where, and what they choose, at whatever rate they pay. As it was, we were responsible for all the permitting, and permitting was no small task. We had to buy our own permits for every state we would travel through, and had to display each sticker on the side of the truck. We worked with a permit agent who handled the mind-numbingly complicated paperwork. We learned that every state is a little country unto itself when it comes to trucking laws, and if your paperwork is not in order they can shut your truck down. Eventually, we would have 102 permits.

It was January 1980, our sheep would not lamb again until spring, the barn was full of hay, tons of Aroostook County oats were stacked in the grain room, and we hired Maurice and Jinx Collamore, who lived in Round Pond and had worked at North Country Wood Products, to handle the daily sheep farm chores. We loaded our sleeping bags, clothing, Nell's dish, dog food, and a camera into the truck. We were ready to begin our first long-haul trucking experience. Nell couldn't climb the steep steps into the truck, but she soon learned to reach as high as she could with her front paws so we could "wheel barrow" her up onto the seat where she could then make her way to the engine dog house or the sleeper berth.

During the weeks we looked at trucks and trailers, a pleasant little piece called "The Music Box Dancer," an instrumental song by Frank Mills, often played on the radio. So I also packed a cassette tape with this song on it. It was a delicate melody and not one to bring forth the image of a truck, yet it had a section of deeper, repeated tones,

that made me think of the rolling beat of a big engine. I also took a
cassette tape that included C.W. McCall's famous trucker anthem,
"Convoy," which just seemed appropriate.

It was the dark of moon on the sixth of June
In a Kenworth pullin' logs
Cab-over Pete with a reefer on
And a Jimmy haulin' hogs
We is headin' for bear on I-one-oh
'Bout a mile outta shaky town
I says, "Pig Pen, this here's Rubber Duck.
And I'm about to put the hammer down.

As we prepared to leave, the four hundred horses in the Cummins diesel roared to life and the mill crew waved as we drove by. We
responded by pulling on the lanyard and sounding the air horn that
called like a freight train. We expected to be gone at least two weeks.
We slowly picked up speed rolling down Route 32 bound for Gloucester to pick up a load of frozen fish destined for California. Our spirits
were high, our rigging was brand new and reliable, and the weather
forecast was good.

Although the day was bitterly cold and windy, we were warm
and comfortable in the truck as we rolled into Gloucester, and bright
sunlight flashed and glittered off the waves in the harbor. The masts
of the broad-beamed fishing boats leaned together around the dock
and gulls rode the winds, their underbodies chalk white and wing
edges translucent in the winter sun. By late afternoon we were fully
loaded with forty thousand pounds of frozen fish, and as we pulled
out, a gold and rose sunset was in front of us. We planned to reach

Los Angeles in five days. The weather was clear and cold and roads pleasantly dry throughout the familiar Eastern states until we hit a snowstorm in the mountains of Virginia. Stops are limited to where seventy feet can be tucked away, so most stops by necessity are at large nationally branded truck stops where restaurant, showers, fuel, and facilities are available. We found one when it was time for supper. At night there were nearly always one or two hundred trucks lined up snugly together at some of these truck stops. Table space is typically reserved for truckers with schedules to keep who needed prompt service. In general truck drivers are hard-working, kindly people, and share a nearly universal rich, dry humor. Mealtime breaks the long lonely hours for many of them. It was fun to see their comfortable western clothing, and listen to their soft drawls as they swapped stories of inconsiderate drivers on long hills and hard-shelled inspectors at weigh stations and talked about gear ratios and horsepower. For me it all seemed so exotic and exciting. I loved to watch people and see the new sights.

New York City won the prize as the least favorite place, and I remember one driver remarking: "Took my wife on a trip in there with me once, traffic was wild, and she was so scared I thought I was going to collect her insurance. Bridges was terrible low, too. My trailer was 13'4" when I drove in there and 12'6" when I come out!"

Climbing into snug sleeping bags in the padded area of the two berths was a short but welcome rest time. In cold weather, our engine ran all night and the soft rumbling roll of our "Hummin' Cummins" diesel, along with the warmth it provided put us quickly to sleep. Part of my subconscious also listened for the different tone of the Thermo King refrigeration unit, because if the reefer quit, our twenty-ton load of frozen fish could be lost. Nell spent most of the day in the lower berth and was also welcome there at night with me, but she seemed to prefer the doghouse—its warmth and gentle vibration was probably soothing.

Each day began before daylight and I joyously looked forward to the sunrise. The sun quickly melted the night's light snow and we continued down Interstate 81 through Virginia's Shenandoah Valley along the edge of the Appalachian Mountains. We drove up hills and down hills all day. This part of Virginia is like West Virginia and Kentucky, all humpy hills so closely connected that houses, tiny hardscrabble farms, and little villages sat nestled in small valleys and creases or perched uncertainly on a hillside. Some lovely old mansions appeared occasionally, and sleek, classic horses grazed within white board fences.

Tennessee's hills had more space between them and handsome herds of Herefords and Appaloosa horses roamed the hilly pastures. There were no evergreens, but it was a tranquil scene of rolling fields. The small villages had imaginative names like "Bucksnort," "Bull's Gap," and "Crab Orchard." Radio stations from Virginia westward seemed to play mostly country music, which had a peaceful way of fitting the scenes as they rolled by. In Tennessee, the radio news announced the arrest of forty moonshiners and the destruction of their stills after a long investigation. We hadn't realized that this hill country tradition still thrived.

Soon, we didn't have to consult the map anymore as we picked up Interstate 40 in Eastern Tennessee, just west of the Great Smoky Mountains, and would follow it all the way to California. On Interstate 40, we passed through Nashville, home of country music, and Memphis, home of Elvis and the birthplace of rock 'n' roll before crossing the fabled Mississippi River into Arkansas. The country on either side of the river was very flat, while the river itself, like all the southwestern rivers we saw, was so muddy it appeared thick. As we crossed the river, we could see groups of five or six barges moving up and down stream that were shoved along by a laboring tug. We thought about the tons of freight that had floated along this highway of nature.

Arkansas along Interstate 40 had no particular character other than country that was obviously flattening out. There was some crop farming, but miles of scrub oak made up the scene along with poor-looking houses and mobile homes. We later saw areas of Arkansas that were quite different. The state had some interesting town names like "Toad Suck" and "Pickle Gap."

Menus at the truck stops began changing somewhat as we moved south and west. Fried catfish and hushpuppies became a popular offering, although I felt catfish just didn't measure up to the thick, flaky haddock of our Maine waters.

After a few hours sleep beside some other trucks in a rest area, our fourth day took us over the border into Oklahoma, and to still another "chicken coop" as truckers called the weigh stations, or scales, used by states to ensure the weights, widths, and lengths of the trucks didn't exceed their particular laws. And laws were all different. We could adjust the overall length of truck and trailer to nearly seventy feet. Virginia inspectors found us eighteen inches over length and fined us. Minor length discrepancies are fined, but an overweight reading meant the truck got shut down until the driver arranged for another truck to come and take off the extra load. All very expensive.

Some weigh stations don't remain open all night, so truckers would wait at a rest area until word came on the CB that the upcoming weigh station was closed and then drivers would proceed so they could avoid stopping and dealing with inspectors. Perhaps this seems dishonest, but as time went on we learned that many drivers were in desperate situations with heavy truck payments and expensive repairs on the near horizon. In some cases fines were zealously imposed for infractions so minor it bordered the ridiculous. It seemed to us that if a truck length is acceptable in forty states, it shouldn't be outlawed in the other ten.

We met a truck driver from Maine who told us that one time he was hauling a load of potatoes from Aroostook County to New York City. Trailer boxes are rated for a limited number of pounds (depending on the construction) or have a capacity limit of so many cubic feet, which would be used when hauling a bulky load of lightweight goods. So the terminology is that the load either "weighs out" or "cubes out," whichever comes first. In the Maine driver's case, he had plenty of room and kept asking for more potatoes to be loaded—the heavier the load the better the pay. There were no scales handy, and he didn't expect any to be open before he reached New York City.

However, when he got to Massachusetts and was crossing some rough construction, his trailer literally broke in half scattering tons of potatoes all over the road. He had to call the potato farm to send two more trucks, because it was estimated that he had weighed more than one hundred thousand pounds.

This same driver told us about going to Hunts Point in New York City, where there was a large wholesale produce district. He wasn't having a good day. He said, "When I get in there I'm about as ugly as if I'd slammed my hand in the truck door. I was going in there down one of them narrow one-way streets and they had allowed cars to park both sides. Well, once I was committed there weren't no way to turn around, and my rig wasn't fitting very well. I cleaned off about every door handle and side mirror all the way through, and then when I got to where I had to make a wide right turn there was just one empty parking space at the corner that might let me make it.

"Well, just when I'm getting ready to shift down and swing right, this little sports car pulls around me, parks right in that spot, gets out, and locks the door.

"I gave the air horn a tug and hollered to him that he'd have to move; I couldn't make the turn. He gives me a smarmy look, raises his middle finger in salute and keeps on going. Well, that pushed my last button. I dropped her into the low hole and proceeded. I swung as wide as I could, but my first axle of trailer wheels went over his left fender and the last axle crawled up over his hood. I took a look and he was standing there with his mouth open and his eyes so bugged they wouldn't have fitted in a bushel basket."

The Oklahoma terrain was notably flatter, although deep gullies and washouts marked the land, and the weather became warmer. The wind blew fiercely, and at a rest stop I picked up a dry tumbleweed, the first I had ever seen. These nearly round, shallow-rooted, brittle bushy things roll everywhere from Oklahoma on, stopping only to pile up at fences. Crumbling their dry twigs, I found they had a delicate sage-like scent.

Nell delighted in all the new smells, but soon came limping with something in her paw. We pulled out a little burr that we were later told was a Mexican Sand Burr. Apparently a wretched weed sends its tiny weapons flying into the wind, for later we were picking them off ourselves after they become painfully entangled between skin and sweaters. We dealt with them all the way to California, and Nell soon became accustomed to voluntarily holding her paws up so we could remove the painful burrs. We moved through Oklahoma, past the Ozark National Forest and through Oklahoma City as we raced toward Texas.

The grasslands of the Texas Panhandle certainly must have been an inspiration for the word "flat." These stretches featured no trees or mountains and were mesmerizing, but to me, almost depressing. When darkness closed in we saw the lights of Amarillo at what we took to be perhaps five miles away. I don't know how far it really was, but it took us an hour and a half to reach it. We began to think it might be a mirage.

The rangelands were broad enough to allow truck parking almost anywhere at the few towns that bordered the highway, and we weren't captive customers of the national truck stops for a while. A Texas steak was a fine treat at the end of a long day. The ladies at the restaurant were quite elegantly dressed and bejeweled, as befitted the Texas oil wealth. Or so I thought until I noticed the wearer of one stunningly lush sable coat wearing a pair of dirty sneakers.

After a few more hours driving in the bright starlight, we stopped to sleep in Tucumcari, located in eastern New Mexico, not far across the Texas border. We were so tired we took little notice of our surroundings and just climbed gratefully into the sleeper berths. Before dawn we noticed that the attractive rest area was surrounded by a large and beautiful growth of cactus. The land was still flat, but in the distance we could see a large, level-topped mesa.

As Jim worked through the gears and we began rolling through the half-light, I caught up on our daily log and said to Jim, "You know in the last twenty-four hours we had breakfast in Arkansas, lunch in Oklahoma, supper in Texas, and slept in New Mexico."

Behind us the sky lightened to rose, blue, and apple green. A great overhead stretch of wrinkly clouds began to catch the first rays of the sun. Sunrise unfolded around and behind us. Streaks of creamy peach became warm apricot, and then clouds turned to vast streams of glowing rose and fiery flame. It was everywhere, changing brilliantly by the moment. The flowing fire became a burst of blazing splendor until I expected to hear trumpets and see winged angels descending.

We stopped the truck and stood outside to be a part of it, and to pay the reverence due such a mighty display of glory put on to announce a new day. We were blessed after spending so many years grinding away day after day in Round Pond to experience the glories and vastness of America. We had already seen so much, and the mystery of more new land lay ahead. We had always wanted to see the West, and what a remarkably strange and wonderful place we found it to be.

Chapter 35
California

On one of the many nearly flat stretches in Nebraska where traffic is far apart and trucks in the distance looked like pinpoints dissolving into a mirage of flatness, Jim said, "How about it, want to drive her awhile?"

I replied, "You really mean it?"

"Sure," he grinned, "I know you can do it."

It was this very attitude of trust and confidence through the years that encouraged me to do things I would not otherwise have dared. Although initially intimidated by the size of our new truck, as we drove I increasingly yearned to sit behind the wheel. Of course, each time I stood on the ground and looked up at the truck's length, height and width, courage began to whimper a bit. Yes, I was at ease driving a five-speed standard shift truck with a thirty-two foot trailer and a single-axle tractor with a ten-speed shift, but this was a thirteen-speed truck with a much bigger load. Standing beside it, I felt like a rabbit next to a draft horse.

I decided it was now or never.

I had watched everything Jim did very closely and decided I had some idea of the extra shifting range. After Jim ran me through the gears and made a few key points, I was ready to go. I gripped the oversized wheel and began rolling, but she didn't seem to be picking up speed.

"Horse it," Jim said, "you've got to horse it!"

He was right. The pressure I exerted on the accelerator was fine for a pick-up truck and trailer, but it wasn't going to move this beast. So I leaned harder and worked through the gears, while trying to line up the white line just next to the left wheels, the only way I could judge the width on a vehicle without a long nose and keep from riding the ditch.

The tired phrase "thrill of a lifetime" doesn't begin to describe the joy and adrenaline that coursed through my body. I was delivered to a different dimension. My respect is profound for the engineering of a machine so mighty, yet could be operated with levers, pedals, and switches. This truck was a symphony of balance and design. It was smooth and gentle to handle, but not for a moment can one relax and forget the massive destruction that could occur without constant, clear judgment.

After crossing into Wyoming I didn't want to stop driving, but I didn't have the experience or confidence to deal with traffic yet. And we had to make about eight hundred miles every day regardless of conditions. Because of the load weights, momentum, and shifting of gears, trucks try to maintain a steady speed as much as possible and it does mean passing each other often. I wasn't ready yet to do this at sixty miles an hour with only eighteen or so inches between rigs.

Wondrous as was the New Mexico sunrise, I believe it was outdone by the Arizona sunset. It seemed to last for hours, its reflection from the clouds was sky-broad. It illumined the valleys and bronze rock battlements in a radiance that did not seem of land or sea. Tangerine shadows gathered in canyons and shaded to veils of smoky red, then lavender, until an oval moon, haloed in lilac, rose above the dark rim of the earth and sailed the black mountaintops. The miles we spent traveling through that sunset was a holy experience.

Gear ranges went lower and lower as we climbed through the clouds to Flagstaff, Arizona's highest elevation at 12,633 feet above sea level. Here in the San Francisco Peaks, a volcanic mountain range, we were in the darkness and mist when we pulled into a truck stop. It was a pleasant surprise to drop down from the truck and find myself surrounded by tall pine trees. Apparently, the soil was richer in the high country. So were the offerings of civilization.

We weren't there long enough to learn about Flagstaff's economy, but it must have been healthy for even the truck stop restroom was opulent, completely carpeted in thick, rich red, vast marble wash basins with gold faucets and dainty gold and white armchairs upholstered in plum velvet. I was impressed. Many truck stops are clean with excellent provisions for professional drivers, but not like this!

Early dawn travel through the clouds afforded few vistas, but the CB radio contact with eastbound trucks kept us informed of hazards ahead. Signs beckoned us to visit the Grand Canyon, but we could only wave at these signs to keep on our tight schedule.

When we dropped back out of the clouds we saw rich grazing lands and beautiful forests, enough to support occasional sawmills. Suddenly we had come out of snowy winter into a land of warm, green spring. Unlike the cattle on desert ranges, these cattle were sleek and plump. Before long we again found ourselves looking at bare rock mountains with sharp turns, drop-offs, and gorges. Cactus of infinite variety sprouted from the rocks everywhere. I had heard praise of the desert when cactus are in blossom, but the amount and variety must make it a magical spectacle.

Vegetation ran out as we crossed into the desert land of California. The rocky earth was bare. We traveled through a strange region of steps and slopes, slants, flat areas, then starkly conical peaks strung together by knife-sharp ridges. All were covered with boulders waiting to become avalanches. Here had the storms battled, and in past ages earthquakes and volcanic fires had ravaged the once noble peaks. They appeared ruined and ready to crumble. It was plain to see why science fiction movies about landings on burned out planets were made here in the wide spaces and the wild places of the earth as it was in its beginning. Or, if the earth is now dying, this is where it has started.

Between these strange dead heights of rock, gravelly, lead-colored desert stretched to shimmering infinity. We thought of the brave souls in wagons who toiled over this hopeless area to reach the fertile lands of the coast.

In the late afternoon we began to see signs for Los Angeles and we eventually passed the hillside featuring the famous HOLLYWOOD sign—it was a long way from Round Pound.

The truckers' landmark for arrival to the coast is the well-known Cajon Pass, a pass between the San Bernardino Mountains and the San Gabriel Mountains in the Mojave Desert. The seven-mile downhill drop on Interstate 15 connects the mountains and the coast. This is a long grade trying to hold back forty tons of payload, and a pall of brake smoke hangs at the bottom.

As the sunset was fading, we reached the outskirts of Los Angeles. I had never seen real palm trees before and was delighted by their slender trunks and fringed fronds. The spiky Joshua Trees, like little stunted pines were also new. Weather was warm and pleasant, and our summer clothes came out of the small closet. We no longer needed to run the engine for heat when we slid into the sleepers. Setting the alarm for 3 a.m., we studied the city map. We had a cold storage warehouse to find in a city that stretches for fifty miles.

Our pre-dawn start gave us a fairly quiet time on the freeway, and with a map and advice from others drivers on the CB, we were backed up to the unloading dock early enough that we could take a short nap before the warehouse opened. Swampers, the men who load and unload the trucks, gather early and vie with each other for jobs. Our swamper, Pasadena, was huge, quick, and efficient. Like some other swampers, he bore facial scars from having been on the losing end of a broken bottle fight.

Heading out of Los Angeles, our next and last stop was San Francisco, four hundred miles up the coast to Northern California. We crossed the Sierra Madre Mountains and descended from an elevation of 1,499 feet known as the "Grapevine Grade," yet another truckers' nightmare. A special turnout is provided at the top so drivers can check brakes before continuing the several miles downhill at the northern end of the pass. It was comforting to hear our Jake brake growling as we rolled down easily with the restraint it provided by working under engine compression, thereby saving mechanical brakes. This pass also was thick with brake smoke, and we passed a driver who had prudently stopped by sliding into the side of the mountain because his brakes had overheated and failed. He was unhurt, but his tractor was going to need expensive repairs.

It was still January, but spring harrowing and planting was in progress, along with the all-important laying of irrigation piping. Groves of still-bare apricot trees were common, tremendous open trailers mounded with golden carrots sped by, and to our delight there were many acres of winter rye being grazed by hundreds of lambs. This territory appeared to be the salad bowl of the west.

The flat terrain had a certain monotony, but listening to other truckers on the CB was always entertaining and broke the long hours. Truckers discuss family and the trucking business, but most of their tales are about their city driving experiences. Typical was one I overheard on this long stretch from a driver whose CB handle was "The Fugitive."

"Couldn't find that produce market. Made a wrong turn and there I was going the wrong way up a one-way street. Before I could find a place to turn around, sure enough Smokey stopped me. He said, 'And where do you think you're going on a one-way street?' I says, 'Well, I ain't sure but I guess whereever it is I must be late because everybody's coming back.'"

A second driver, "Tasmanian Devil," laughed and said, "It's the bridges I have trouble with; was in a little town when I come up to a bridge. It wasn't marked, but thought it looked okay. Wasn't, and I stuck her, good and solid. There I am, can't move either way and, of course, Smokey comes alongside pretty quick, leans in the window and he says, 'Driver, looks like you got a problem!' I says, 'Yeah, Smoke. I'm trying to deliver this bridge, but I've lost the address.'"

And so it goes. Facetious or not, their stories passed the time.

Outside San Francisco we left the highway to travel about thirty miles through two-way traffic and too many stop signs and traffic lights. It was dark by then, but the pungent aroma of onion fields stayed with us for miles. Roadside stands (closed at that hour) proclaimed prices of ten cents each for avocados, seven cents per head of lettuce, and thirty oranges for one dollar. It was too far to go shopping, unfortunately.

Again we studied our city maps and entered "Shaky City," as San Francisco was known to truckers, in the wee hours of morning. Four thousand miles and our load was finally off at last. Jim made our final daily call to the dispatcher back in Gloucester at the fish freezing plant. The company shipping the load must know its whereabouts each day. We were now free until our broker found us an eastbound load. Since produce is not loaded on weekends, we had a couple of days to explore.

The broker told us to head toward Indio, California five hundred miles down Route 19 southeast in the Coachella Valley, a desert valley in Southern California that stretched from the San Bernardino mountains to the Salton Sea. There was a lot of citrus to be shipped. Heading back south we saw the territory we had missed the previous night, high round hills and flat stretches with miles of grape vineyards, the home of Gallo and other wines. Not a tree or bush grew on the hills and they were too steep for planting, but they were covered with lush grass and cattle.

Indio's colors were a pulsing azure of the sky, shimmering purple of the mountains with peaks of opal snow, and tall emerald topped palms with heavily hanging bunches of dates. The Coachella Valley is the nation's largest date growing region. It was stunningly beautiful. We found a small motel with a parking space for Pine Tree Express and a big, walk-around bed. Having our own bathroom and shower felt luxurious. Nell, too, seemed happy with the walking space, but she was always content.

The desert with its low growth of mesquite and arrowweed, came to the very edge of the carefully cultivated lawn of the motel, and in it were the little creatures of the desert. Luckily, I learned the ones I would like least, such as rattlesnakes, hibernate at this time of year. Looking out our window in the morning, we saw brown cottontail rabbits playing, leaping six feet into the air and landing in the same spot. Most engaging were the roadrunners. They were partridge-colored with crested heads, a bright red-and-blue patch above their eyes, long legs, and long tails. They were rightfully called "the clowns of the desert." As their name suggests, they can run like the wind. We were told they have the courage to attack, kill, and eat a rattlesnake, yet they are nearly tame and comical to watch, their long tails bobbing up and down constantly like a small plane struggling to take off against the wind.

We had Saturday to spare, and Disneyland, only an hour away, was celebrating its twenty-fifth anniversary. We unhooked the tractor, left Nell in a nice kennel for the day, and spent hours with the children of all ages roaming the fairy-tale land the great man created. It was a memory book day of childhood relived.

Toward the end of the day we were weary from walking and sat down on a bench to relax. We were right near a building featuring wax figures of famous people, so we sat very still pretending to be one of the wax people. Soon a group of giggling teenage girls were heard approaching the curved walkway. We stiffened ourselves and didn't blink. The girls stood in front of us trying to figure out who we were. Suddenly, we smiled and waved and they jumped back, exclaiming, "Sheesh! We thought you were stuffed." It made our day.

Jim checked with our broker early Monday morning, but it was not until nearly noon when the broker told us he found an available load in Nogales, Mexico bound for Montreal. There was a hitch. (As the years went on we found there to be many hitches such as this one.) This was the only load he knew of coming east for at least a week and he knew that trucks connected with other brokers would want the same load. The gist of it was: "If you want the load, you'll have to make a run for it." Jim told him we were on our way.

A quick check of the map showed us that Nogales was located just over the Mexican border, adjacent to Nogales, Arizona, and about four hundred miles southeast of where we were. The loading appointment for whoever reached Nogales first was 8 p.m. that night. We couldn't afford to sit out West for a week waiting for a load, and although we weren't in this business to play *Smokey and the Bandit*, both Jim and the Kenworth were capable of getting us there if we applied ourselves. Nell had her run and was now good for hours, so we fired up Pine Tree Express and were in serious rolling mode as we headed through the desert for Mexico.

Crucifixion trees, the Salt Sea, miles of gravel desert, dry washes and black lava beds sped by. We rolled past the Chuckwalla Mountains, with the Chocolate Mountains looming in the distance, then whizzed by miles of orange groves. We circled Phoenix and turned sharply south at Tucson on Route 19. Miles were now kilometers, and the higher numbers made the distance seem longer.

Nogales proved a squalid little border town, but when we reached the warehouse, we were vastly relieved to see no other northbound trucks in sight. The hard push had been worth it. Stepping into the produce center warehouse was a treat. It contained hundreds of tons of huge bell peppers, plump garlic, satiny cucumbers, and green tomatoes. The aromatic fragrance of all these together was delectable, like being surrounded by a giant salad.

All this produce was from Mexican farms, and our share of it was forty thousand pounds of green tomatoes that needed to reach Montreal in five days without fail.

Because this was Mexican produce being transported to another country through America, United States laws required that we be under bond not to unload anywhere else. Our load was sealed and even the hinges on the trailer doors were spot-welded. This procedure was known as a "Canadian weld." We never saw the inside of the trailer again until we unloaded in Montreal. We were told to set our refrigeration unit at forty-seven degrees and to maintain that temperature. The tomatoes were a bright, hard green when we loaded them, but between the temperature and the darkness in the trailer, they would become a deep rose pink by the time we arrived in Montreal. After a 10 p.m. supper of bacon and eggs, the safest menu item in an unappealing eating place, we were sealed tight and eastbound. Coming west, the only part of The Lone Star State we saw was the Panhandle, but going back over Interstates 20 and 30 we saw 980 miles of Texas, crossing through the Apache Mountains and driving through Pecos, Abilene, Fort Worth, and Dallas. Oil rigs were prevalent and we spent one night among a forest of tall derricks, the air thick and heavy with the smell of oil.

We just rolled on and by the time we were once again among the tall and thickly-growing trees of the East, I realized fully just how much of an northeasterner I really am. Our California to Montreal schedule was in order, and at Plattsburgh, New York, on the Canadian border, we turned in our paperwork and bond. We, and the forty thousand pounds of tomatoes, were on the final leg of our five-day journey.

Never having been to the Montreal wholesale market before, we talked with other truckers going through customs and found two headed for the same produce center. Neither of them knew the way, but one, whose CB handle was "Professional Tourist"—PT, for short—thought he had some pretty nice directions. "Carolina" was behind us, and we were in the middle of the "rocking chair" as it was known. We set off in a small three-truck convoy along a dark snowy road to the market forty miles away. Unloading was not scheduled until 5 a.m., but it was good to know we had all night if necessary to find our destination.

Sparkling frost crystals blurred the lights of Montreal as they rose from the ice-choked waters of the mighty St. Lawrence River. All the signs were in French, a language none of us understood save for four compass points: "Sud," "Nord," "Est" and "Ouest."

Montreal is a large city with complicated elevated highways. A recent snowfall had made the streets slippery and clogged with snow. It seemed every driver in the city was obsessed with reaching a destination at record speed, and the whole traffic pattern was horrendously confusing. We three stayed tight together, waiting if one or two of us were left behind at a change of lights.

PT found that his directions were not ringing true, and as we slogged along in the ice, slush, and frost misted air, it became apparent that we were hopelessly lost in the midst of this sprawling city. Traveling along a major boulevard with eight lanes of two-way traffic, PT decided that we all needed to make a U-turn in the middle of this wildly flowing river of cars before things got even worse, if that was possible.

It does take a certain amount of sheer gall, grit, and determination to swing seventy feet across eight lanes of traffic—a "no-no" anywhere, anytime. We each had to back and fill twice to clear the curbs, and we followed closely enough so that we could accomplish this without being separated. We would probably have been put away for the winter if the Mounties had caught us.

On we poked through the murky Arctic-like atmosphere, trying vainly to read what we could not understand, and keeping in constant, comforting touch with each other by radio. Finally, a wonderful Irish accent came over the CB and announced himself as "Polecat." He understood from our conversation that we were three lost truckers looking for the produce market. He had just left his trailer there and was going home "bobtail" (tractor only), until unloading time in the morning as he lived in Montreal.

Polecat asked our location and told us to wait until he came to guide us in. A short while later he led us along the river, across the railroad tracks, and to the loading docks. We thanked him and he called a cheery goodbye, saying he must hurry home for supper. He was a great guide.

We hadn't seen snow for a while, but it was all around us now and very cold. Ice crunched and groaned with the motion of the river, and trains called their lonely notes before thundering past on nearby tracks. Through the miles, Pine Tree Express had been revealing her wonderful personality, and she became our mother ship. Abundant warmth, individual reading lights in our snug bunks, a 12-volt coffee pot, a small refrigerator, and the great purring engine that lulled us to sleep.

At dawn, our Mexican tomatoes, now looking just right for market, were off-loaded, and we were bound for Maine, the final short leg of our first trip to the West Coast.

We drove past Lake Champlain. And through the hills of Vermont and New Hampshire. For all the wonders of the sights crossing this great country, and the magnificence of the West, it was a revelation to learn that Maine still looked so glorious, not just because it was home, but because there is just no place that can match the eternal evergreens, the vast rich forests, the coast, the islands, and the sparkling sea and rivers. Our trip was inspiring and the beauty magnificent, but never have I seen stars more radiantly brilliant and bountiful than in Maine on that crisp January night as we poked our way back to Round Pond—back home.

CHAPTER 36

Connie!

EVERY TRIP ACROSS the country in Pine Tree Express was new in its adventure and experience. The loads were sometimes different going west such as a load of wooden tongue depressors from Skowhegan to Los Angeles instead of frozen fish. But we nearly always pulled produce back to Montreal or New York City. We pulled lettuce, strawberries, tomatoes, melons, and even frozen fish from west to east.

We found long-haul trucking a rewarding way to see the United States. In total, we crossed the country to California thirty-five times. A typical run saw us unload in Los Angeles and reload in Bakersfield. It typically took us five days out and five days back with two days waiting for a return load. To make our destinations on time with refrigerated loads, we had to drive an average of eighteen hours per day. Log book rules, of course, don't allow one driver to do this, so I quickly learned how to drive the Kenworth and would relieve Jim for a few hours at a time. On average, we were on the road at least three months per year, and would gross a few thousand dollars for each round trip. It required tight schedules to earn a living, and it was far from luxurious. However, I think if given a choice of truck or tourist travel, I would still have choose to stay at "The Hotel Kenworth" because we saw the country's true inner beauty—its people, its industry, and the every-day struggle, not just stereotyped attractions with people trained to display them. We experienced and witnessed many small dramas on the road, some comic and some tragic, and sometimes both at once.

One morning in Little Rock, Arkansas, I was performing my morning ablutions as usual in the good old truck stop when I was star-tled out of my early morning privacy by a plain, round little lady in her middle years who slumped into the rest room. With a tired sigh, she flung a complete change of clothing alongside one of the washba-sins near me. She removed all of her clothes, which were black with oil and grease stains, and, tearing off big wads of coarse brown paper towels, proceeded to take a bath of sorts. Heaving another sigh, she remarked: "Three days on the road, and this is the first time I've even washed my face!"

Feeling called upon to say something, I asked, "Was your truck broken down?"

"No, we're driving a car, but it had engine trouble and squirted oil all over us. We've been sleeping in the car and then we ran out of money and couldn't even buy meals until my husband wired his fam-ily for a small loan."

I murmured sympathy and hoped that was the end of our con-versation, but as she continued scrubbing, she leaned toward me and in a whisper said, "I'm not traveling under very pleasant conditions."

I gave her a polite questioning look, and she said with a fatuous grin, "My husband and my boyfriend are both traveling with me!"

Mulling this over in my mind, I thought of nothing more clever for me to say than, "Oh, really?"

Powdering herself generously with talcum, she continued with barely concealed glee, "Yes! It's just terrible! They're both so jealous they're fighting all the time."

She went on to deplore, although somewhat happily, her precarious position and the fact that there were four hundred more miles to endure this enthralling love triangle.

Eventually I became compelled to ask, "How ever did you get into such a situation?"

She replied, "Well, I decided to leave Alabama and go to Kansas to find work and leave them both. But my husband insisted on going with me to see that I got there safely, and my boyfriend came along so he could stay with me after I got there. Guess when I get a job it had better be for twenty-four hours a day!" She giggled delightedly.

Folding my towel and closing my travel case, I smiled weakly and said, "Well, good luck!"

Later I saw her at breakfast in earnest conversation with two men. I thought of her last remark to me as I had turned toward the door. Her wet hair straggled about her plain face, and all that came to my mind was a line from some silly poem I had read long ago, "her hair hung round her pallid face like seaweed on a clam."

But her eyes sparkled as she said, "I know it seems like I'm bragging, but really, they are both so fond of me I just don't know what to do!"

Obviously she didn't. I wondered how their plight would resolve, but I was never to know more because the fuel desk loudspeaker announced that the Pine Tree Express of Round Pond, Maine was fueled and ready to go.

The greatest and most joyous experience we enjoyed on the road was managing to fit in an overnight stop with Connie and Tim in Provo, Utah, where they had bought a house. Although our correspondence was close and regular, it had been six years since they had left Maine. Tim was working on a sheep ranch and Connie was assisting at a veterinary clinic. Their precious little daughter, Megan Amber, had been born a few months before our trip that would take us through Utah.

The prospect of seeing our family was so exciting that every mile seemed to drag and drag. Dropping down through Wyoming toward Utah, the strange, dark-skied terrain seemed to have at least five horizons that stretched to relentless distance. Alkali-crusted dry basins appeared in this country of rock, but the eerie scenery was relieved by miles of sage brush that was inhabited by beautiful herds of what are thought of as antelope, but are apparently pronghorns. There were twenty to thirty in a herd and they bounded gracefully alongside us, their sides half-white and their backs a soft fawn color. Jackrabbits sprung everywhere using their long hind legs.

We pulled into a cliff-sided rest area just over the Utah line for the night. The stark beauty and height of the rock formations was intriguing. Giving Nell her evening walk, we picked a few pieces of sagebrush and I gloried in its richly herbal scent, later tucking it under my pillow as a fresh and spicy sachet.

Before dawn, the Kenworth's engine was tuned to sweet song and we descended the mountainside. Through the day the great beating heart of this diesel engine sounded like the steady background throb of "The Music Box Dancer," and it seemed to call out to me over and over again, "I'm taking you to Connie. I'm taking you to Connie."

Anyone who has been reunited with family after an absence of several years knows that supreme joy and emotion can overwhelm the senses, especially when it includes a first grandchild, in this case an angel-faced little granddaughter. In their pickup truck, Tim drove us to the nearest nice restaurant fifty-three miles away, no distance in that country. We could hardly eat for all the catching up to do, and just holding sweet little Meggie was a thrill. Early the next morning, Connie made a memorable breakfast, including eggs from their own small flock of hens. Tearing ourselves away from the family to continue on our journey was one of the hardest things we had faced for a long time, but we left with the delightful news that they were considering returning to Maine and would be looking into the possibilities of a farm somewhere near us that summer. Joy!

Their western experience had been successful and rewarding. It proved an important building-block adventure in life that served them well. The old theory holds, I guess, that somehow we are compelled to return to our roots.

That summer, Connie and Tim did find a beautiful, productive farm with plenty of acreage, a large and charming farmhouse, and even some lake frontage. It was only thirty-five miles away from Lower Round Pound. In the fall of 1981, they sold their Utah home, and moved with Megan Amber and their fine flock of Suffolk sheep to their own farm in Nobleboro. As the flock continued to grow so did their family, when our second grandchild, Travis Ian, arrived in 1984.

CHAPTER 37
Your Truck is On Fire!

AFTER LEAVING CONNIE, we eventually arrived on the outskirts of Los Angeles on a steamy hot day. We had been using the air-conditioner throughout the day, something that had not been necessary for months. Jim went to call dispatch and make an appointment to deliver our load. I was comfortably curled up in my seat reading a book, and Nell lay stretched out in the lower berth enjoying the cool air in the cab. These calls often took quite a while so I really settled in. At least I thought so.

About ten minutes later my attention was drawn to a man and woman, perhaps in their thirties, approaching our truck. I knew that drivers can look road-worn, need shaves, haircuts, and clean, mended clothes, but these two were so ragged it didn't seem they could be anything but hooligans. Suddenly they began running at top speed straight for our truck and my mind started whirling. The truck was locked, but what if they had a gun and wanted to hijack it? I would have no choice. The man tore up to the cab, pounded on the driver's door and said, "Open up quick! Your truck's on fire!"

This brought Nell to attention, and although she didn't bark, she gave him the border collie "eye" and jumped into the driver's seat.

I opened the window a crack and said, "It's just fine, there isn't any smoke." Thinking to myself that this was probably a tried and true way to get into a truck and steal it when it was occupied only by a woman. The man insisted, screaming, "I mean it, your truck is on fire! There is smoke coming out from under it. I can save it for you if you'll just open the door and let me help you!"

By then I could smell something burning. I searched the distance in hopes of seeing Jim, but I knew he wasn't due back for a while. Quickly, I considered my options: Sit here and burn up with the truck; open the door and get shot while this wretched-looking bum steals the truck; or hope the man is honest and can prevent a disaster. I decided to walk the road of faith. I opened the door, and the fellow leaped up the steps, seeing Nell, he said, "Will he bite?" I said, "Only if I tell her to."

Which, of course, was nonsense, because I knew that in another moment Nell would probably be licking his face. Nell slid back into the berth with a quick command, and the fellow jumped into the seat, leaned over me toward the map compartment and said, "Is it locked? Can you find a screwdriver there—FAST!"

My trembling fingers located a screwdriver and he worked feverishly on the dashboard fastenings, dropping the cover and revealing masses of wiring. Smoke could definitely be smelled and seen by now, but it was not in the dash wiring; apparently it was somewhere below. The man was frantically trying to locate the source, and I was convinced by now that he meant only to be helpful. His scruffy-looking lady was standing outside the truck. I saw Jim coming at a dead run. Leaping for the cab he yelled, "What the hell's going on here?" I could see his thoughts mirrored my original ones, but I quickly assured him, that the man was trying to help with a real problem. The man also gave a fast explanation, and shortly he and Jim were under the truck.

To our great good fortune, the source of the smoke was only a stuck belt on the air conditioner. It hadn't been used for a long time and had seized. All we needed was a new belt. We thanked the man and his lady profusely and apologized for our original suspicion. They understood, as they also knew some of the horror stories and dangers of the road. They were just a hard-striving young couple who were trying to make a living trucking with an old and tired rig that was eating up everything they could make with its constant demand for repairs and tires.

Finding a full load home was slow going. Finding Less-Than-Full-Load or LTL jobs was easier, but more time-consuming because they required many stops for delivery and could leave us in an outpost with no return loads unless we dead-headed (empty) for perhaps hundreds of miles. We had learned early on that the first rule of successful trucking was that "the load had to be on, and the wheels had to keep turning." The payments do not stop while you wait for, or run after, a load. For this trip, we had a "salad bowl" of lettuce, peppers, strawberries.

The strawberries were loaded outside of Los Angeles. After being palletized they were wrapped in plastic and gassed inside the wrapping with nitrous oxide. This was not dangerous to human health. It is actually the "laughing gas" used by dentists, and it put the strawberries to "sleep," keeping them from further ripening until they reached their destination. The lettuce and peppers were loaded in the middle of the night in Bakersfield, California, famous as birthplace of the Bakersfield Sound pioneered by Buck Owens and Merle Haggard in the 1960s. From there we made our way across the white-hot Mojave

Desert. I used to stand on the doghouse and look out the two upper windows at the surrounding scenes, dust devils in the distance and shimmering mirages.

We spent that night in Ogallala, a one-time stop for the Pony Express in southwestern Nebraska. We were due in Montreal on Easter Sunday, for early Monday morning delivery at the market. We now had less than four days to make it. As we left Nebraska and crossed into Iowa a green Volkswagen Beetle pulled in behind us, and stayed with us as if on a towrope. The car passed when we passed, and travelled at exactly the same distance behind us across the lumpy hills of Iowa.

The Beetle driver had no CB radio, so there was no contact. Jim said he was drafting us, as many cars do. Our draft helped pull him along and he saved fuel and could relax also knowing that we weren't exceeding the speed limit. We only spoke with him once and that was after we pulled into a weigh station at the Illinois border. He came right in behind us and when Jim stepped out of the truck with his log books, the little fellow came up to him and said, "Why are we stopping here?"

Jim explained the state laws for trucks, and the man just said, "Oh," and returned to his car ready to follow for another hundred miles or so.

As we approached the Northeast, spring was emerging, and it was heartening to think that the best of all seasons was coming again. We would hire a relief driver to run the truck for us during lambing season and again for the fall fair season. We now had on average about eighty-five sheep to care for, which included two rams and about fifty-eight ewes that were lambing each season. We loved the trucking life, but it was intense and allowed for no real home life. By now we were becoming familiar with Montreal, and late Easter Sunday afternoon found us ready to settle into a truck stop near the market. At dawn on Monday we would slide into the unloading docks. Or so we thought.

Going into the truck stop and talking with other drivers we soon found out to our extreme agitation that the market would be closed for Easter Monday.

We had always known of Easter Sunday, of course, but nothing in our upbringing had prepared us for Easter Monday. One of the drivers summed up the attitude for all of us: "Here we busted our asses wide open to get here for Monday morning, and now we're going to sit on our thumbs for a whole day."

The next morning an eighteen-wheeler that had suffered the grief of covering more miles than she had a right to clanked in and the driver, whose face was gray with exhaustion, slid to the ground from his cab. His clothes were worn shiny, but age was most evident on his boots. The left one had a decent heel, but the right one that slid all day between accelerator and brake was worn on one side to the thinness of a coin—a graphic picture of how his days were spent. In a weary, but mild-mannered way he told us about stopping at a rest area in New York near the border. He said he had pushed so hard he just couldn't drive another mile that night, and figured that he could still make the market today with no trouble.

He had just gotten to sleep in his berth when a state trooper pounded on the door and ordered him to appear. He was informed of two things: First, eighteen wheelers were not allowed in these rest areas, and, second, he was going to be fined for three tires that were too smooth. He told the trooper he planned to replace them as soon as he was off-loaded and had the money. The trooper was not an understanding sort, and so this poor fellow could have been saved this hassle and expense if had known about Easter Monday.

None of us could understand why our brokers and dispatchers had not told us of this holiday, but we took advantage of the good side of it by taking long and welcome naps and playing our favorite waiting-for-a-load game of Othello. This is a tricky little exercise in strategy that leaves me wanting to hang by my tail from a tree, for I can win about one out of twenty games while Jim grins like the Cheshire cat.

One of the trucks waiting out Easter Monday was driven by a lady, white-haired and probably in her sixties. I didn't get a chance to speak with her but did observe her interesting companion. I had just brought Nell back from a walk and was looking around when I saw the lady with a little creature that was wearing a red leather body harness. It rippled along on tiny legs, and I knew it was too narrow-headed to be a cat, and its movements were definitely not dog-like. As it approached her truck, I could see it was a ferret with shoe-button bright black eyes. It went to the truck step and sat up with its paws on its chest knowing that it couldn't reach, but this was the approach. She slipped off its harness off, and placed him on the seat, where he then undulated along the dash and back to the inner regions of the cab.

CHAPTER 38

In Praise of Cats

It should be blindingly obvious that we loved all animals, but we loved cats as much as any of them. Jim especially had a passion for cats, whether it was Joe who lived with us back in our original cabin or the many barn cats who joined us over the years,

Some people less enamored of felines will point to the independent and self-centered nature of cats, which is true, to a point. But like us, cats are all individuals with complicated little personalities and characters. Ours were always so capable of giving us boundless affection and comfort no matter where they came from.

For example, we acquired a pair of four-year-old Siamese cats because they were about to become homeless. We called them Cleo and Si-Ling-Chi. Cleo was a female and lived with us until she was twenty-one, while Si-Ling-Chi, the male, passed away several years younger. They were inseparable, and arranged themselves on furniture like decorative ceramic pieces. Their favorite spot was the top of the television. Throughout life, they formed a circle, nose-to-nose and tail-to-tail, around the lamp centered there. They would sleep in this position without a movement. One evening prospective sheep buyers were visiting the house. The lady and her husband were seated on

Two kittens enjoying the heat from the woodstove.

a couch facing the television (which was not in operation), and after an hour or so the lady clutched her husband, and with a look of disbelief on her face asked him, "Did you see that cat move?"

Cleo had just stretched a little, and we smiled at the woman's dismay.

"I thought they were china," she said. "They were so perfectly arranged and still."

Cleo and Si-Ling-Chi slept with us. They would flop on the pillows in a semicircle around our heads, grooming our hair and ears a little before going to sleep, and purring a soft song that lulled us to slumber.

I would be seated at the typewriter, or desk, for only a few moments when Cleo would find me and drape herself around my neck to take a long and quiet nap. In those days when the checkbook balance showed only tens of dollars as opposed to the hundreds of dollars needed, the warmth of this silken fur neckpiece, her velvet paws stretching into starfish under my chin, and the contented rumble of her purring soothed my financially tortured mind. Although the eyes of these cats had the brilliant depths of sapphires, they were not crossed. Nor were they noisy cats. Their meows were distinctive but only offered up occasionally. Never did they bite or scratch, they were loving, gentle, and intelligent beyond any felines we had ever experienced. A life shared with cats is not complete without at least a Siamese or two.

Sandy, on the other hand, was big, heavy, and a graceless but lovable slob. He was short-haired and sand-colored with black striping and emerald eyes. Sweet, attentive, and stupid, he ate anything that he could get past his jaws. He was a fine mouser, but tinsel from the Christmas tree held a tasty fascination for him. During this season, he would amble around with the shiny tinsel streamers he had ingested reaching the floor from under his tail. Removal was accomplished by stepping on them as he walked on leaving them for our disposal.

Sandy was also a quavering coward. Once a small but pugnacious tomcat hung around the farm for a week or so. He viewed Sandy as competition in his search for romance, and Sandy looked upon him as a threat to his existence. There would be a great crash against the side of the house as if a large stone had been hurled, but it would only be eighteen-pound Sandy cowering in the window box he had just thrown himself into and looking desperately through the glass for rescue.

Sandy chose places to sleep that could, and did, only result in his falling to the floor. A favorite was on top of an old iron kettle placed in a special opening of a brick chimney. He loved paper bags, and if one was hastily left on a tabletop or chair he would crawl inside to nap, first rolling around in an effort to settle until he rolled onto the floor with a mighty *thunk*.

One day, when a little tom cat was around, I heard some pitiful caterwauling and ran outside to locate the problem. We had a massive maple tree, probably well on its way to two hundred years old. At its very topmost and outermost branch, Sandy teetered and bobbed on mere twigs, screaming in fear because the small tom was coming after him and this was his last stand. Intermittent streams of liquid were falling from Sandy's branch and I realized that his bladder was emphasizing his terror. I waved my arms and yelled at the tom, who scuttled down the tree and ran off. Sandy carefully crept down and heaved himself into my arms, his pupils large and black and his big body shaking.

Blackie, who knew how to gain nightly passage outdoors by walking on the piano keys until someone let him out, was a miniature black panther. His sleek ebony coat and topaz eyes belied his gentle nature. Like most cats he was a natural hunter and often roamed the far sheep pastures for field mice. One morning Jim was taking the tractor down the dirt road to the largest pasture, and on his approach he saw Blackie in dire trouble. He was out in the field lying on his back, a posture of final desperation, using all four feet in an attempt to claw the underbelly of a large red fox who straddled him trying to dodge the claws for a hold on Blackie's neck. Jim sped up and

A Maine coon cat, Friday, sleeping by the fire.

rattled the tractor bucket in an effort to scare the fox off. The fox was reluctant to leave its prey, but Jim and the threatening clatter of the machinery convinced him his best strategy was to escape. Blackie was unhurt, but frightened and exhausted; he purred out his happiness during the ride home tucked under Jim's arm.

We inherited Baby, Blackie's mother when a sweet lady had to leave her home to go into elderly care. She belied her name. She was a large and magnificent example of a calico cat with three clearly defined colors of black, yellow, and white. Her most distinctive feature was a small black mustache right under her nose. She was never friendly except when she was having kittens, only then would she climb under the bed covers purring as she burrowed her way to our feet. And then we would awake to tiny, wet, and warm wriggling kittens among our toes. We did eventually catch on and realized that when she was friendly, she was not allowed in bed with us.

Through the years we had many memorable cats on the farm. All colors and varieties, calicos or "lucky money cats," tigers, and shorthairs, Angora mixes, and beautiful Maine coon cats. Legend tells us that Maine cats are varied and lovely because so many sea captains lived here and brought home these fine examples to their families.

We were never without cats and never had to go looking to obtain one. It seemed that summer cottage tenants would provide a kitten or two for their children's amusement during the summer months and then decide there was no place for kitty in their winter abode. However, there was a big old farm up on the hill with a nice sheep barn that should be full of mice, so why not? Mysteriously, around Labor Day we always found at least one new pussycat had been added to our family.

Each of them had a special way of enriching our lives, and as they passed on through the years, we buried them on the farm. During some waking hours one night the cats we currently shared the bed with brought some words to my mind.

To Touch a Cat is:
Warm softness
Icy wetness
Hard sharpness

Vibrating happiness
Brittle whiskery

All true; and we loved them each and every one of them.

CHAPTER 39

North Country Sunrise

As ANOTHER YEAR sped past, our outlook and our plans continued to evolve. Stays at home remained brief until lambing season and the necessary spring and summer work of shearing and haying. Pine Tree Express was stable as a boulder, reliable and forgiving through thousands of miles. But she did require repairs occasionally and new tires regularly. Summer heat in southern climates nearly melted tires into submission, while the ice and snow was sometimes so bad we had to "ride the ditch" so the right side tires traveled in rough territory. If snow fell overnight in a rest area, we poured Clorox on the tires to keep them from spinning, which created enough heat on the rubber to get us out, but caused wear on the tire.

But all of this was necessary maintenance, part of the deal, and thus was not the basic problem with running an independent refrigerated trucking business. Increasingly, obtaining a decent paying load was a problem. Meanwhile, fuel prices kept increasing, while our gross pay remained the same. Waiting for the right load cost us money in time lost, and as I said, a truck has to be loaded and rolling to make it all work. So we found ourselves, like most others, taking what was available, always believing that the next load would be better. Our profit margin was slowly, but surely decreasing. Then the real crunch began, because some of the major loads, which always had to be provided by a broker, were from companies that started taking a month to six weeks to pay. When some of them didn't pay at all, we had to resort to collection agencies.

The delivery of refrigerated loads was numbingly demanding. The nature of the cargo required prompt delivery, for the load could be refused if it did not arrive in good condition. Whatever company we were pulling for provided cargo insurance, but that only covered the cargo. Timely delivery required eighteen hours a day of driving, and as we grew older it was becoming too much. Hiring a relief driver at times was helpful, but that was costly and cut into profits.

Long-haul trucking had been a great adventure and a fine way to earn a living together and seeing America, but the day finally came when we had to face the reality of this business and our ability. We did not want to give up trucking, although we were increasingly finding that the roots of home and its way of life were reaching out for us, especially with Connie and her family back in Maine. We talked with other drivers and did some research, and the picture emerging seemed to show that refrigeration trucking was too expensive for us to operate, but pulling more regional flatbed loads might work. Chiefly, there was no reefer fuel, and a load of lumber, steel, or oil drilling rigging was not going to rot if you had to pull over and wait out a bad storm. We found some brokers who were encouraging and we came to a hard decision— we would sell Pine Tree Express. It was too costly a truck to keep just for flat bed work, and the Great Dane refrigerated trailer would need to be traded for a flatbed.

The dealership where we bought Pine Tree Express was eager for our resale, because they knew she had been well cared for and looked as fine as when we first took her away. The same was true of the Great Dane trailer dealer. All that remained was choosing the day to deliver them.

It was the right decision, but still difficult. Changes in life are divided between those one is glad to make and those we must make but are difficult to accept. We had travelled this glorious country, and we had seen it in all its moods and conditions. We had noted the places we would someday like to return to for leisurely exploration. I have heard many a truck driver say that part of the mystique his work holds for him is his love of the Lord's natural world and all that he sees in it in such great diversity. Most of them have a strong respect and love for the Almighty as they have an extra need for His daily protection.

Yes, white line fever was still with us. It's a strange malady that makes you want to be out on the road when you are home, but yearn to be back home when you on the road. We cleaned our 1980 Kenworth Aerodyne inside and out, and she shone in response. The cab still had a new and fresh smell. This was going down very hard, but it had to be done. Jim hooked her up to the Great Dane for the last time and we drove to Boston. I followed in the pickup truck so we would have a way home. Pine Tree Express had a personality, just like *Spindrift*, and she had faithfully taken us tens of thousands of miles and been our home on the road. Once again, I listened to "Music Box Dancer" on the truck stereo as I drove along behind her. It was her song.

Although we had many photographs of her, I knew we could always see Pine Tree Express by merely closing our eyes. She would be with us always, powerful and beautiful, rolling forward across the mountains and deserts, on and beyond through all the strengths of the elements. She had stood for something mysteriously wonderful but unattainable. She was no answer to our longings, only a brief vision of what lay forever beyond our grasp. What she stood for was more important than the things that actually were. It was the quest and the dream that had mattered.

My tears were too heavy to say goodbye to her again, but Jim spent a little time in the cab to make his own private farewell. She and he had a fine understanding and had worked together in interactive harmony. Just as I had. I knew how he felt, and our shared handclasp when he returned to the pickup was our only comment.

—❦—

With Pine Tree Express sold, it was time to find an affordable truck and flatbed trailer. We made enough money on the sale of our truck to pay for the next one. We soon came upon a used but well cared for Freightliner with a long nose, formally known as "conventional." While not as luxurious as Pine Tree Express, she was a truly handsome truck with a big sleeper berth. We named her North Country Sunrise because of her bright but tasteful yellow and orange stripes along the center of her shining black cab. She also possessed a four hundred horsepower Cummins diesel engine and thirteen-speed transmission and could pull up to twenty tons.

We always found Maine lumber that needed to be delivered, and many of those runs were to docks in New Jersey or Philadelphia, where return loads of steel were usually available to pick up.

The runs were not as exciting as driving cross-country, mostly just overnight trips, so I stayed home to care for the sheep lambing when necessary. Our new rig was ideal for hauling oil-drilling rigging, so we did occsionally make trips from Nova Scotia to Louisiana.

The good news was that North Country Sunrise work paid much better than refrigeration work and allowed us some home life. We found a dedicated and reliable middle-aged man to drive her when we had to show our sheep at the fairs (We were still earning about half of our annual income from the sheep farm). Flatbed trucking seemed to solve our trucking issues and all was going along very nicely. Most of the summer our driver was carrying massive single blocks of granite from Stonington to Newport, Rhode Island to face a new bridge. Each block weighed thirty-thousand to thirty-five thousand pounds, so one was a load limit. At Newport, the blocks were cut to needed sizes. It was fun to think our truck had a role in building an edifice so permanent.

The truck did need new tires and as every load paid, we bought a new one. By late fall of 1985, she was sporting seventeen new tires and had only one to go for a complete set. We were definitely on a roll. During November and early December, the Christmas tree market was booming and we regularly pulled loads from Maine and Nova Scotia to southern states. As the days shortened, we were looking forward to a happy Christmas at home.

Our relief driver was single, had no local family, and preferred to keep driving right up until Christmas. He loved the truck and took excellent care of it; like Pine Tree Express had been to us, she was his temporary home. Four days before Christmas, the driver, Bryan Stanton, loaded lumber in Bangor to deliver south. He had an uncle in Cherry Hill, New Jersey, so he left early with the load and stopped at a truck stop in nearby Paulsboro. He left for a few hours to visit with his uncle and then he returned for the truck shortly after midnight.

To Bryan's horror, North Country Sunrise was gone. In a panic, he called the state police. The trooper arrived and told him to get in his car so they could tour the truck stop. The trooper explained that with more than two hundred trucks parked there, Bryan might have

North County Sunrise.

gotten confused as to just where he had left his truck. However, repeated searches for the truck stop availed nothing. The truck was just gone. The trooper told Bryan that all they could do was report it missing and put out bulletins on it. Then the trooper said very matter-of-factly. "Well, I have to tell you, that makes the twenty-first truck stolen out of this truck stop this year."

Bryan said to the trooper, "But I've got the keys right here in my hand!" The trooper laughed and said, "They can get into those trucks quicker without keys than you can with them!"

It was three days before Christmas when Bryan called us and told us what had happened. He was nearly hysterical with grief. He knew the truck was our living, and also much of his. Most of his clothes and personal belongings were in the truck so he was bereft. We comforted him as best we could, assuring him that we did not hold him responsible, all the while looking into a black pit of shock and despair ourselves. What was it about Christmas? Big Babe blew up at the mill just before Christmas. Once again it was, Merry Christmas to the Davidsons!

We didn't bother with our own Christmas tree. Except for spending the day with our family at Rivendell Farm, we stayed near the phone, hoping that the truck would be found.

The lumber company that owned the load, of course, was unhappy, but cargo insurance covered their loss. We were in touch with our insurance company, and the agent, due to his experience, seemed to have some answers. He said that the Paulsboro, New Jersey truck stop was not far from international shipping docks in Newark, and because the truck was ideally suited for hauling oil drilling rigging it was probably already on a ship bound for the Middle East. This was a crushing thought, but our constant calls to the New Jersey State Police yielded no good news.

Our insurance agent was helpful, but the carrier was not overly cooperative. There was a great deal they didn't want to pay for, including tarpaulins, cargo chains and straps, and the seventeen new tires. All tires were considered at a flat minimum rate regardless of condition, even though we had the receipts to prove their purchase. It was many months before settlement was made, and then it fell far short of the truck and trailer's combined worth.

Well, I guess every endeavor we had made in life had to be looked upon as "Grist for the Mill." When a truck could disappear this easily, getting back into trucking was unthinkable. We were in well into our fifties, and once again, we sat down to figure out just how we were going to earn a living, let alone save any money so we could retire one day.

CHAPTER 40
The Fair Life is a Good Life

THE ONE CONSTANT in our lives starting in the early 1960s was agricultural fairs. Even as we evolved from chicken farmers to rabbit farmers to shrimp peddlers to sawmill operators to long-haul truckers, we always set aside time to show our sheep at Maine fairs. Ever since we won that first blue ribbon at the Union Fair, we had loved every minute of it.

What did change over the years, thank goodness, was our means of travel and lodging. We moved on from sleeping in the back of the truck and tenting as quickly as possible. Our first pop-up camper, which was basically a tent on a metal cart with wheels, was a major step up from our traditional canvas tent. There was inside storage, a table, a built-in ice box, and sleeping quarters that folded out on the end and were off the cold, hard ground. The roof was still canvas, and when it dried after a rainstorm it would shrink to such proportions that we would awaken looking out upon the world from our sleeping bags while the passersby looked in upon us. When traveling a rough road we feared the pin on the icebox door would break and let out all the contents and the ice itself. It didn't. Instead, one time, the entire ice box left its casing and slid around the interior of the camper.

Jim pulling "barn" stock trailer, May pulling "house" camper trailer.

Through trading and watching for affordable bargains, we soon progressed to travel trailers starting at nineteen feet and working up to a thirty-two foot fifth wheel. These trailers featured gas refrigerators, cook stoves, and a small lavatory and shower and were self-contained, meaning they had holding tanks for waste until it could be disposed of at a dumping station. We never had time to use our trailer anywhere except during fair season, but the security and easier living were deeply appreciated after the hardship of living out of wet cardboard boxes and donning wet clothes.

All herdsmen and shepherds traveled this way, the wives typically pulled the trailers and the husbands drove the big trucks or stock trailers. We found a good old five-speed, standard shift pickup truck and traded the car in for it. Jim always encouraged me to believe that I could do anything I wished to try and patiently helped me with all technicalities. At the time (before we were long-haul truckers), I loved driving but had never pulled a trailer. He said, "Just remember it's going to take longer to come to a stop, and make your turns wider to allow for what is following you." I quickly came to enjoy the challenge and became comfortable with it. Jim always said, "May pulls the house and I pull the barn."

One of my favorite memories of our fair years occurred on October 8, 1987. That day, the livestock superintendent of Fryeburg Fair visited us at our sheep pens and asked Jim if he would spend a half hour or so putting on a sheep-shearing demonstration. We had done this twice a day at the Union Fair for many years. Jim did the shearing on a small stage and I had a microphone to explain his moves and to give some facts about wool. Jim said he would be willing to shear one of our North Country Cheviots. The superintendent smiled and said that he was pleased, as this demonstration was for someone special.

We didn't ask who that special person was, but when we appeared at the end of the barn with our sheep and shears, we found mobs of people milling about and saw people from several Maine television stations setting up and positioning themselves with cameras. We looked at each other askance until the livestock superintendent brought forth Vice President George H. W. Bush for an introduction.

The previous night Vice President Bush, who served two terms with President Ronald Reagan, had announced his plans to run for President of the United States. He and Maine Governor John McKernan were visiting the fair. Vice President Bush said he wanted to get into the real spirit of an agricultural fair, and one of the things he most wanted to do was see a sheep being sheared, and perhaps participate in it. For us, this was a time to hope the sheep didn't act up and that the shears worked well!

Secret Service were everywhere, their keen glances taking in everyone in the crowd. It was all very exciting, but Mr. Bush put us at ease at once. He was so friendly and genuine in his interest, his questions

George H. W. Bush watching Jim during the shearing demonstration.

were pertinent and all went smoothly. Jim explained the procedure, then began shearing the ewe, while Mr. Bush watched and talked with me about sheep raising in Maine. Then he said he wished to try it with Jim guiding his hand, which Jim did when it came to what is known as "the long blow." This is when the sheep is held on her side for the long strokes from shoulder to rump, and is the easiest part of the animal to shear. Mr. Bush was on his knees beside Jim who held his hand above the shears to help him. Mr. Bush smiled delightedly with his progress and talked with us for a while after the twenty-minute demonstration. He was sincere and down-to-earth. It was a fine experience and we felt honored to be part of it.

Each fair season felt like a family reunion. We saw and camped with many of the same people year after year and considered them our fair family, while some also became year-round friends. We also stayed active in 4-H. We hauled the 4-H sheep from Maine to Western Massachusetts for the Eastern States Exposition, or the Big E as it was called, for many years. Jim helped supervise the sheep and helped sharpen trimming shears and offered advice on feeding and showing. He also judged the 4-H shows after Connie and Debby Jo were no longer participating.

In fact, we attended fairs for so many years that we were honored on our fiftieth anniversary of attending the Fryeburg Fair. We were driven in a convertible at the parade and our picture was placed in the fair's hall of fame. We also were inducted into the North Country Cheviot Hall of Fame for our success and promotion of the breed at fairs and at North Country Farm.

It is all a part of my life that I will always cherish. It not only helped provide income, but also provided us with joy and happiness even during the hardest times in the 1960s and 1970s.

CHAPTER 41
Like the Ringing of a Bell

BEFORE WE WERE married we had looked at all available options for making a living in Maine. What presented itself was lobstering, lumbering, farming, and making crafts to sell at gift shops. Over the years, we tried some offshoots of the first three, plus long-haul trucking. It seemed that making crafts was the only road we had not yet walked down. As we sorted through our talents, I had nothing to offer that would provide a ripping late-life crafting career. Cooking, cleaning, mucking out barns, delivering lambs, driving trucks (because I had a Class I driver's license the state occasionally offered me jobs driving trucks) typing, bookkeeping, and being willing and handy rounded out my abilities.

On the other hand, Jim could master almost anything he decided to try, and especially loved working with steel and welding, which he enjoyed even as a hobby.

We were in our mid- to- late fifties by this point, and during our thirty-five years of marriage we had worked together nearly every day at a variety of jobs. We were still not ready to give up that togetherness and take eight-hour jobs drawing paychecks from a company and work for a boss. And besides, we didn't really think there was much market for people our age and with our type of experience. We knew that at our ages our next career move would be the last, especially if we ever hoped to enjoy any type of retirement. To this point, we had not saved any money that would allow us to enjoy our later years and time was passing quickly.

As we discussed our options, we kept coming back to crafts. What, we wondered, could we make that would appeal to tourists and, by extension, gift shops? Not only that, but what could we make in enough quantity that we could earn real money? We reviewed some things that Jim already created in the past taking advantage of spare moments and when he might say referring to his farm equipment, "I'm going to spend an hour or so welding something that isn't rusty junk." Welding was his way to relax.

Making wind chimes was perhaps Jim's favorite creative outlet. Through the years he had made many different types of chimes using old saw blades and scraps of steel. They were mostly strung from a bar so the pieces would swing together in the wind, but like most chimes of this sort the strings tangled easily. Then one day in the mid-1970s, he was daydreaming about the 1950s and thinking about one of his many fog-bound days lobster fishing without the benefit of any electronic navigational equipment. He had relied on a compass and depended on a nearby bell or gong buoy to help him identify his position. This method allowed him to set his course from the compass and head for safety or find his way home. When lobster fishing, there is no particular direct running course. Hauling lobster traps requires constant circling and when a sudden fog shuts in, it can be confusing. More than a few times he was thankful for Maine's iconic bell buoys.

Jim always said he wished he could make something that sounded like those bell buoys and finally he did. He wanted the bell to have substance and deep meaning, it couldn't be "tinkly," and it should be rugged enough to hang outdoors year 'round without rusting and it should not tangle in the wind. So Jim went to work. Cor-Ten steel never rusts out and it was great for farm equipment repair. The pieces left over from this work were often triangular. He took the triangle pieces to design a three-sided bell and hung a chain with a clapper down from the high point where all three pieces met. It was not truly a chime, but the tone was resonant and pleasing, the string couldn't tangle, and the metal would not rust through in weather. Once the design was finished, he experimented with the tones and discovered that by varying the gauges of the steel, lengths of the weld, and tweaking a few other things, he could produce multiple tones in the same bell.

The sounds produced by these bells were reminiscent of the bells and gong buoys on the ocean. But similar was not good for Jim, he wanted the tones to be spot-on accurate. He went back to sea to record the sounds made by each buoy. By listening to them repeatedly and cutting different lengths of steel, he took advantage of his love of music and his understanding of tonal qualities to reproduce those haunting sounds of the sea.

For a handful of years, as he had time to make them, he gave them away as Christmas and wedding gifts but it never entered our minds that these bells could be sellable or could be produced on a large scale. Making them was just a hobby that Jim enjoyed.

So now in the mid-1980s, following the theft of North Country Sunrise, we were casting about for something to supplement our sheep farming income. I was sitting at the desk one afternoon trying to do some bookkeeping, when Jim walked in carrying an old bell he had unearthed in his workshop. He held it up by the chain, swung the clapper, and as always, I drifted back to *Spindrift* when I heard the sound.

He asked simply, "Do you think this would sell?"

I told him I would surely buy it. Although to be honest, while I believed in the beauty of the bells, I wasn't sure if they were something other people would want. As we sat there, neither of us had any idea how to market such an item nor how we would produce it on any kind of scale, even if we found sales outlets.

Finally, we discussed the bells with a friend, who remarked, "Why don't you do this for real? These would sell!"

She told us that Maine had a fine organization for handcrafters called United Maine Craftsmen and that if we joined this group we could participate in craft shows at armories, malls, and convention centers around the state. It seemed like a logical way to test the waters so we sent for an application. Their rules were strict, and rightly so. For the good of all members who produce excellent quality crafts, any potential new member must have their crafts "juried" or approved by an experienced committee made up of organization members.

If we were going to try this, we had to do it right. To make a quality product, we could no longer work with scraps and partial pieces of steel laying around the shop. We needed a real steel shear and standard sheets of steel, which come in four foot by ten foot dimensions and weigh 450 pounds each. Before getting into this too deeply we thought it best to try some road selling with our samples to see what gift shops might think. We traveled along the coast of Maine doing our due diligence and we were heartened by the response to our buoy bells. Our enthusiasm mounted as we took orders for the following summer. One shop owner told us: "These will sell beyond your dreams."

We returned satisfied that it was time to gamble on yet another way to make a living in Maine. Scanning newspaper advertisements for used fabricating equipment, Jim found a Miles Wysong four-foot

Jim working in the North Country Wind Bells shop in the 1990s.

steel shear. It was in Massachusetts, so with the dump truck and plenty of chain we went after it. We had saved what little was left after the payoff from the truck insurance, and this would get us started with some machinery and steel.

The Wysong was a very old and top-heavy monster, but it could chop steel as if it were a block of butter. With the farm tractor loader, chain falls, rollers, and patience, Jim got the shear placed in his workshop. Then we drove to Augusta to buy several sheets of steel and again with patience, gritted teeth, and straining muscles, the two of us managed to bully 450 pounds at a time from the strategically placed truck onto the shear to be chopped into proper lengths.

It was work more properly fit for oxen, but we had done lots of that in the past, and we were elated that we could still "muscle up" when necessary. The steel plates were sanded on a belt sander to smooth the edges, and chains and wind catchers also had to be cut. Jim put all the pieces together. We wrapped the bells in newspaper for shipping and scrounged cardboard boxes anywhere they could be found to contain them.

Our first United Maine Craftsmen show was at the Rumford Armory shortly after Thanksgiving in 1986. The retail show launching experience of our bell business had begun. The show was timed for Christmas shopping and we were amazed at our sales. While talking with other crafters we soon learned that some of them made an excellent living this way. The Christmas season was best, but with the exception of mid-winter, all the seasons could yield a good income. It appeared that we just might be onto something.

We continued successfully with Maine shows until after Christmas, selling essentially to individuals looking for gifts, and soon learned of organizations that booked craft shows throughout the eastern states. We also soon learned that the dead of winter was hard going for craft shows. At a show in Hanover, Massachusetts we sold only three bells and did not sell our first one until 7:15 p.m. after starting at 10 a.m. A fellow crafter said, "It took me three terrible days just to have one bad day."

There were not many winter shows, but we kept making bells and by spring had enough to fill the wholesale orders for the gift shops. In our zeal we had sent a couple of samples to L.L.Bean, who returned them with a polite letter saying that they "had tried wind chimes in the past without success." Oh well, we felt that we had at least tried.

A knowledgeable craftsperson we had met worked as a sales representative and for several months during the summer took our buoy bells on the road and made some valuable wholesale contacts. So while we were busy with lambing, haying, and attending fairs, orders were still being generated.

———❧———

Before we started attending craft fairs again in the fall of 1987, we tackled a project that had to be done. Our old, original barn—our first chicken barn—had to be torn down. We could not afford its upkeep, and the thousands of tons of water used in washing it down after each flock had taken its toll on walls and floors. We found someone to tear off the roof for salvage, and together we dismantled most of the rest of it. This was another job better fit for oxen.

The final part of the old barn, built in 1902, was torn down by a local young man who used its wonderful old pegged timbers to help build his home. We were delighted to think that some of this historical piece was used by someone in the community. The most difficult emotional part was filling in the basement floor that Jim had dug out with pick and mattock through a winter of bone-crushing cold. It had served its purpose, and in the inexorable passing of time that which has been built must sometimes be removed. We left a one-story section large enough to make a good equipment shed.

When we returned from the fairs that fall we found that our sales representative had done excellent work. I wrote in my diary: "Bell orders coming out of our ears—panicky! No time for anything except to make bells and go to bed for a few hours!"

A few weeks later I wrote: "Working like mad on bells, but if it continues, the bell business will be the best thing we've done yet besides the sheep. Desperately tired nights, but happy!"

Over the next few years, except for the summers, we continued exhibiting at craft shows, expanding our sales territory into New Jersey and Pennsylvania. Many of these shows were on a "turn around basis," meaning we would return home just long enough to make bells. If the show was out of state, which most of them were, and lasted a few days, we would try to make seventy-five to one hundred bells to take with us. When time was short, Jim would chop the steel and I would sand the edges on the steel, and while he welded I sanded the wind catchers and then we both cut the chain. We then wrapped them up to head back out to the next show, packing all the heavy equipment into our pickup truck and camper. We owned a Ford F-250 and truck camper, which slid into the bed of the truck. It was small, but livable with a bed, tiny bathroom, propane stove, refrigerator, table, and padded bench. The truck camper arrangement allowed us to tow a two-wheel utility trailer filled with bells and display equipment.

We were still selling almost exclusively to individual customers at these shows, but we felt we were headed in a good direction. The positive comments about our bells kept us on a constant high. At a Cherry Hill, New Jersey craft show, a lady stood listening to the bells that were ringing gently with the help of a fan. Tears were running down her cheeks as she said, "I was born and grew up in Maine, but I've been stuck down here for the last ten years. Those bells are just like the bell buoys at home and they make me so homesick."

When late winter lambing time began, I stayed home to ensure safe deliveries and give extra care, but in between farm jobs I sanded the bell plates that Jim chopped between his trips. Connie came to help when she could, and we shared many happy hours. One day while we were working together, we both did the hourly check of a ewe expected to lamb that day. She was a prized producer and had been showing signs of labor, but just didn't get down to business.

By this time, we still had nearly eighty sheep, but had added a small flock of Southdowns in an attempt to bring in more prize money at the fairs.

As the day and the ewe's labor went on, it was obvious she was not dilating and the only way she could be saved was by a Cesarean delivery. The other times we had needed to resort to this we had taken the ewe to a veterinarian. This day was a Sunday and no vet was available; we were surely going to lose this ewe. Connie said, "If you have any scalpels, alcohol, iodine, a needle, and some silk thread I can use for stitching, I'll be glad to try it." While she had never performed it, she had assisted several times with this operation while she worked with a vet in Utah.

We sometimes needed to lance infected wounds on sheep, so a doctor friend had given us some scalpels, and the other equipment was also on hand. So with soap, hot water, towels, and assorted surgical items, Connie and I trotted out to the barn. I was concerned about the lack of anesthesia, but Connie assured me that where she was going to cut there was very little tissue with nerves. She was right.

For the best results, Connie wanted the ewe standing upright, and although the sheep was in some discomfort with labor pains, she patiently stood while I held and stroked her head. Connie used electric shears to remove wool from the operating site, and then, on her knees, she executed an orderly and wondrous surgical feat. Layer by layer, she laid back skin and tissue, skillfully wielding the scalpel. There was virtually no blood, and the ewe stood calmly unaware of what was occurring.

Connie brought forth a fine and vigorous ram lamb, and stitched the ewe together in a manner to make any surgeon proud. We liberally applied antiseptic and began a series of antibiotic shots (always kept on hand) to ward off any infection. The ewe never went off her feet and happily licked her offspring clean while nickering soft love talk to it. We named the ram lamb "Stitches," and he was our champion ram at fairs the following summer and went on to become one of our finest stud rams. His mother delivered normally for the remainder of her long life. Connie has never been afraid to attempt any task, and I admit to being a proud mama!

All of the craft shows were retail, and to make them work as income, Jim, or both of us, were on the road weekly rushing back to make more bells, then heading out to another state. The wholesale business was growing slowly, as our existing accounts kept ordering, but we didn't have time to generate new wholesale business. We were becoming acutely aware that we would need to stay home more and ship to wholesale accounts for two reasons. One, so we could take proper care of the sheep, and two, because the pace for retail shows was just too demanding physically. This was now the late 1980s, meaning I would soon join Jim in his sixties.

To make a change we needed to find and enter wholesale shows that were designed to attract the gift trade. We knew one in New York City called The New York International Gift Show that brought in

A North Country Wind Bell in the foreground with the buoy bells that served as inspiration in the background.

worldwide business. We did not know what was required to enter it, nor how to go about it. But as we headed for a retail show in Nassau County on Long Island we believed we would find some leads there.

At our first craft show we had used a clean and quietly colored bedspread over a table. We had now developed a more serious presentation. Jim had created a metal frame that enclosed three sides of our booth, and we purchased yards of forest green velour that I had sewn into drapes to hang from the framework in soft folds.

This background gently, but effectively set off the attractive, wrought-iron look of the bell stands. We completed the first day of the show with good sales and were now able to spell each other so we could talk to someone about the New York show. We were soon told that one lady stood above everybody else in her knowledge of that show, and that she was absolutely the one to see. This lady heard about our interest and when she was doing a walk-around of the show stopped to see us. After introductions we expressed our interest in the New York show.

She was probably in her thirties, clouds of dark, curly hair swirled about her face, and she was dressed in a skintight shirt and toreador pants. Black leather boots rose to her knees and were topped with wide swashbuckling, buccaneer cuffs. She kindly gave us information about the New York show, but standing with hands on hips, her head cocked to one side, she brayed in a nasal, Bronx accent, "Trouble is ya see, looking at this display, I just don't think you've got enough clay-uss to get into the New York Gift Show."

She didn't enlighten us as to how we could upgrade our class. Our clothes weren't fancy, but they were neat, clean, and quiet. We puzzled for a while, then Jim said, "Guess we'd better have a look at her booth so we can see what 'clay-uss' is. You go first, I'll handle this for awhile."

I was not impressed. I returned to report to Jim that I didn't believe that "clay-uss" was going to be a big problem for us—unlike her, we kept our shoes on our feet, brought no food into our booth, and counted our money in private.

We soon found our way to the promoter of the New York Gift Show, and booked a spot for the following winter. The show took place at the massive Jacob Javits Convention Center in New York City. Over five thousand exhibitors from all over the world participate in the five-day show, and there was seven miles of carpeting in the exhibit area. It was overwhelming, but the orders were good, and we were able to start dropping retail shows.

Jim and May selling North Country Wind Bells on the QVC network in 1997.

The overall products for North Country Wind Bells were called Maine Buoy Bells. We named each one to match the tone that Jim created that matched the actual bell. Early on these were: Island Pasture Bell, Boothbay Harbor Bell, Bar Harbor Bell, Pemaquid Bell, Camden Reach Bell, Pemaquid Bell, Nantucket Bell, Cape Cod Bell, Chesapeake Bell, and Outer Banks Bell.

With a few other craftsmen, and a University of Maine small business association program, we began a State of Maine Craft Show in Portland at The Holiday Inn by the Bay. When the show started, L.L.Bean buyers came to look at Maine products. They stopped to listen to and look at our bells and ordered a few samples. What

happened next is beyond pleasant history. L.L.Bean placed an initial
order of several dozen and sales exploded immediately. The Maine Buoy
Bells have been in their Home and Camp catalogs and in the Freeport
Flagship Store for years and in some seasons are a runaway item.

It is not an exaggeration to say that L.L.Bean changed the course
of our business and our lives, dramatically boosting sales with orders
sometimes in the hundreds. We had to hire extra help in the summer
and before Christmas to meet demand.

It was all so dramatic. Over the next few years, sales continued to
grow as Jim and I began attending almost exclusively wholesale shows
(those attended by resellers) and we traveled from New York City to
Miami, as well to Philadelphia, Chicago, Atlanta, and other places.

It certainly was all a long way from shoveling chicken manure.

Chapter 42
Fire!

It was exciting to work hard at something that paid us for our labors. We were happy and grateful, and it seemed our hope for the future was finally on a solid base. But the Davidson Christmas season jinx was not through with us yet. Big Babe's spectacular demise and the theft of North Country Sunrise both occurred during the Christmas season. We felt two Christmas disasters were enough, but a third one was coming.

By 1993, business was excellent. Jim had expanded the factory and warehouse and we now employed ten or more workers depending on the season, including two who had worked with us at the sawmill. We also had to hire a welder in addition to Jim to meet production demands as the wholesale business continued to boom.

Our means of travel also evolved. As business grew and we attended big city shows, we would ship a large show box ahead and then fly to the destination and stay in a hotel. This proved expensive and was not our preferred means of travel. We still enjoyed seeing the countryside. So, we bought a forty-foot motor home that could carry the bell samples and show materials and give us a place to stay. We also used the motor home during fair season.

The motor home also allowed us to, in some ways, relive the joyous days of long-haul trucking. When we traveled we would sometimes stay overnight in truck stops, just to be part of their sights and sounds again. Our sleep was again soothed by the running truck engines—the familiar roll of Detroit, steady humming of a Cummins, and powerful clatter of a Caterpillar—was all so lovely.

In late 1993, we planned to attend the gift show in Miami scheduled for just after Christmas, so we were in town staying in a campground on a Florida beach in our motor home. It was the first time we had ever relaxed in this style and we were loving it.

The day was December 24, 1993, a blissful Christmas Eve afternoon. As we were swimming, a campground official waved us to shore to tell us there was a message from home, "extreme emergency, call home immediately."

Our hearts turned to cold stone; we could only think of the family. Rushing to the nearest pay phone, we stood together shaking as Jim dialed our Maine number. All I could hear were Jim's words as he uttered, "Oh, my god! Is anybody hurt?"

Then, "Thank God for that! Is it completely flat—nothing left?"

It seems that about thirty minutes before quitting time, a flash fire started and swept through our bell shop. It was so swift and intense that the crew barely managed a call to the fire station before fleeing to safety. The winds were fierce and the temperature bitter. Our great Bristol fire department and its dedicated volunteers worked hard to save the shop, but it wasn't possible. Certainly, our wonderful old farmhouse would also have gone up in flames without their valiant efforts. Even the farm pond helped as firefighters chopped through thick ice to replenish fire truck tanks. The fire's cause was never identified.

It would take at least a couple of days of hard driving to get back to Maine with our motor home, so flying out on Christmas morning was the only solution. Our second Nell, also a border collie who traveled with us but had never flown, stepped into the sky kennel purchased from the airline and laid down quietly. Connie and Tim met us at the Portland Jetport on Christmas afternoon and tried to prepare us for the sight we would soon see. Our precious workshop, the root source of our income and as well as that of our crew, was a grim pile of charred rubble covered with fresh snow.

I stood and wept at the desolation.

Later that night huddled in bed, Jim and I held each other and tried to form the needed plans. As we lay there, I was sixty-four years old and Jim was sixty-six. After all the years of stress and hard work, all the years of building and struggling, now we just couldn't seem to raise the spark one more time to dig ourselves out of a sinking despondency. But the next day, the sun shone on the sparkling snow and spruce forest. Our wonderful crew came to us with heartwarming sympathy and concern for their jobs.

We never had been able to save any money for retirement, so now we had to think of future income. At our age we weren't remotely marketable in the job market that we had so adamantly avoided all these years. But this fine group of people offered themselves and their friends to help us rebuild. Their enthusiasm and hope was so great we soon found ourselves in the throes of plans.

Maybe this was our Christmas miracle. We rallied again.

The one-story section of the original chicken barn that we had torn down and now used to store farm equipment would serve as the nucleus of a new beginning. It was January 1994 and the weather was brutally cold. Jim was on the telephone and out on the road at all

The remains of the North Country Wind Bells shop after it burned on Christmas Eve in 1993.

hours hunting down rental equipment and guiding its placement in the farm machine shed. Our crude operation was akin to running a large restaurant with only a two-burner hotplate, but we had orders we didn't want to lose. With the seeming unquenchable enthusiasm and dedication of crew and neighbors, we got a big catalog order shipped only two weeks late.

Jim and the crew literally worked night and day putting the last of the roofing on in a blinding snowstorm. My job was handling the endless paperwork that goes with such an incident. There were long visits from fire and insurance inspectors and adjusters and perpetual lists of lost equipment to itemize. We had many conferences with our crew trying to remember everything we lost, going at it wall by wall and floor station by floor station. I still think of things that went up in smoke.

Our insurance was inadequate, although the insurance company was fair. We will ever be grateful for the fact that nobody was hurt. Our new building, encompassing the old remains of the chicken barn, is mostly lined in steel, and every method of fire prevention known to man resides in it.

As friends and neighbors always have in Maine, ours came through with the love and beauty of all good people. This made it possible for our crew, who are our friends, to continue work without the loss of a day's pay, and each crew member provided input into the design of their own bailiwicks. At Christmas, what had seemed like a black hole we couldn't summon the will to climb out of, had been conquered after all and, like a phoenix, North Country Wind Bells rose again to even greater heights.

CHAPTER 43
Back to the Sea

THE STARTLING SUCCESS of North Country Wind Bells not only solved all of our pressing financial problems, but afforded us a chance to slow down and live life in a more enjoyable manner, including doing things we never thought possible.

The ocean always remained a vital element in our lives even after our lobstering days ended. The yearning to return to the sea never subsided. And with joyful hearts we were able to do it, but in a boat very different from *Spindrift*.

In the summer of 1994, we began cruising the coast in *Come Spring*, a 45-foot, live-aboard boat, a yacht really. We truly felt blessed. It featured twin diesel engines, a flying bridge, wraparound couches, a generator, television and music center, as well as a full kitchen, two bathrooms, and a comfortable bed. Given all the years we lived basically broke and in debt, it was hard to believe this all wasn't just a dream.

Jim named the boat with my delighted approval. After we bought the boat, all winter long we had said, "Come spring, she'll be in the water," so one day Jim said, "Why not call her that?"

The name fit so well with our annual longing for spring, and it also harkened back to our happy days at Union Fair, the area so

Come Spring, *1997.*

beautifully described in Ben Ames Williams' historical fiction novel
of the same name. We used to take walks with sheep from the Union
fairgrounds to the cemetery where Mima and Joel were buried. In the
book, which described their hard, pioneering winters, these principal
characters often began sentences with "Come spring." They always
ended with a prophecy of life improving.

And so, in our golden years we were able to wander the coasts,
the Maine coast being the best, of course. I don't believe its magic and
splendid beauty can be equaled anywhere. It changes constantly in
mood, season, weather, conformation, and color: The salmon-hued
cliffs of Acadia, the steel-gray ledges of Fox Island Thoroughfare, and
the smooth, creamy roundness of Stonington's rock-walled shores.

From headlands foaming with raging surf to remote and tranquil
coves, silent except for the gulls' and ospreys' cries, the plummeting
splash of a hunting eagle, or sometimes the lowing of cows in a pasture,

its edges shadowed by great oaks, the scenes are always new. In May or September there's also the soul-reaching call of gathering loons.

Awakening on board the boat you can look out on a luminescent dawn streaking the dark waters of a harbor with silver, delicate opal clouds, and often the vivid colors of lobster buoys suspended on the still surface like wildflowers in a floating pasture.

Of course, there can be the famous Maine fog. We could go to bed at night with skies so clear even the Milky Way was reflected in the water and wake to fog so thick the boat's bow was barely visible. Often this fog would lift with the warming sun, but sometimes it would linger for days or even weeks. Charts, or no charts, Maine's coast is famous for its submerged ledges and rocks, and I do have a fondness for seeing where we are going. Jim was comfortable with fog, whistling and humming as he enjoyed its challenge.

Come Spring was born in the age of electronic navigation and she had radar, GPS, a foghorn, VHF, and other standard equipment. We would run in fog for hours at a time, and through these instruments, and Jim's instinct, our destined harbor suddenly appeared out of the silent banks of oblivion. I was always happy to cast the dock lines or grab the boat hook to gaff a mooring buoy when we emerged from it. There is a sensuousness to fog though, soft veils of cool moisture, richly redolent of the sea, caressing the skin. Tiny beads of it glistened on hair and eyelashes. It even tastes good. It subtly promises, "What you can't see won't hurt you." A fallacy, yes, but fog is also an enchantress. We traveled in her hushed world where even the seas sweeping the bows dared only whisper.

Our favorite islands and old haunts of our early years were revisited. Some of them were even more beaten with forest blow-downs from line gales and Northeast storms. But nature replaces, and once open pastures were now thickly beautiful spruce forests. Harbor Island in Muscongus Bay—we had once dreamed of owning and lobstering from it, and raising sheep on its pastures—was still much the same.

Coming into the harbor in June or early July, a veritable presence of fragrance from the wild rugosa roses suffused the senses. They, along with pungently spicy bayberry, grow profusely on the shorelines. The delights onshore are a constant discovery—raspberries, wine-colored in their ripeness, striped gooseberries, plum-dusty in their readiness to eat, wild strawberries hiding succulently in the field grasses, and big blue-green juniper berries, smelling delicately of gin and so flavorful in a chicken casserole.

Island nesting ospreys searched the waters from dawn to dusk to feed their eager young, calling all the while. Guillemots, tiny black, perfectly sculpted bodies with snow-white wings and bright red paddle feet just under their tails for expert diving, flap their wings happily in the water, drinking the sea as they hold their heads high in the pleasure of it. They seem to be paying homage to the sea by immersing themselves so full-heartedly. Watching them, I felt like expressing my feelings in almost the same way.

We walked from the quiet shores of the island's harbor through a soft, brown needle path lined with nodding ferns, under a canopy of sun-shadowed spruce boughs. There were wafts of balsalm in the air, and the deep woods absorbed all sound. Old tumbling stone walls attested to the farm animals that once grazed the island when a family made its living here. We were so touched by this evidence of the past that Jim once remarked that perhaps it was us who once settled this island since we loved it so long and so well.

Coming out of the forest on the island's westerly side, it became a different place. Surf boomed on the headlands, and great ledges and

Jim and May in 2003.

boulders were a jumble everywhere, with a small, shingle beach or two interspersed. Huge mussel shells, bleached to an exquisite shade of lavender, adorned the beach and there were sprinkles of bone-white and bright-yellow periwinkle shells. Most intriguing, of course, was the search for unique pieces of driftwood. We looked for small wooden barrel heads to paint a scene on, or big, sea-battered beams and planks, ideally with a rusty ring-bolt or two, that Jim used to make coffee tables and plant stands for the house.

We sat and watched the soothing roll of incoming surf or the lobster boats daring the rocks as they rode the swells to haul their traps, just as Jim used to do. One day we sat mesmerized by the sight of literally thousands of monarch butterflies feeding on an abundance of flowering plants at the shoreline. It was late summer and they were gathering for their great migration.

There were many adventures on *Come Spring*. One time, we were caught in a sudden microburst that created a water spout with us at its center. *Come Spring* maintained her stability, but the top was twisted off the fly bridge.

One midnight, while moored in a quiet harbor, the lobster boat swinging fifteen feet from us caught fire. Jim saw the flickering through the porthole and then, always in control at dire moments, he gently shook my shoulder and said, "I'm sorry to wake you, but the boat next to us is on fire."

Emerging from layers of sleep, I couldn't quite take it in until I went up into the galley and felt the intense heat. At that moment the flames broke through the lobster boat's cabin roof and shot a pillar of flame thirty feet into the air. We didn't know if this boat was fueled by diesel or gasoline, and if it was the latter I could only see us going up with it in a Hollywood-type explosion. I shouted this thought to Jim along with the desperate suggestion that we jump into the dinghy and get away quickly.

But he was doing several things at once: He had the engines running, was on the VHF calling the Coast Guard to notify the local fire station, and was sounding out an SOS to surrounding boats on the air horn. He went out onto the bow and groped his way through heavy black smoke to release the mooring and backed us out quickly. Meanwhile, I was searching for my clothes. I always put them in the same place, but in my panic I simply couldn't locate them, and pictured flinging myself into the dinghy wearing only a sparse nightgown.

A wiring problem had caused the boat's fire, and unfortunately the handsome vessel burned to the waterline, but she had a diesel engine, so there were no explosions, and no one on board to be rescued.

On a long trip down to Newport, Rhode Island, we were running ninety miles offshore to keep a direct line and didn't see land for fourteen hours at a time. But there were wonderful sightings of whale pods and even an eighteen- or twenty-foot shark alongside the boat.

On the return trip a long while later, we engaged ten- and twelve-foot seas for hours putting the rails under. Even a table it took two of us to lift went over in the salon, but *Come Spring* plowed on until one of her engines began to falter. Apparently the constant heavy action of the sea had loosened some crud at the base of the fuel tank and although the fuel filter caught it, it became fouled in the process. Jim had no choice but to go down into the tight quarters of the engine room and change the filter.

We had been taking beam seas because that was our course, but I held the bow straight into the oncoming seas to try to lessen the pounding Jim was taking in the engine room. He accomplished the mission but sported some bruises. As someone once said, "A long boating run can be hours of boredom interrupted by several moments of sheer terror."

Although we got six months out of it, the Maine boating season was still too short.

When we went up the Sasanoa River and came down the Kennebec late in the season and saw the huckleberry bushes lying like crimson lace on the ivory ledges and the marsh grasses turning gold, we knew the oaks would soon be russet against the dark evergreens and the waters more often pewter than blue. In the harbors, the sailboats pulled at their moorings like horses on lunge ropes. The winds shrieked mournfully in their shrouds, and their halyards slapped against the masts in a sweet and monotonous song. These were signs that winter was coming. The season was at its end.

When I prepared meals in the galley, I was sometimes watched by the dark, soft eyes of a harbor seal twitching his scrubbing brush whiskers. Another season over, but my being yearned to hold it forever.

On those last trips in October or November not all the saltwater on my face was from sea-spray. But as soon as the boat was hauled out, I would again daydream about what we would do again *Come Spring*.

CHAPTER 44

May and Jim: A Love Story

It was a day in early spring in the mid-1990s, the bell business continued to great success. The softer days of April, and the land's breath promised that the air would soon be warm and sweet once more. New lambs were springing around our pasture in evening's lilac dusk awakening to the first joys of their life. The loosely starred and pure-white blossoms of the shadbush hung in a delicate raggedness of light against the soft dark of pine and spruce.

Our way of life had improved beyond anything we had dared dream. We were able to pay bills as they arrived and were able to enjoy life with some luxuries. It didn't seem that this could really be us. We were grateful beyond measure. On this spring day, we were also deeply tired from a long winter spent attending wholesale shows in New York, Chicago, Philadelphia, Atlanta, and Miami. Luckily with our excellent crew of twelve to fifteen working with us, many of the physical pressures were off.

This day began with the sunrise setting the dew afire with diamonds on the grass. The breezes caressed and were filled with scents of spring. The day was so perfect that Jim reached for my hand and said, "Let's play hooky for awhile!"

I grinned happily and said, "Lead the way!"

As we walked down the pasture road, we noted the snowflowers, dogtooth violets, and trout lilies and wandered through the sheep pastures adrift with tiny bluets like lingering snow. On through the intertwined branches of tall and solemn spruce, while golden sun rays filtered through them to the ground.

As we came out on the cream and amber granite of the shoreline, the rich smell of surf-washed kelp and the sea surrounded us. Finding an inviting ledge, we sat to worship this glory in humble thanks and with hearts full of joy. This was what it had all been about, what our lives had been about: The ability to walk out into this, our own little kingdom, any time we wished, and soak in the great beauty and majesty of Maine. For more than fifty years, we had done it all together— and it had been love, literally, at first sight.

On June 4, 1945, with Jim's eighteenth birthday approaching in August, both he and I knew he would soon be drafted. While the war in Europe had ended, World War II continued in the Pacific. Jim had a Scottish great-aunt whose resources were small—she was a retired school nurse but she had always been his mentor and they enjoyed some fine times together. When he was a boy she had taken him to Yarmouth, Nova Scotia, several times. Now, not knowing what his future would be, he wanted to return her kindness and bring her to the Maine coast for a week-long vacation. He had time due him from the railroad where he worked.

My Scottish mother and Lithuanian father, Jo and John Banis, ran a small farmhouse inn. It stood on a hill overlooking Greenland Cove, and a few minutes' walk through a tall forest of pines back of

Jim on furlough from the US Army in 1945.

the house led to Webber Pond. The setting was beautiful and they had owned and run the little inn for many years, struggling long and hard to establish it.

I was sixteen, and until this particular spring, we had never had electricity. All was wood stoves, blocks of ice from Webber Pond in the icehouse full of sawdust, kerosene lamps, and a water system powered

413

by a gasoline pump, which did provide running water. The house was situated nearly a mile from the main road, Route 32, and bringing in power lines had just been too expensive until now.

Jim had seen an advertisement placed by my mother in a newspaper and responded to it. He and his Aunt Clara were our first guests of the season. Something he said in his letter of inquiry indicated that he was young, and I was looking forward to having a young person around the house for a week. There was little time to spend with my schoolmates at Lincoln Academy, and because of the distance from my home to the school, and the need of my help at home, extra-curricular activities were not possible.

I did not regret this. We had no near neighbors, and my childhood days had been spent in the woods, fields, and shorelines exploring and discovering. I cherished my surroundings, and they, along with books and cats, were my happiness. In addition, I enjoyed the cows, chickens, and farm animals my folks raised, and I swam and rowed, fished, skated, and skied.

This particular year, school was almost over, my exams were complete, and the remaining days were mostly for putting in an appearance. Each morning I rode my bike three miles each way to meet a schoolmate who drove several of us to Lincoln Academy in his car. When I came home on the afternoon of June 4, Mother had left a note saying that she and the new guests, Jim Davidson and his Aunt Clara, had walked down the field to the brick landing. The field was a half-mile or so from the house and nearly surrounded by water. The brick landing was like many old crumbled stone docks that had once been used to ship bricks made from local clay, which had abounded in the field. This field was a lovely and a scenic spot, nearly surrounded by the waters of Greenland Cove and looking out to sea and the heavy

May as a teenager in the 1940s.

spruce forest of Hog Island. My father pastured his cows there after he had mowed the hay from it.

As I walked down the driveway to meet my mother, I saw the three of them returning and standing under a big pine tree just beyond the railed pasture gate. I saw a tall, dark young man in a simple suede windbreaker, speaking and smiling animatedly with my mother. I approached and Mother introduced me. My mother and I were very close, and although I did not have her Scottish accent, some of her speech stayed with me, and Jim claims that as we shook hands—(he had a great, firm handshake, always a measure of character to both him and me)—I said in a very dignified way, "Hello, there!"

I looked upon thick, dark hair, a shock of which had escaped to just above his eyebrow, and into soft brown eyes, so deep and sincere, they still tug my heart to this day. I believe there is love at first sight because something sprang to life between us in that moment that remained with us forever. The evening was pleasant as we all got acquainted. I played the piano; mother loved to sing and had a lovely voice (her mother had sung in a London theater briefly as a young woman). Jim joined in and did a wonderful deep-voiced rendition of "Ol' Man River," one of my favorites.

That night, I formed a clever little plan and executed it the next day. I dawdled around on the lonely and wooded road on my bike a sufficient length of time that I missed my transportation to school. I reported this to my mother with a properly straight face. She said, "No matter, you can help entertain Jim!"

Exactly.

Entertaining him was not a problem. He didn't think of vacation as a time to be idle, and he never ceased being busy while he was there. He helped my father milk the cows and weed the gardens, and he mowed the big lawns himself. My mother had bought some used electric lamps in anticipation of our electricity coming in, and one of them refused to work. She was going to throw it away, deeming it unworthy of paying to have it fixed. There was no point in asking my father to deal with it. He was a hard-working master gardener and livestock man, a hunter, and woodsman, but his talents didn't reach beyond that. He called objects that required small tools "dinglets," and he left them severely alone.

Jim told my mother he would like to take the lamp apart as long as she was just going to throw it away. Since I hadn't seen anyone work with something of this nature, I was fascinated. With screwdriver, snippers, and connectors, he soon had the lamp working perfectly. Mother happily found other items around the house that needed repair. She also insisted that we take time to go rowing, swimming, and fishing, which we did, finding with every passing hour how much we liked the same things and had the same beliefs and philosophies. So important to me also was how Jim could make me laugh. His humor was keen and spontaneous.

Dad had killed some chickens for the following day's dinner (he always believed in hanging them in the cellar overnight afterward). Jim and I took them into a chicken-plucking spot in the big pine woods behind the house. Sitting under a tall pine, that sighed gently in the spring breeze, we contentedly plucked chickens and exchanged our short life histories.

Our barn was built on a hillside in such a fashion that its three levels could be entered from the ground. On the top level next to the haymow were three roughly built rooms, one for my parents, one for summer help, and one for me. In this way, we did not occupy rooms in the house that could be rented to the summer guests. I loved this room; it was large enough to hold my old piano, had a big window that looked out into massive pines, and was next to the sweet smelling haymow. At night, I could hear the cows humming as they shifted to comfortable positions, and in the mornings I heard the milk hissing into the pails as my father milked them before taking them out to pasture for the day. And I heard the heart-haunting cry of the loons as they yodeled or called flying overhead from lake to sea.

In this barn room was an old wind-up Victrola that refused to work properly anymore, and so mother had retired it from the living room where the guests had once been entertained by it. There were a number of records with it, including Tchaikovsky's "Piano Concerto

Jim, May, and Mundy rowing in the dory, 1945.

No. 1," which I adored. To my joy, it had also long been Jim's favorite, along with Rachmaninoff's "Piano Concerto No. 2," to which he introduced me.

The Victrola just would not maintain speed to play a record all the way through, but Jim tackled it and before long it was performing as if it had been newly built. We listened to Tchaikovsky's "Piano

Concerto No. 1" over and over, and its powerfully magnificent strains became our love song forever more.

We were surrounded by the lushness that is June, the rich greens of grasses and ferns, yellow-enameled buttercups, daisies that smiled into the sun, showers of delicately scented apple blossom petals, and the lilacs, dew-laden and intoxicating in their rich fragrance. I managed to avoid school most of the week, and we dug clams at low tide, rowed across the cove for lobsters, went fishing for perch on the lake in soft apricot sunsets, and rowed in Greenland Cove evenings marveling at the sparkling chains of phosphorescence created by the oars.

The week went quickly, and suddenly there was only Saturday left in Jim's stay. That Saturday was one of June's perfect days, and mother suggested that Jim and I take the dory and have a picnic on Hog Island. She made sliced chicken sandwiches and a delicate, moist gingerbread, as only she could make it, poured a thermos of milk, and we were off. Mother enjoyed Jim's Aunt Clara and they had a great time together drinking endless pots of tea and talking about their beloved country of Scotland.

Our day on Hog Island, we were two free spirits released into a world of beauty where literally nobody else existed. We were castaways who had found a huge and glorious island just waiting for us to explore its beauties and discover its treasures. We walked every trail, examined the wonders washed up on the shores, climbed the ledges and rocks, waded on the beaches, and built elaborate sandcastles. We ate our lunch leaning against spruce trees, smelling the sea, and watching its diamonds glinting in a June sun.

We talked and talked about what we wanted out of life and what our values were. There was no question that our hearts were securely bonded. Over all of this hung the certainty that Jim would soon be drafted, and the somber uncertainty of when, how, and if the war would end. Like everyone else of our generation, we would have to deal with this through hope, courage, and faith.

As we returned to the mainland in the late afternoon, curious seals came alongside our dory, bristly whiskers dripping and dark liquid eyes blinking softly. The tide was too low to get the dory into the cove, and so as was always done in this case, we tied it safely at the brick landing where it would be secure until a future high tide. There was still a beautiful walk along the field road and through the woods. With no spoken word, Jim took my hand, the first time we had touched, and we continued holding hands as we sauntered toward home, discussing the beauties of a day spent in an island paradise.

The following day Jim and his Aunt Clara had to leave on an early train. In a private moment, Jim held me and kissing me tenderly, promised me that somehow, in some way he would return, and he hoped that I would wait for him. Silently I nodded assent, and then he was gone. The painful pangs of my first (and only) love went with him. When she had time, my mother and I walked the mile to the mailbox together and shared some wonderful conversations. But this was spring with so much to do indoors and outdoors toward the coming of summer guests, so riding my bike for the mail was my duty and one I loved. Three days after Jim left there were two letters from him, one for me and one for my mother and father. There was an old moss-covered pine stump at the top of the first hill after leaving the mailbox, and I sat on it to read Jim's letter. It was a beautiful, simple, and sincere declaration of his love for me, and the fact that he was writing to ask my folks if he could return and work for them for the summer.

His birthday was in mid-August and even if his draft notice came on its heels, it would likely be fall before he would be inducted into the army, so he would be able to complete the season at the inn. His railroad job would have been finished anyway when he was drafted, but at least we could have this time together. I was ecstatic, the rest of the road home was downhill to the shore and I'm not sure my bike wheels touched it very often.

Each year my mother hired a girl, usually in her teens, to work with me doing chamber work, waiting on tables, dishes, house cleaning—all the work that goes with running a small inn. She had not yet arranged for anyone, but reasoned that if Jim was willing to do this, which he enthusiastically said he was, it should work out just fine. He had certainly proved, even as a paying guest, that he was a hard and willing worker. To my great joy, it was agreed that Jim would return as soon as his notice had been worked out with the railroad.

My mother was not a prude, but she was brought up with many strict values in Scotland, and in a gentle way had instilled them into me. Actually this was true of Jim also, as his parents were Scottish and English. She had seen that we were two young people who enjoyed each other's company immensely, and although we had not demonstrated romantic leanings, my mother was a keen-witted observer of people and knew in her heart that a spark existed. She knew Jim was a gentleman, but she also knew what it was to be young and in love. She expressed her concerns about our knowing he would be going to war, and that we would be working together all day every day, not just dating occasionally.

True, I had just turned sixteen, but throughout my childhood my parents had often spent winters in New York, Connecticut, New Jersey, and Pennsylvania. It was during the Depression years and they were trying desperately to build their farm inn into a paying business, and there was no work in Maine in winter. They worked in wealthy households as cook and butler, because with room and board included they were able to save nearly all they earned. Most times it was possible for me to be with them, and I had a most enlightening glimpse of how "the rich are different."

There were also times they could not find work where there was room for a third family member so I boarded with relatives, and in some cases strangers who had been screened by my parents but were still strangers. It was all a valuable learning experience, and as a result my inner self had matured considerably beyond my sixteen years. Also, I came to the firm conclusion, at about eight years old, that when I was grown up and on my own, I would live in Maine no matter what it took.

I assured my mother that I had always been proud of the trust and confidence that she and my father had shown me, and that Jim's character was such she need have no worries about us. We both believed in the sanctity of marriage.

It was a halcyon summer. We worked long and hard hours together, even though there was now electricity there were few affordable conveniences and certainly not a dishwasher. Fourteen paying guests and the four of us made lots of dirty dishes three times a day. There was daily chamber work, animal chores, lawns and gardens, pitching hay by hand at haying time, picking and cleaning vegetables and fruit from Dad's mammoth gardens, and spending many nights helping to can and preserve the extra harvest for winter. Churning butter by hand was a nearly daily performance. It was a seven-day, dawn-to-dark workweek.

Still, Jim found time, mostly in our afternoons, to realize a dream of my mother's and build a log cribwork pier filled with big stones and decked over. The tide went out long and far in the cove, and guests using the skiff and dory had to plan on being back before the water left or they had a long, over-the-knees walk in mudflats. A pier would at least lengthen the time they could go rowing. My father had always said he didn't have time for it and he claimed a pier wouldn't hold there anyway because of the tidal pull and the heavy winter ice floes. So when Jim began building it, he didn't participate because he considered it a waste of time.

Jim had the pier completed by mid-summer to the delight of my mother and the guests. Fifteen years later, in 1960, my folks sold the old farm inn and moved to the shore near our farm. The pier was still well and whole then and for many years thereafter.

There were no days off, but my mother believed in efficiency and nearly every afternoon we were free from 3 to 5 p.m. Being young and resilient, we still found plenty of energy to swim in the lake or saltwater, go rowing on the lake, fish for mackerel or perch, and ride bikes. Jim had brought his bicycle, and we could cover many miles in an afternoon along the lightly-traveled roads.

We were deeply happy and full of future plans, and talk of marriage came naturally. We were both of one mind about living in Maine and didn't care how simple our life or belongings would be. The sole goal was to continue living in this freedom and beauty. Jim had a finely tuned sensitivity to the glories of nature and great tenderness toward people and animals, traits we shared. We didn't plan to live like bums, but we weren't driven toward the accumulation of material things either. We would build a log cabin, Jim would go lobstering, and we would raise and catch our food.

Barely a week after Jim's birthday in August, he received notice that he would be inducted into the army, and should plan on

Jim and May on their wedding day, October 16, 1948.

appearing at the Custom House in Wiscassett on October 22, 1945. We knew this would happen, but the notice and an exact date made it all too real. Fortunately, the war ended before he left, but there were still unknown years of possible post-war occupation ahead.

The gray dreariness of October 22 matched our spirits, but we encouraged each other with all the happy thoughts we could muster.

We promised to write daily. When boot camp ended, he would have a pass; perhaps he wouldn't get shipped overseas. We would concentrate on time passing quickly until he was discharged. Then just like that, he was on the troop train leaving. I was bereft as my mother tried to comfort me.

We wrote daily, continually cheering each other, or attempting to. Eventually weekend passes were granted and Jim would hitchhike home through the night in snow, cold, ice, and rain. I would sit and watch the road until I saw him coming up the hill in his uniform, his duffel bag slung over his shoulder. The passes were usually just two days, and one of those days Jim would work with my father in the woods helping cut the winter's supply of firewood. They got along well together and sometimes went hunting. One of the two days was ours, and if it was winter we skated, skied on the hilly, unplowed roads, or went sledding. The four of us would play Monopoly in the evenings.

We dreaded the possibility that Jim would get shipped overseas; fortunately, it didn't happen, although he came close. He was moved all over the country, though, and at times could only get home by train.

Through all this, I was still in high school. One day during English class at Lincoln Academy, I happened to look out the window and saw him standing under a tree, tall and slender in his uniform, waiting for classes to end. I had just heard the train come in but hadn't dreamed he would have a last-minute pass and be on it. From that moment on, I changed my seat in English class so I could faithfully watch the train station.

Jim's time in the army was productive. He learned to weld, drive trucks and heavy equipment, and became a tank instructor. All of these experiences proved useful in our future. I had no intentions, and there were no funds, for college. My school courses were strictly practical—typing, shorthand, and bookkeeping, all of which proved a vital help in the future.

The longed-for day of honorable discharge from the army finally arrived. Although it was a foregone conclusion, Jim honored tradition and dropped to one knee to propose to me. Then he and my father sat together on the flower garden wall while my mother and I watched from the window as he asked my father for my hand. There was no question. Although my dad was not much for words, he did say that he knew we were meant for each other.

On the morning of October 16, 1948, I wrote in my diary, "Today at noon, out on the lawn, Jim and I became one."

The day was warm and clear, the sky so vibrant blue it shook the heart, and topaz sparkles danced on the October-indigo of Greenland Cove. We were married under a big cedar tree on the lawn before thirty friends and relatives. We had too many plans to invest in an engagement ring at this point, but we had bought two exceptionally wide gold bands.

When I had been piano accompanist for Lincoln Academy's glee club, I had bought a long white dress with satin bodice and a tulle skirt. There had only been a few occasions to wear it and, along with a veil, it served perfectly as a wedding gown. Several years later, visiting my parents, Jim and I stood under the tree remembering. I looked down and saw a little scrap of white tulle peeking up through some washed away earth. I must have stepped on the dress and torn off a tiny piece that then got tramped into the ground. We pushed it back into the earth.

My mother's cooking was legend and she served an elegant dinner. My father had given me away with dignity, but with a small choke in his throat, which made me a little sad and yet happy for his caring.

The hour came to get into the old but good Ford coupe Jim had bought with some army savings, and as we drove up the Shore Road headed for our honeymoon, I had never felt so utterly free and filled with adventurous spirit in my life. That feeling would last a lifetime.

In the early days of just the two of us laboring in the workshop making bells, we often listened to a favorite FM radio station that played soft music. A piece we especially liked was a piano version of "Ballade Pour Adeline." It is a lilting, delicately ethereal kind of melody, joyous in the pictures it evokes. One day when it was playing, Jim left the welder and came over to hug me and say softly, "When I hear that, I always think of you and me dancing in the pastures."

Yes, we certainly did dance. And somehow, somewhere, I believe that will always be true.

Requiem for Jim Davidson, 1927-2017

The Ways of My Love for You

The deep and enduring love you brought to me,
Your spirit that never stopped dreaming and working toward wonderful events to come,
Your sense of humor, the laughter from your keen wit, a constant source of joy to me who loves to laugh.

I loved your fearless judgment to meet the elements, sea, winds, fog.

Pride in you surges into my heart when I think of all you accomplished through brutally hard work, and when I see the respect and love for you in those around us, and the help you gave so many.

The word "miss" cannot describe the lonely emptiness without you.

Over and over again I read the hundreds of daily letters you sent me when you were in the US Army during World War II, so full of love and plans.

You were, and are, all my dreams of love and romance, for romance is eternal in you, showing it to me through every stage of our lives together—best friends, lovers, working partners.

For sixty-eight years, four months, and eight days we were so close that each could be said to have passed beyond the boundaries of self and to live in the other.

As you once envisioned, we will be dancing together in the pastures.

You are my star in heaven, Jim, the music of my soul. I love you. Love never ends.

Epilogue

As you may have guessed, Jim passed away in 2017. He was 89. I loved him so and miss him terribly. As I have recounted in this book, we lived an amazing life. Always together.

A lot of things, of course, that I discussed in this book have changed over time, and I will bring you up to date on a few.

We officially and fully retired in 2012 and moved to Whitefield.

In 1998, Connie joined us in working at North Country Wind Bells. It was her choice and we were thrilled. She took over the company in 2008 and we steadily reduced our role until retiring. Connie now lives on our old farm, and it still has its one hundred glorious acres of beautiful land, loved and cared for.

Debby Jo now lives in Illinois, and although she has a full-time job, she still has a small sheep farm and shows them at some major events. She has loved sheep since she was first old enough to toddle into the barn.

North Country Wind Bells now employs up to twelve people during peak seasons. The company produces five collections of bells: The Original and Authentic Buoy Bell, The Wilderness Bells, The Lighthouse Bells, The Compass Rose Bells, and the special Themed Bells. The bells are available in more than fifty sizes and sounds with 125 windcatcher designs. The bells are sold in more than five thousand retail shops.

Our North Country Cheviots are now owned by Bill and Stacy Webster of Windham. When the bell business and age became too much for us to care for our sheep, we passed them along to the

Websters, who show our former sheep along with their own. They are professional shepherds and are pushing the flock forward beyond our dreams.

The Mayfair House and Ocean Reefs Inn are both now private homes.

Our dear old log cabin is still standing in the woods and is rented seasonally.

The Browns Cove house was torn down long ago and replaced by a lovely new home.

We sold *Come Spring* in 2005.

North Country Wood Products continued for a few years after we sold it but eventually went out of business. We bought back the land in 2003 and reincorporated it into North Country Farm.

Often I am asked what the secrets are to a marriage that lasts sixty-eight years.

Enduring love is the first ingredient, but I believe that common goals tighten the bonds, teaching that you must work together. The result of this is a "oneness" that creates a need beyond want for each other. Being a solid "one" helped us reach our dreams, withstand the hard blows, and embrace the joyful successes.

Faith is also a binding force. You cannot work on the sea, or with the earth, or witness the innocence of animals and the goodness of fine people without recognizing the work of a great creator.

Be kind, respectful, and above all, laugh and love each other well. These threads are the true fabric of that precious tapestry we weave known as marriage.

About the Author

MAY DAVIDSON WAS born in 1929 in Damariscotta, a charming fishing village located in midcoast Maine. In 1947, she graduated from Lincoln Academy, a private high school in the nearby town of Newcastle. She married her teenage sweetheart, James, a year later. Determined to stay in Maine, Davidson and her husband experimented with several entrepreneurial endeavors—from creating a lobster trap building facility to raising purebred sheep—before finding worldwide success with the design of the iconic Maine Buoy Bell. Today, she lives in Whitefield, Maine, and is known for her column in *The Lincoln County News*.

Photo by Dean Lunt.